I am My Father's Daughter

WINDS OF TIME NOVEL

B G SIMPSON

ISBN 979-8-88945-134-1 (softcover)
ISBN 979-8-88945-136-5 (hardcover)
ISBN 979-8-88945-135-8 (ebook)

This book is a work of fiction. Names, characters, places, and incidents are the product of the author's imagination or are used fictitiously. Any resemblance to actual locales, events, or persons, living or dead, is purely coincidental.

Printed in the United States of America.

Brilliant Books Literary
137 Forest Park Lane Thomasville
North Carolina 27360 USA

PROLOGUE

The small, framed girl with the long blonde curls draped around her shoulders carried herself quite effortlessly. She had learned to be quite the clandestine girl in almost eighteen years of her youth, a pure heart according to legend, hidden into the newness of being a leader. She was the best trained to one day to take her father's place. Danica had made the trip across the universe along with her parents. Their group, referred to as the Circle, was isolated in their new world out on the edge of the constellation Libra, 21.3 light-years away from where they had come from. Danica's parents were away making a name for themselves on some persistent quest assigned by the Aquerian fellowship, beyond the other side of the planet was what they were told. They were doing an important search to improve their world. Find new ways of preserving their culture or other finds of life. Too far from home was Danica's opinion, yet not too far from reality. Their parents pushed them to always to do their best in their studies, and training, and setting of personal goals. Danica would drift off dreaming about conquering her enemy of that darker world, dreamed of memories on certain days hence. She was the leader of these six youthful, gifted Circle members, seven, including herself. They were prepped to become a second-generation Circle to take their parents place. Many years had passed since dealing with those devils of that other world. Danica had memories of dark angels, and battles from prior conditions, even though only being three years old at the time. And there were visions of chaos that had brought her to understand those blacked winged creatures left of Earth. As far as she understood, everyone else was gone from the blue-planet—far away never to return to that once beautiful place. This second-generation Circle was in an ascetic form, giving most of their grueling hours of dedication to a cause they weren't quite sure they were ready for. They had won the backing of a king of realms, most likely sitting in the distance, watching and waiting or taking notes to improve them as warriors they were to be. Then this young girl came along, who had dreams like her father. She was quickly chosen, small in stature, but big on ideas of supporting the members of these teenage second generation of gifted students. And then there was Amen. He was the baby of the bunch, yet stood out like no other, without the accomplishments of his older brother given as an example, Ismael, who ignored him when at all possible. Yet the two boy's father always leaned in on the older to do a better job at watching the younger. He'd try to keep Amen out of trouble, if that could even be possible.

And then seeing them as a unit, Danica realized they had nothing to do with that other world of their parents. It troubled her to even think of trying to make a connection with the other world. They didn't want anything to do with those creatures of before, long ago on some distant shore, past ancient history, past the ability to understanding earth now gone, through the mistakes of others, loved by some king far away not of their present world. This was their lives now, this was their home—where they sweat and toiled in the heat of a red-dwarf star, not too far in distance, yet close enough to leave a lasting impression on the inside of each ones heart. Orbitus was where they learned to be warriors, taught from the hands of the Aquerian fellowship. They were taught to love those things of character in this new world of hidden secrets. Of course, not held to the dreams of their parents, who'd at times appeared lost as their minds would quite frequently drift back to that other world. They were too young to understand their parent's motivations. Facing the ultimate fight between good and evil, as they were told by the leaders of realms, but why now after all these years? They were just children chasing after their own dreams in a world set apart. From first impressions, they didn't look like much to the eyes of their parents. Their deficiency of years showed a lack of experience, moral judgments, or inconsistency.

Tory was the second in command, after Danica. She was the only adult of this second Circle of seven. She had been parented by Jake and Angela for the last fifteen years. She held an endeared role of the seven, being well trained and proficient in the talents that were given to her, as all retained a certain gift given. She was there navigator facing most of their circumstances of moving as a team from one place or another—that's where the hovercraft gave them an edge. Where edges were quickly learned of, as shear drop offs bringing them to their current situation. In her quiet emissions she'd avoid the ill-wills of today's youth's immaturity, being older and put together more efficiently from an emotional standpoint, she had experienced shooting across the galaxy on a wing and a prayer that they'd get to the other side in one piece, before falling into a world they couldn't avoid being a part of.

Argon, now fifteen, was the boldest, not the smartest of the seven would quite frequently show off, never holding back from youthful regressions. He'd shoot half the food sources if not stopped by the others from his overplayed exportation's of bravery—yet his other members viewed him as a manic-depressive only looking for attention from the rest. His father, Randy, and mother Janet, had taken his privileges away on several occasions, trying to keep him focused. He was like an over-heated puppy on steroids from Amen's point of view…don't figure… Amen thought. They tried to point the boy in the right direction, while still showing some signs of worthy affections as parents when dishing out awards or punishments. Not upsetting the natural order of a boy with stranger surroundings than those left of earth, minus a few elements of comfort swaying him to be challenged by certain rules and regulations. His father wasn't bending to his non-conformance of bad behavior had brought them at a loss. And yet still, Argon was a day dreamer, thinking he could change almost any circumstance without having repercussions from his way of thinking in the things he would do. His father wanted him to grow-up in a well-respected manner, without showing mistakes of his youthful ambitions. The Aquerian fellowship had endured enough of him and was leaning toward further discipline. And he was set to spend many a moment of confinement to think about engaging his brain before his mouth. It had gotten him in quite the trouble so many times over. He lacked the patience and discipline needed to endure this new world, even if taught the hard way. They'd get him to conform.

Now going back to Ismael, who was parented by Tommy and Tilla, the older of two brothers, left behind to sort out his differences with the younger. Who had been born half-human and half- Aquerae, like his brother the younger of a distant mother minus the affections of what a mother could give. Their mother was fully Aquerae, not by right but by birth. They had a diverse way of viewing their children. Ismael exhibited a little more self-control than little brother. He was soon to turn sixteen coming up on the next weekend, while the younger would turn twelve next month. Little brother was more prone to do a father's bidding to win a father's approval on any given day of the week. Amen would reflect an awkward walk full of playful confidence, along with an insurmountable lighthearted faith that the others couldn't imagine having. He glowed from his innocence. According to certain parents he was the glue that would hold this group of young adult's altogether. Amen was set to make history one day through a connection he had with Danica. She had watched over him like a little brother. Ismael couldn't imagine being as gullible as the younger, all bug-eyed and out of control, with his mouth and his emotions. He knew a long talk was imminent, of little brother getting under his skin. Amen had a way of constant prodding bigger brother to no end. Ismael wanted to reach down and slap him on the back of his larger-than-life looking alien head. Ismael was finished dragging Amen along on any further reaching expeditions given of their parents or the Aquerian fellowship. He was too young to be a part of his Circle of friends, was his thought, yet Danica kept insisting he come along. She wanted him to feel he had his part in their company. Even noting, all too often, Amen had become very vocal of his own personal opinions—running back to dad to tell him everything that had happened in his day. This had to stop. They had to have some secrets, was Ismael's way of thinking, but the boy was relentless. Where was his self-control? Ismael was done telling little brother their secrets, only to hear his father return words said in the strictest of confidence. You have to understand that Ismael was partial into doing the right thing too, when it came to doing what dad wanted him to do. Yet sometimes he felt the need to not share certain items of secrecy which were held to upsetting the natural order of a father's best intentions. Amen was emphatic about not leaving out details that he thought dad needed to know of right up front. Ismael believed a certain amount of dignity was formed by holding certain items of dad's disapproval in secret, he thought it was a natural order of growing up, forming his own opinions without dad's nose into everything they did. Yet Amen felt this to be dishonest as taught by the Aquerian fellowship. He wanted to follow the codes to the letter. Then after being exposed, big brother would take on most of the punishments dished out. Ismael was frustrated, hotly heated and sometimes depleted of patience. Yet he still pressed to spend most his emotional life chasing after dreams of an intellectual mind. Ismael was eager to prove his advancement of manhood, without little brother tagging along, causing more than his share of awkwardness or God-awful gawkiness. Amen looked like the small thin boy that he was, with big feet and long arms, with a peach-fuzz scratch-and-sniff routine that caused Ismael to cringe. Big brother was set to lean toward educational resources brought on by the Aquerian fellowship, trying to find his niche in the world, of course, within the settings of a normal environment, yet what was normal about anything in this new world of theirs? He tried to compete with the locals like he was the lone Robin-hood of Loxley, stealing ideas from the Aquerae to give back to his crib of conservators. Now Jacob, named after his commending father, called Jake by family and friends, and Angela being his mother were a part of the original Circle of membership. He had been empowered with a gift through touching someone else. He could feel or sense the effects of a spiritual setting that the others would find quite uncomfortable. Jacob was the literary writer like his father, yet still in training through the Aquerian fellowship and the gentle guidance of his father's assistance. He would turn sixteen in two months from today of this given story. He lived like each day ahead of him was still too far away. He wanted to be an adult before his time, as all boys live with obstinate moments of growing up.

Moving on, in remembering the first Circle of membership, reminding us of Bella's friend, Toby, had finally won the affections of Bella's heart and had become her husband. Through the years he'd always stayed by her side, showing patience, holding back his opinion had left a mysterious door open leading to Bella's heart. He wasn't sure if her commitments to him had stemmed out of guilt that Bella had held on to, but he wasn't willing to judge her for her actions or her choices of the heart leading to him, only accepting it as a positive way of direction when finally winning her affections. He had many memories of their youth together. They enjoyed a lifetime of friendship to think about for the rest of their lives. Toby figured from his warped way of thinking, if the steer was running toward you, you either got out of the way or went for a ride, and a ride was okay with him. Bella had learned to tolerate his way of thinking, as he had put up with her constant inward struggles. He loved Bella, even with the flaws in her character he looked past them and loved the girl of his youth without following an agenda. He knew she had a tough life, living without others around her on most days of the week. Uncle Buck was the closest of any given parent, but that was another world now gone, never to be seen again. She was molded with a disconnected life, losing her mother at fifteen and having a father who worked away for weeks at a time. She grew up with horses and steers, and chickens and beer, listening to country music while repairing barbwire fences, wearing her cowgirl boots and gloves and hat with a bit of attitude carried on her shoulders. She snubbed her nose at most of the boys from school, rolled up her sleeves and did dirty work around the farm, from early in the morning until past dusk. That was living to her. She felt invigorated by sweat and the beating of her heart. She was cute, then beautiful, and then a complete knock-out, while her friend Toby had his fair share of rejections from the girl with her misconstrued ways. He didn't judge her too harshly by what she did. He stuck around and became her friend. He saw past all her broken dreams that needed to mend. She mimicked a cowgirl with straight brown hair, freckled face of a gentle kind. She was a girl that had grown up in the heart of Texas. Yet she was nothing like her mother, when it came to personality. If she meant it to draw attention—it worked. That's what made her so interesting. Bella gave birth to a beautiful little girl she named Renee. Drew wondered about the name calling of children was about, but then he knew that could be her way of getting Drew to remember his past. Yet young Renee had no such dreams as her mother, but she did see things of the future. She would turn fifteen in just a few days. All had come to bear witness that seven was the perfect number of acceptance. They were the gifted, appointed by a king of realms, to someday shortly go traipsing across the universe trying to change the past. They had to find a way to repeat themselves as leading Oracles, like their parents. Not that their parents had given up their leading roles of yesterday. They were to learn from their mistakes. Yet still set to chase after those creatures of a darker world of fading memories. Face it, their parents hadn't seen or heard of them for fifteen years.

So, to re-count those of a second generation—there was Tory, being the oldest, and Danica named by her deceased mother as their leader. And Renee, don't confuse her with the first wife of Drew named Renee. And then to the young men, there's Ismael and his brother Amen, and don't leave out Jacob whose father became that lone writer on the planet, and Argon who seemed to be the fearless of the boys, always getting himself in trouble every day, that makes seven. They would begin this inept journey to find their parents—who weigh in the balance of this mystery just up ahead. Setting to take a journey across the universe as their teacher, Dr. Zimmerman had informed them. They as a group, would come next, maybe one day the group as a whole would bring back the world to better conditions. Soon to be visited by those creatures fallen of heaven.

1

Second Generation Circle

Starting with Danica, who was the perfect daughter under the perfect circumstances of how a parent would want a daughter to be, yet knowing her father and stepmother, she was more than the best of what a mother and father could want from a young lady that adored them as excepted parents. Danica lived in a community closely scrutinized by an Aquerian Fellowship. They expected the best that each member could give of their intelligence and strength. As a girl she dreamed of success in a way that others didn't quite understand. She breathed in air and walked on the land as if it was feeding her soul, filling her with ideas and dreams that would never let go of a girl of such innocence. Even being somewhat isolated, in a world not ever imagined from a normal earthly sense, once experienced. She was a far cry from being the average teenager back on earth. She soaked up knowledge in a daily fashion that drew the attention of these gifted degenerates she faced every day, as they watched her every move, leaning in towards her leadership. And those elite alien types that she'd rub shoulders with loved her like one of their own. Condac, watcher of the Aquantice range, guarded her like he was her own personal bodyguard. Danica would reach up and take his big hand, walk a trail of her training with the big guy at her side, on some usual plain. He would look down and smile at the girl gifted of her youth. Danica completely felt her life of the future was something of great responsibility. She was ready to make her mark on her world or on one of a future yet to come. Saddened by the memories left behind by her parents had nothing to do with her life as it was now. She was on a personal mission, living without the embittered experiences of the Circle of her parents. Although loneliness from time-to-time would visit her, she still had her part to do in her world yet to live. She'd kept busy preparing for a journey beyond her seventeen years of training, taking her to reach beyond the stars twinkling past the heavens. Her parents had felt helpful in molding her into an exceptional young lady of leadership. She was self-reliant in a way that others of her age would never understand. Noting, they were sure to miss out on opportunities passed on by that world of their parents—things that teenagers did back on earth that was a part of that world. Bearing in mind, no Saturday night football games, and definitely no M.T.V. or You-Tube streamed video's through the internet. There wasn't too much of ranting and raving going on for the weekends. The movie-theaters were a no-go, and bond-fires at the beach were out of the question, yet somehow the newness of these Circle members would survive and find purpose in their lives up ahead. Just to point out—they were pure of heart, but the name given to them from their own accords was the Circle of Trust, yet chosen by those of a scholarly mind, Dr. Zimmerman. For short, called themselves the Circle, as the others before them, for saving time, and quick reference for those of membership. In as much, Drew's daughter, Danica, read everything that Anna, her stepmother, had ever transposed from Dr. Zimmerman's personal library. His picture was plastered up on the wall in his formal wear from the early 19th century, of a black and white image shown of years never imagined from a girl of her stature. Many of the well-worth stories read touched her heart, even though she couldn't feel for people that she didn't even know. She tried to put herself in their place, with the trauma of the blue-planet left behind of past history. She read where it was already gone from a newspaper clipping from Dr. Zimmerman's personal library. Nothing to salvage from days gone by accept the memories of those who once lived there. And many a good story told by aged writers of the past, not all was lost, yet faded of what a good life use to be like. She couldn't quite find tears to shed for such people known by her parents past. Only sensing that these people were connected to the ones before didn't directly connect with them. What Danica did do was make a connection with her current surroundings. It wasn't a mystery that her heart was full of love just like people felt of earth, but different, not like the past. She was a particular young lady, with an extreme intuition in knowing the answer before being told by others, just like her stepmother Anna. Since most of what she learned came from her. It began to make sense. Danica was stronger than most when it came to doing the right thing among her peers, but even more than that. She had learned to develop skills of a gentle heart like her father, but with the intuitive mind behind it like her stepmother Anna. Yes, she did have that picket-fence type of life with the outstanding garden, and the alluring countenance about what looked good in the house when it came to furnishings, or how well she could cook or entertain guests—yet Danica wasn't just a refined young woman of her youth. She was well-schooled by the Aquerae and taught of a warrior's heart about stuff of survival. She even spent many a day with the watchers of the Aquantice range, who had learned with time to love the little girl with the golden locks that found joy in the smallest of belongings that seemed to draw her attention.

She was beauty incarnate as so widely spoken by her father, yet he trusted his daughter as much or more than he trusted himself, and what that really meant, was that Danica had learned about her future at an early age without being forced to change. What Drew and Anna went through was different. She had a dissimilar road to travel that didn't make much sense to her parents. Her life was grand from Danica's perspective, and for no particular reason she wanted to remain in this place she considered home, and nothing was going to convince her to be anywhere else at the moment.

Drew and Anna Lighter, along with the rest of the older Circle of membership, were exploring the other side of the planet, trying to find livable conditions of land. Most of the land was barren, leaving little to culture toward improvements for use in agriculture. Danica's father insisted on calling this new planet, Gliese 581 C, so named by scientists left back on Earth.

Earlier, a month or so ago, earth days, the year 2038 to be exact, during the summer months, on a warm cloudy day with a breeze coming in from the west, an Aquerian team, with a few of the humans, were invited along on this sort of expedition. To distant land, hopefully to shortly have positive feedback from the local Aquerians. Whatever was out there beyond the borders of their quaint little city, and whatever Danica's parents hoped to find out there, seemed a little bit far reaching as far as she was concerned, yet somehow it didn't rank that high on her list of importance. Only the safety of her parents was her deepest concern, and then, everything else became second fiddle. Unfortunately, her parents had been gone already a month, with lost radio communications seven days before. She lost the last bit of her faith she had saved up was now faded. They, not making it home without some type of acknowledgment that they were still alive, still seeking a mutual bond with their previous world behind them. Then the younger members of new membership was okay with it when Danica brought it up in conversation, at their present-day meeting, even though, Danica might take it upon her own accords to seek after her parents alone, she knew she better not try such a trip solo. The younger Circle of membership was set to go after them once getting everything together as a group, after speaking about taking such a journey on a whim that they needed assistance—of course, without the council's approval. Danica was done sitting home worrying and wondering, biting her nails down to the quick, checking the rooms in the morning to see if they were there. They'd agree that their parents needed their help. So that was it. They were going...

The first of her conspirators to hit her up was Argon, more than up to the task of making emotional gestures of bravery beyond what a teenage boy should do. And then there was Ismael following suit right behind him. He was more of a controlled citizen with a little more substance between his ears than Argon, and thus continuing, Ismael's younger brother Amen, yet not wanting to include smaller brother within mixed company. Amen didn't always hold his best interests at heart and became disruptive to say the least on certain occasions. Moving on, there was Tory and Renee, who were definitely in for the adventure. Furthermore, Ismael had his work cut out for him. He wanted to leave quickly without young Amen finding out, considering it a chore within itself to keep watching him. So then, Ismael wasn't sure if he could trust the little scoundrel coming along. He remained too much of their father's shadow, which cast doubts upon the Circle's coming adventure. The thing was, Ismael's father Tommy, was on the expedition too, lost like the others, leaving little to doubt that Amen would want to find his father leaving no stone unturned. Consequently, he wanted his say in the perceived trip to come. According to Danica he was one of them. Then Danica, got this fantastical idea early that evening, and decided they needed a little bit of supervision from their slow aging teacher, Dr. Zimmerman. The good doctor appeared to get along with the use of a cane. Even though he was already older when first landing on such a far-out unequipped place, eons from earth. He still had the ability to carry his own weight. Now, almost seventeen years had passed since leaving the blue-planet, and Dr. Zimmerman remained quite healthy. Danica loved her teacher as much as any other person she had known in her few years of her youth, yet also, he had been a guide exposing wisdom to a young girl's mind that others might not see as fitting to a child with overactive senses of the human species. In many areas that surpassed anything the Aquerae could comprehend, by not being human. Danica, well trained, and focused had referred to her beloved teacher as grandfather, knowing the personal title had suited him well. Out of respect for her teacher, she had given him such title and because he was good to them. He was more than devoted in all of his connections to these children pointed in his direction. Dr. Zimmerman took up residency and dug in, for his purpose of life remaining was in the guiding of these children. Knowing each member of both Circles had come to face the same facts of their changed environment. He was looked on as if being family. Danica had learned about the saddened stories told of his past by her father, in closest of confidence she'd never share. In losing one's life and family was the toughest for their well-respected teacher. She decided he deserved such a title by his many years of dedications towards these people he considered his own. So, it was final, he was grandfather.

Now, Ismael cast his doubts on telling anyone at all, but Danica knew deep inside, from hidden intuition not telling anyone could turn out to be the worst of disasters. She had finally talked Ismael into telling

Dr. Zimmerman would hold the best of attentions toward their youth and their mission—but to tell no one else. The professor did have his ways of convincing the innocent-of-heart about doing the right thing in life was always the better road to take. But somewhat, this time, the professor wasn't quite sure if he should do just that, because for some reason he had felt the same intuition that his seventeen-year-old granddaughter had felt. Something was wrong. The expedition that the first-generation Circle was on felt to have run amuck somehow, and something needed to be done. They had to find their parents. Dr. Zimmerman's advice was so simple that Danica felt silly at first. Then she knew wisdom was given to those of years, his advice was truly measured. So, they began to prepare.

Ismael was in charge of all the gear and Argon the weapons. Argon was more than pleased with himself to arrange the placement of weapons in the hovercraft. Tory became the one who would be the tracker, reading maps and checking prints left behind. Jacob was blessed with the same hallowed curse that his father bore so adamantly. He was able to see vividly those things of any future events by touching the braver. Danica inherited two gifts, one of being the door that opened up into other worlds, in gaps of time where she could slip through spaces, like her father. And two, she learned of the intuition of her ways taught to her by Anna. This almost made her feel like she had twice the responsibility than the others, but that part, at the moment, she was keeping to herself.

Ismael had powers to be able to move objects like his father, telekinesis he'd been told. He also was told being of the alien mind and body had powers not considered by those who were fully human. For example, he could swim underwater and breathe underwater because he had gills in his neck and webbed feet and hands. Also, able to withstand extreme temperatures of the water. And little brother had the same abilities for he was half of both worlds too. They were able to avert such causes of hypothermia and having striated-cat-like-eyes they could see in the dark. They could also communicate with the watchers of the Aquantice range telepathically, like their Aquerian leader Torack could. So, they were gifted, from that point of view, but not full-fledged seers like Renee. Tory had a new gift that the others had not experienced, which was the ability to move water, massive quantities like in a storm. Ismael's little brother, Amen had the heighten gift of smell, besides having his Aquerian traits.

He was always willing to give advice even if not asked in the least to try and gain a little advantage. He could smell effects in a peculiar way just like his aunt Angela. At times the meaning of what he could smell remained a bit confusing. At one time, big brother thought to get even with the little scoundrel and convinced him that he probably had the same ability with his tastebuds and offered him a scoop of something found on the ground, quickly spitting it out when finding out it was Dinosaur doo. The older, but wiser, brother had a field-day with that little stunt and constantly was there to remind him of it. Amen didn't find it humorous as the others stood and laughed.

"That poop is full of bacteria!" Amen said, "And dad might think you're a bit cruel!" The others couldn't help but laugh. Amen couldn't find the humor in the cruel gesture of Ismael's sense of humor. Ismael shook his head and dropped the smile that had so graced his face just seconds ago. Danica didn't find it funny either as she glared back at the older.

As time progressed, Danica proved she could make intelligent decisions to earn such a title as their leader. Her father taught her well about making the right decisions when it came to the safety of each member. She'd been tested by the best of the Aquerian fellowship and trained with the watchers on certain days of the week. Being she did possess two gifts. She might think the Aquerian fellowship would expect more from her than someone normally of her position. She was strong and lean and quick with her reflexes. One day, the leader of the watchers knew she'd shine. She'd set an example for the others to follow, a blossoming warrior that she was. Furthermore, she was stunning like her mother. And she had most recently caught the gentle eyes of Jacob and Ismael staring back at the most awkward of times. They had quickly noticed her changing physically with age, from a little girl to a woman. She'd developed into quite the beauty queen by what her father could tell. Yet these boys were too intimidated by her to even consider trying to get close, and besides, she was their leader, who'd been set apart from all the rest.

Danica wasn't the princess type from her own point of view, but she did have her delicate features. And bearing in mind, young men of youthful hormones weren't allowed to show such feelings. She was too intimidating for either of them. Dr. Zimmerman was betting her life would be filled with more important issues at hand than the awkward stares of two strange looking boys slowly becoming men. Jacob was definitely a fan. His worst fear was to catch her looking. In his frame of mind, he'd remain a devoted follower, and keep his feelings to himself. Like most days she had dressed more for comfort than for personal appearance as she'd been pictured as a warrior, set for leadership for a not so easy life in the future to come.

They were all set to make treks across barren land of low-lying fields with rolling hills frequented by storms from the coast. An ocean, going west was just a few minutes away by hovercraft from where they had first started from. The hovercraft would make pretty good time provided and made by the Aquerian intelligent mind, while those of a youthful heart would skim along on some distant shoreline to make up time by flying quite effectively through the air. If nothing was heard from their parents in the next few days, then Dr. Zimmerman would give advice on what to do next. Condac, the watcher of the Aquantice range might come in handy if they ran into trouble, so he'd make his presence known at just the right time. Ismael would load extra solar cubes in the hovercraft, taking that as sound advice from their teacher Dr. Zimmerman. Danica knew that traveling by day would be safer. She felt Condac would be accompanied by his trusting Condorsorous of dragon-like-fashion, being a surprisingly enormous beast that soared through the air on wings with a body mass quite unexpected.

Jacob, being the only son of Jake and Angela Drake had turned fifteen three months back. He had a few skills taught by an Aquerian fellowship also, and those of leadership from a Circle of members well familiar to the art of war. They were all exposed to grueling exercises, pushing their bodies to the extreme. Danica taught daily sword-fighting and shadow boxing to the youngest of their group. Jacob had the usual eight-pack and protruding trapezium muscles when flexing. He looked the true gymnast. He would expose his muscles quite frequently on the parallel bars. Doing flips and circled turns, plus walking on his hands, and don't forget one handed push-ups. Jacob spent most of his days with his shirt off. Ismael thought him to be a show-off and wondered when the boy was marked to grow up, keeping his hormones to an all-time low. Argon was excited about the mission to come without even noticing Jacob. He was game. Even though Argon's curiosity pulled him toward weapons, more than showing the others a physical presence. He was taught by an Aquerian fellowship geared to get it on while keeping his head in the game. And having advanced training with a particular weapon called an Element gun. Rather than spending wasted time learning from uncles who were more into spears and chucking big rocks at each other. Argon had this impetuous habit of always finding trouble without knowing of its cause. He was one card short of a full deck, one less good idea to lean back on, but he was game, and ready for fame if given the chance. He was a bit entrusting of seeing anything of a metaphysical nature and stuck to only believing what the eye could see and the mind could understand. Yet their journeying hadn't even begun, so knowledge to come of that other world weren't even on the menu. The trip to come would change his attitude, especially of journeys not yet comprehended. Argon's imagination took him to chase after fantasy villains left unseen by any watchful eyes. He'd think of rescuing stranded victims hanging out on a limb with nothing to save them or knowing why. He only trusted the Aquerian soldiers in training, not as pen-pals or buddies to bunk up with. Nothing of sword or danger had been experienced by the young lad as of yet. He would be new to the world they were getting ready to embark on, by closely examining those apparitions to meet of that other world. To him, it was all poppycock, and wise tales, not connected on their own. Danica thought him like a big child. He was fascinated by weapons from ancient history that he had read about in Dr. Zimmerman's personal library. At first, hearing the stories told by Dr. Zimmerman, he'd then experience present-day weapons that the Aquerae had produced. He was glued to the screen when seeing impressive battles left behind in fields of massacred and dismemberment. Stories quite unbelievable, yet Argon believed his teacher as if it was fact. He held this to the highest of importance—to be a warrior like no other. It made his heart stir to even think of such glory. How were such men made into these incomprehensible beings? He wondered of the teachings from an Aquerian race that measured all circumstances, never thinking one had the upper hand, unless wiser and better prepared, geared with unexplained emotions. But even then, the enemy standing across from you, in a simple field of battle, always seemed to have as much a chance of success as any other, especially if motivated in the right way. So, emotions ran high of each warrior seen of rage and death of the other wasn't taken so lightly. Yet there was something hidden beneath the ranks of those already protected few, guarded unnaturally of something stronger and greater than all those of history, prepared for battle to come. There was something amiss by the boy misconstrued of reasoning, something eternal was barking at their door.

And Renee. She was a true seer, being raised by her mother Bella. Taken to see a better way of living through simple attributes of a young girl growing up and getting along with the few children glued to her side. She didn't appear so impetuous about her mother's cowgirl boots or attitude, but only grew to love this physical world she was connected to. She wanted her life to be about being sophisticated in elegant gallantry. Even though she had been sported in several difficult forms of martial-arts, self-defense. She'd prefer a gentler way of expressing herself. A soft beauty graced her face as seen from Anna. She wanted to experience love as the many stories told learned of her by her parents. She knew her mother had a connection with their previous leader but didn't know how. She was intrigued by how Drew and Anna fell in love. This gave her a bit of hope that love could last a lifetime, then on to the next.

Renee had turned fifteen just two months earlier. She was way ahead of a girl normally of her age. She would dream as her mother had in the past, yet those dreams took her places that didn't include the two moons lighting a pathway across the sky. Her dreams took her places that she had never been too, possibly mapped out from an imagination that pulled her heart toward an eternal draw of love—like a mighty undertow causing her heart to reach for something never experienced or wished for. Bella had wronged her daughter of this retched curse by not sharing too much of what she was to experience later in years, not letting on that it would increase with age. Bella didn't want to bring up a past that almost ripped her own world apart. This was something young Renee would have to learn on her own, or from the professor who might assist in explaining her future.

Danica, Tory, Renee, and Ismael, younger brother Amen, Jacob, and Argon were the children of a race of people, left out on an edge of a forgotten place to far from the second generation's motivation. It was the second planet from the red-dwarf-star, in the central part of the universe, in the constellation Libra, 21.3 light years away from what used to be normal, but what was normal from their perspective couldn't be explained by an ordinary human that walked this earth. It was a mission planned and prepared for those of the gifted. Their lives were about to make a turn that would take them across the cosmos to a place with an indebted history—a small blue-planet that stood in the distance, as once before had been called home. Only a flicker of light stood out to give one last glimmer of hope towards humanity.

2

Distant Shores

The morning was early, before the sun rose to the lower end of a new beginning of the next day. Danica rolled out of bed prior to any evidence of the sun peeking through her window. She lived with her parents, taking a back bedroom across the hall from mom and dad's master bedroom. The room was dark from being early morning pre-dawn, and the sky was clouding over quickly as it moved in over their community. A low fog had settled in making it almost impossible to see more than thirty feet away. Danica could hear a faint knock on her bedroom window. She was dressed in sleepwear with a faded Aero Smith T-shirt and tightly fitted shorts, handed down from her mother was of thought as she tenderly held things of value with a deeper meaning. She moved the blinds just ever so slightly, bringing in view the shadowed figure canvassing by the light reflected from the streetlamp. The awkward face in front caused her eyes to widen. Jacobs's sullied grin cast a fog like breath with incomplete viewing. He'd looked goofy and annoying from her angle of perception. Danica rolled her eyes with a slight movement of her head relayed her disapproval. She couldn't believe he was here, at this dreadful hour, and at her bedroom window no less, hoping to be her grateful prince, was the thought. His persistence made her wonder of his true intentions, always hanging around, always at her side, innocently looking at her with that deep penetrated stare. Danica slid up the window to let him slip by. He couldn't help noticing her skimpy attire while raising an eyebrow.

"What's wrong with coming in through the front door?" She said.

Jacob lost the grin. "I didn't think you would hear me, and besides I thought knocking would wake others?"

"What others…my parents aren't here? Only Fluffers is sleeping in mom and dad's room." Fluffers was an old sheep-dog dad had rescued one night back home. Well, not her home but the blue-planet left behind. The dog was one that reminded dad of another he used to have from his memories of youth.

Danica looked out past the window to get a view of the streetlight just after letting Jacob pass by. He could see her long beautiful legs when turning to look at her. She caught the glance of her admirer and narrowed her eyes. She cast a stare of disapproval his way as he turned away and walked toward the hall.

"Are you looking for something or are you being your usual rude self!"

Jacobs's complexion turned a crimson red, yet couldn't be made out from the lighting, lucky for him. He thought. But it was too late. He'd gotten a good look. She was beautiful in a way he'd never understand, was his second thought.

"Sorry—it's just…I'm not used to seeing you dressed like that."

Danica's eyes narrowed further. "You think…that's why there's a front door, so you don't go traipsing through my bedroom. Next time show some manners and knock on the front door!" She said with an attitude. Jacob turned quickly as Danica slammed the door behind. A cushion of air blew passed him that caught him off guard causing him to stumble.

She brushed off his rude intrusion of personal space like he was her little brother. She dressed quickly and prepared for the journey to come. Putting her slender frame into blue jeans, then socks and boots, and a tanned colored t-shirt with a picture of a Barbie doll holding a machine gun. Then she wrapped her hair in a ponytail and grabbed her gloves and leatherjacket after using the bathroom. Her shadow cast a stunning reflection down the hall yet went unnoticed for those of a growing consideration weren't around to view such a girl.

Jacob sat up when hearing a back bedroom door closing. Danica made her presence known. It wouldn't take her but a few minutes to meet the day head on. She rolled her eyes and looked toward Jacob. She wasn't amused by his ill-timed conduct. She looked past him and went straightway to the kitchen and retrieved a few items of necessity. She filled a backpack with water and food. She grabbed a pack of matches, a box of granola bars, some beef jerky, a couple of pears, two apples, and sunflower seeds from a top shelf. She looked around for anything else that seemed appropriate for the trip to the other side of the planet. Then she went back to her bedroom to retrieve the healing-stones. She knew they always came in handy on certain occasions. They were a gift presented by the Aquerian fellowship when she first made rank of Circle leadership. Jacob watched her silently with a besotted expression on his face. Suddenly, she jetted from the back bedroom to make her way back to the front of the house. She turned and glared in his direction. "Come on—we don't have much time before we're found out!"

Jacob shot up from the chair and looked at her, and then quickly followed after. Then he thought of what he'd been doing just before knocking on her bedroom window.

"The hovercraft is prepped and ready to go." He said. "Everyone is there except Ismael and his little brother, Amen. I assume Ismael is dealing with his little brother, at the moment because no one has seen him." Danica turned her eyes quickly in a flash.

"And you assume his brother is keeping him from being here on time and ready?"

"I don't know. I think he might have had some trouble…you know how Amen is sometimes…"

Danica whipped her head back in a parallel gaze and pushed her lips toward their corners.

"I knew he wouldn't be able to convince him to stay home! I should have handled this myself." Jacob wondered if Danica would have a problem with leaving Amen behind.

"We should take him with us." She said. "Besides he's one of us. Just because he's not ready doesn't mean we should leave him home on his own. He feels the rejection you guys keep feeding him. It's not right." Danica said. "And beside he's, my responsibility. He's going with us." She flashed her eyes Jacob's way before continuing. "Isn't that what Dr. Zimmerman mentioned?" She turned to look at Jacob straight on while stopping on the street corner. Jacob's face had flushed a slight crimson color. He knew she was right.

"Yes, I see your point—but he's still too young to do what the bigger kids get to do, and way too small to have any effect on…" losing his words. "Well, he's always getting into trouble. It's bad enough that he and his brother are always fighting." Jacob paused to look into Danica's eyes. "They can never settle on making the right decisions. And their dad…he's kind of left field in his way of thinking…lacking common sense, and always missing from the scene when needed."

"Yes, I know what you're saying, but he's still one of us." She turned to view his expression. "You guys need to start excepting him for who he is. Not judging him by what his father does or says. Give him time to grow…he'll be there soon enough."

Jacob saw the flare of anger in her eyes as she quickly responded. "I'm sure his father wouldn't want us to leave him behind either. He's a big responsibility I know…he just needs our understanding and support," then suddenly stopping her train of thought. Danica's expression showed a look of worry as she moved toward the light up ahead.

Jacob had a serious wrinkle cross his forehead when thinking of the youngest of members.

"This place makes us who we are," Jacob said, "and nothing is going to take that from us. I've had my reasons to feel the way that I do about what is to come ahead of us and have prepared as the others…but Amen sees everything as a game. He doesn't take anything serious."

Danica looked over. "And that gives you the right to cast a child's earned blood-right to the wind." She waited for a response, but none was given. "Our enemy to come has been trained by a different type of soldier that we could only imagine. You can't compare your measly few years of training against those of a heavenly host." Jacob's eyes watched her every move as she talked. "We have no right to pick or choose between us, who'd be right to face an enemy we haven't begun to imagine." She said, "Don't you get it? We don't stand a chance against those fallen of that other world, unless we stand together as a unit." Danica looked parallel of her vision showing a touch of doubt in her eyes. "Your age shows your lack of wisdom, Jacob. Don't you see…your own demise is in thinking in such a manner leaving the youngest behind is not right—it's even written in your eyes that you are not ready to meet an end still not comprehended of a turning of factors, for we are just ponds in this game of chance. We pick and choose the right movement as a team…not anything less." She looked to get an opinion before finishing, "for what reason are you so willing to leave this Circle short of its members, when we were specifically chosen as a group of seven, not six or five or eight, but seven? We go as a team, or we don't go at all. Tell me what group is efficient enough to face an army of seven hundred thousand legions! Who will lift their sword toward the heavens and shout out victory before its time? No tomorrow is promised by making changes to our group at our own disposal. Keep your head when visualizing this Circle of friends, and not wandering aimlessly on blind ambitions. What worthy blind ambition do you have Jacob, tell me? And I'll free you to do what you will…if not," she suggested, "Then hold your tongue! And do as I tell you to do!" with a flash of indifference in her eyes she continued her walk towards the next streetlamp.

Jacob looked at Danica with astonishment. He raised his eyebrows for a brief moment, and then clicked his fingers together like a light had just turned on.

"The Conquerites!" he yelled while trying to keep pace. "They can stand against them! They're a force to be reckoned with," Jacob caught her eyes moving from him to the view in front, "my father has always said, they were from a time and a place only imagined in our dreams." A flicker of courage was seen in Jacob's eyes. "I'm sure those Immortal's will lead the battle of all battles. Maybe not just three of them, but a host could do it!"

Danica rolled her eyes back towards Jacob, "And who's to be the one that gathers such a host in the heavens?"

Jacob got this misaligned look in his eyes. He crossed her parallel gaze of wonder. "Well, the Indian princess might have a say in this." He said, "She'll stand up to them if need be."

Danica understood him quoting from a father's ambitions and not so much of his own. She didn't know what to say about his comments. They were beyond any acknowledgment she understood at the moment, for they were young of heart and only measured as children. Even though from an elite type of human never imagined, but their numbers were but a few. It had been so long from the time since seeing the Indian princess, and not knowing what she would commit too. She wondered. Would she drop all things of importance and shoot across to some distant world to bail them out of their future miseries?

In the short distance of fifty feet, she saw the hovercraft—hidden in shadows behind the last building, fronting the shuttle port. It was a good mile walk from her house, and Jacob lived only across the street from her, which made it convenient to knock on her door, or window from his perspective. Danica thought of the words Jacob said. She knew he was partially right, but to what part she didn't know and left it for another time. Even though they were light-years away from earth standing as a flicker of light in the universe, she knew there was purpose of being here. That was something yet to learn of the near future. Because of their lack of years and experience they would have to learn to be patient. Something began to stir in the young leader's heart as she carefully thought of all the children connected to her, by words, and deeds, and commitments taught of her parents. Life at times reflected chaos, even if only in her mind, she needed to get control of her new way of thinking. She also wondered if she'd have any luck at finding those that had once been lost. There were no promises written anywhere where she knew to find stability of mind—except from the professor, he'd know what to do from his many years of experience. She had to seek after his guidance on many a day.

Too many questions, too many thoughts clogged her mind that early morning about this trip to come. Danica pushed down a lump in the back of her throat. She thought of the loss of life when facing an over-powering enemy, without first considering Jacob's faithful words. Twenty feet ahead she saw Ismael standing with the others. Jacob and she came closer and noticed they were all there except for the smaller of brother's, Amen. She wondered what had happened to him. Danica's heart was pounding by then as she came within an earshot of the others. Sweat already beading on the back of her neck. Her expression seemed a bit strange to the others as she tried to change her way of thinking, by gracing their presence with a smile, yet nothing seemed to faze them at the moment. She felt heavy of heart and lacking in wisdom. Danica needed a good dose of Dr. Zimmerman's prodding. As her teacher, he would push her along to build her confidence. He would have her best interests at heart, even though he'd expel a bit of trepidation while getting his point across. She needed his advice and strength as a leader almost weekly.

"Is everything ready as planned?" She asked.

Ismael's eyes met with their leaders. "Yes, everything is prepared as we discussed from earlier...it's just I don't know where Amen ran off to, and I thought maybe you two might have seen him? There was no sign of him at the house, and my dad said not to leave him alone for any reason, and I'm at a loss of what to do."

"Never mind about him at the moment." as she looked toward the gear.

Danica trusted no one in packing. She knew they your prone to forget something important along the way. She turned with a glared greeting. "You need to find him before we take off on this trip and check your list again before we leave." She paused to make eye contact with Ismael, "make sure everything is right."

"I told you everything was ready to go!" Ismael said.

Suddenly a force of Aquerian soldiers turned on lights and filled in space around them. From above, the captain's first officer and crew held guns on the small group of circle members who looked like they were caught.

"Where do you think you're going with that Hovercraft?" The first officer barked out.

Ismael responded quickly to the question. "Well...our parents are lost—nobody has heard from them in over a week, and we sense something is aloft...so we were thinking of taking a look. Well...only if you bright gentlemen don't mind us borrowing it, besides there's two more at your disposal right over there."

Most of the Aquerian soldiers were caught off guard by his words and looked in the other direction, which gave Ismael a small window of opportunity to take advantage. With a wave of his hand, using his gift he pushed all the soldiers back relieving them of their weapons. Danica turned around quickly, surprised by the sudden take over.

"Why do you always do that at the most uneventful time? There never going to trust us if you keep doing that!"

Ismael turned around to glance at their misinformed leader. "You have a quicker way—if so, I'd love to hear it," he said while raising a hand.

Danica mimicked him. "No, I don't, but can you warn me before acting on a whim!"

"There wasn't time." Ismael barked out.

Argon picked up one of the weapons and waved the soldiers to get up and move toward a utility shed just off to their left. Tory, being the oldest, left the children to child's play while she viewed a screen in front of her, showing a three-dimensional graph of the terrain just past the cities borders going east. Tory questioned if this was a good idea after all, leaving the confines of a protected city, out into no man's land without knowing what's out there, without knowing they could end up in the same boat as their parents. Jacob stayed quiet, since he had already been bested by their leader. Argon points with the barrel end of the gun.

"Get in—don't make me tell you twice!" He said, "I might do something you would regret later." The five soldiers moved as they were told towards the utility shed. Argon locked the door behind. All the members finished loading up the hovercraft. They slowly made it out of the shuttle port with their lights off in some type of stealth mode. They had altogether forgotten about Amen when distracted by the Aquerian soldiers, and left in a hurry, leaving the little scoundrel behind.

Ten minutes later, they came to the edge of the barrier where Danica and the rest saw the sun making its way up from the lower end of the eastern sky. Suddenly from above, rose a giant shadow startling the others.

"What the…Condac, it's you!"

Danica's heart was pounding for the second time that morning. Her stare, seeing the beast above had startled her, knowing they were in for a thrill with the watcher and his local transportation taking to the sky.

I have to learn to relax like my dad mentioned I can't take much more of this. She thought. Condac shot past them on his Condorsorous.

They kept steady as the giant bird veered past them and landed just in front. Tory lowered the hovercraft and Danica got out. Condac got down and looked at her with a smile. He was ready for a trip of a lifetime, doing his usual by leaning towards testing the weather before traveling, grabbing the dirt and releasing it in the air. Somehow, he'd find the right weather patterns by stirring a few grains of soil together between his fingertips, possibly giving him a clue about what they were in store for. This was a bit primitive, from the others perspective, as they looked back at each other. The tall, green and purple, one-eyed watcher had his way of doing that which looked a bit confusing, far from any normal way of acting as a leader of his kind.

Argon spoke in sync of the watcher's productions of the weatherman. "You sure he knows what his doing?" as Argon stood at Danica's right shoulder. He looked up past the scene while scratching the back of his head. Not giving anyone else time to respond. "Besides, he only has one good eye, where's his depth perception? I can't figure how he can tell the weather by doing that."

Jacob glared at the boy with too many opinions. "Shhhh—he understands what you're saying. Don't be so obvious!"

The watcher turned while shaking his head. He then looked over at Danica. She understood the look. "You boys be quiet, before he leaves you behind!"

"I'm only stating the obvious—he does only have one good eye. Maybe he was in a bad accident and both his eyes got slammed together." Ismael giggled; Danica rolled her eyes. Jacob stared unaffected by the little tussle of words, and Tory was showing Renee something on the screen in front of her.

Danica stepped back into the conversation. "Why is it that every time we need to be somewhere, you can't stay focused?"

Argon's face seemed offended. "And what would that be boss." He said with a pushed out cheesy grin. Danica used her gift to move through a door and came out on top of Argon slamming his body to the floor of the hovercraft.

"Keep it up lug-head and I'll strap you to the back of that smelly creature above us, and you can deal with the dismal flies!"

Argon pulled back quickly knowing Danica had gotten the better of him.

"Dude—lighten-up!" he said, "I was just messin around! Hey man—sorry for the party foul!"

Argon held his hands up in surrender as he lay breached before her.

Danica's face turned sour. "Don't you ever take anything serious, is everything a joke to you?"

Argon displayed a set of wrinkles deeply in the contours of his face, and a dismal look twinkled in his eyes. "I'm serious, what's your problem—I was joking!"

Ismael reached for Danica's shoulder. "Hey, you know how the little screwball is, he's always messing around. Argon, tell her you're sorry!"

The teenage travesty looked confused. "What—it was a joke?"

"Tell her!!! You little twit, before she straps you to the beast!"

The Condorsorous squawks real loud as if he understood. Argon still confused.

"Okay—what-ever man—I'm sorry, okay! Would you let me up now?"

Danica still showing a furious expression helped him to his feet and brushed him off. "I should have locked you into that utility shed with those mutations."

Amen popped his head up from underneath one of the trap doors in the floor. "Hey, stutter brains, who you are calling mutations!"

Danica looked surprised. "What are you doing here squirt—you weren't supposed to be here?"

Amen looked insulted. "Why not—I'm as much a part of this group as anyone else, aren't I Ismael?" Amen turned to look at older brother for moral support.

Ismael cast a depressing look toward little brother. "Look, I told you this trip was only for the bigger kids! But you never listen to big brother—do you?"

Danica shook her head. "No wonder my dad said we're not ready. We're a bunch of freaka-zoids!"

Amen stares down their leader. "Who are you calling freaka-zoids?"

Ismael grabbed his little brother's shoulders and pulled him back. "Hey, little man, put on your brakes—we all need to just calm down!"

Danica couldn't believe their disconnections, while looking at the little soldier with the green-beret uniform on, and a cap almost covering his eyes. She gave a half whimsical smile and grabbed him by the back of the neck. "Like the uniform…Skippy."

Amen lost the smile. "Don't tell me you're going to call me that dreadful name too!"

"That's it," Amen said, "I'm going to be a deserter."

Argon looked his direction and smiled. "Daddy's little soldier wants to kick some butt."

Everyone turned suddenly and looked at Amen's attire. "I'm not daddy's little soldier…freaka-zoids…you're trippin." Amen said.

Danica was sorry she used the word. Everyone laughed, even Amen showed a little smile of comprehension. "You guys are in big trouble if not focused. I'm ready to fight…that's just the way it's going to be." Amen raised his eyes further to see past the baseball cap. "I might even try some harsh language on those blackened winged creatures that seem to come uninvited."

Danica wondered where that had come from. "You better not…I'll drape your tongue with hot sauce…if you do. And you better let us worry about what comes from the sky."

Amen looked over at brother to have his back.

Ismael put his hand on little brother's head. "Look squirt, we're just looking for our parents, it's a search and rescue operation, and nothing else. We're not killing anything on this trip. Besides we're not wearing spacesuits. We're only going to the other side of the planet, not into deep space."

Amen scratched his lip as he looked up beyond the vision of his cap. "Are there any more bugs on this hunt, or are we going to be invaded by some more aliens with green blood?"

Ismael shook his head and cast a dismal stare out of the hovercraft.

"Hey squirt—where did you hear that mumbo-jumbo from?"

Amen looked up like he was confused. "Dad said there are others out there like us."

Ismael squinted an inflection, "And you believe him?"

Amen still looked confused. "Well, have you looked in a mirror lately? If you think the thing in the mirror looks normal you must be smoking that bad weed dad found in the forest—you know that stuff that makes the animals lay around looking all drugged up."

Ismael's eyes narrowed. "Who's been talking to you squirt, that's a bunch of nonsense?"

"Dad said the Aquerae have been cutting that stuff out of the forest floor, because it numbs the senses, and makes you see all funny and stuff. They don't think we know about it but we do."

Danica turned around quickly toward older brother. "Sounds like you have left little brother unattended."

Ismael looked offended. "Watch him!! He's out of control—no mom and dad around—not my job to take on parenting! No thank you, —besides he's a big-boy! He knows better than to screw-up. He does it all on his own, with or without my approval."

"Then whose job is it to watch little brother, if big brother doesn't have his back?"

They all caught the gist of their leader. Ismael tried to defend himself. "Hey man, I can't be everywhere for the weasel. He doesn't listen to me anyhow! He thinks he's that cowboy dad use to talk about…what's his name Skippy?"

Amen's face turned sour. "Don't call me that! I've told you before, and his name is John Wayne. He's from eons ago, not even from our planet. Dad's the one who tries to imitate the red neck from a place called the Rio Grande, somewhere in Texas, I think. He was big, tall, and bow-legged from riding too many horses. And wore six-shooters and talked really funny."

Amen looked up through the army cap that was pulled too low blocking his view.

"Besides I'm one of you guys, and mom told you not to leave me alone."

Amen shoved Ismael lightly. He was offended that big brother would leave him behind, unsupervised.

Big brother showed a frown. "Sorry Skippy—I just didn't think it would be safe for you to go with us."

Amen's face lit up with a sour note of deluged anger. "I said don't call me that—my names not Skippy, its Amen—got it!!"

Amen punched big brother methodically in the chest.

Danica stepped in between the little scuffle. "You guys need to sit down and buckle-up. This isn't some pleasure cruise, most likely our parents have run into a snag, and we need to cover their backs. I'm not babysitting you Amen, so if you don't want to be hog tied and kept in that storage container, I'd advise you to sit down and shut up before I get mad!"

Amen's face showed a hint of hurt, but to keep from causing more due harm to his delicate ego he did as he was told, while the hovercraft took off through the early morning fog.

The Condorsorous trailed behind just on their shoulder. The air was cooler than usual for this time of year, considering it was late fall and the weather patterns were beginning to change with the season. Danica could see clouds slowly moving in from the north, and the sky had a slight purplish color to it that appeared normal as the sun began to rise. The hovercraft clipped along at a pretty good speed of a hundred and fifty kilometers an hour, just to make pace with the giant bird that remained alongside. Condac took the Condorsorous higher than usual to get a better view of what was up ahead. He had sensed something building from what he could tell and took the lead to shed some light from the coming condition. They were crossing over some mountain range they'd never seen before. It was a stunning view of this uncharted land that rose above the present landscape painting a rapturous picture of pre-dawn light. The hovercraft had a glass bubbled top that covered them from the exposed colder air that hit the surface of the craft. Each member seated comfortably, warm and cozy as the heat pushed through the cab. Each member was strapped in and ready to go. Amen took to playing with a video game that he brought along with him. Tory, up until now, had been speechless. She was reading the view finder, trying to map out the right direction they had to go. She could see a three-dimensional graph showing hills and valleys as moving terrain on her video scope, showing the dimensions and layout of each stage of progression. She was pushing buttons and setting parameters that seemed foreign to most of her team, but to her it was like riding in her first hovercraft—not for a simple-minded person, yet not to complicated either. The first leg of this trip would take them about six hundred miles from where they had first started. The land there would be much the same, forest, mountains, and possibly some snow from higher elevations, and lower lying grasslands in the valleys of rolling hills.

The Aquerae nation wasn't too keen about the humans taking off into these uncharted territories, without escorts of the Aquerae pointing them in the right direction. Since most of this land was not without dangers, they had to be constantly scrutinized. Danica was staring out into the distance, while flashing memories crossed her mind. Her heart had finally settled to a normal beat after dealing with her dysfunctional crew. She was thinking of her parents, worried that something went wrong with the hovercraft they were in, and maybe her father was hurt or something worse. She considered worst without really knowing anything. Maybe they had lost their abilities to use their gifts, similar to being cut off in the dead-zone.

Suddenly, rolling clouds up ahead caused Tory to slow down, she wasn't quite sure what she was seeing. A bizarre weather phenomenon was filling up the sky. From her angle of view, it was prolific in form. Usually, mysteries of a scintillating kind were left for the adults to deal with, but now this was their problem. They had to do something. Danica looked over and noticed the puzzled look on Tory's face. "Can you avoid that?"

"No, I don't think so…it's pulling us along."

Danica knew her father and mother had taken a journey past the point of making any sense. No communications, no warnings that they were trapped somewhere, or facing some unknown predator. They lay somewhere between four to five thousand kilometers away, according to the bleep on the video screen. Tory was tracking their GPS. It bounced off one of six satellites orbiting the planet. Danica had heard the stories told of places seen by the Aquerae, to still be searched, not on any map they'd ever seen, set out past the borders of this unnatural world they lived in. Too far away from home was her train of thought. She was just a baby back then, who had been thrown into the heat of chaos, remembering doomsday from several newspaper clippings. Death of a planet wasn't anything they'd ever wanted to happen. She knew that other world left behind was spinning out of control. Now the memories had followed them to this new place, where a small group of members had gathered to find a new life, the last bit of hope remaining was here now, not somewhere else so far away. Only a flicker of light showed in the distance of memories. Danica had a lump of emotion rise up in the back of her throat. She held it back, thinking, showing weakness in front of the others would set a bad example. She had to be strong where they were weak. She had to get a hold of herself. Danica's mind was racing. Wondering if there were others like her parents. Looking for new discoveries that would help improve their world—by searching their own worlds, hiding in the mountains, or some hollowed out place far away from here, maybe living on one of the many moons of the bigger planets, or surviving somehow on one of the many hot Jupiter's. She wanted to stand up and scream at the top of her lungs, but then the others would hear her and not understand. Most of them were too young to know about misconceptions of living a full life without love, without sharing your soul to another. Only Tory, being the oldest might understand, knowing memories of her father left behind were a blur. They had been protected from the confusion left back on earth. They had broken part of the covenant by leaving without permission. Danica was beyond the point of leaving her parents behind in the dust to settle from a week passed since. She understood more than the Aquerae knew. She always felt this home to be temporary, not being able to explain what that meant to her. How she was going to figure that part of her life out was still a mystery. Tory turned to look at her. Danica was staring aimlessly in the sky beyond, in a direction she couldn't go, far away in memory, was the look. Tory sensed her stressed, under classed, living on the short end of making the grade, and definitely not inside the hovercraft—comprehending her disconnection. Everyone else in this group of misfits were left to their own devices. They were still too young minded and only seen as children by their parents.

Suddenly, Tory and Danica noted with widened eyes an opening in the clouds ahead. The sky in front parted above them and a celestial trail of clouds billowed around taking them by force. It pulled them toward a whirlwind of a building mass, creating a magnetic wind-tunnel. This form grabbed the hovercraft and wouldn't let go. The Condorsorous was pulled along behind without having a choice of direction. They spun forward into madness. Danica yelled out.

"Hold on—something's taking us!"

3

The Great-Gulf

Danica, once awakened, blinked to bring focus her surroundings. After realizing that everyone was still in the hovercraft and the Condorsorous was with the watcher just outside, she took a deep breath and let it out slow. She sensed something was different about where they were. The land was flat and without form, as if salt-flats or solid beds of a barren land, with jigsaw puzzled cracks of ground colored gray and black and spots of white. Even the colors of the inside of the hovercraft appeared to have changed. They were pulled through an alternate dimension, but they actually didn't go farther than just a few hundred miles from home. The area was void of any type of water, and there were no clouds or wind. It appeared they were enclosed inside a big sound-proof beaker from what she could tell, held as a specimen. She paused to take notice of the others, slowly showing signs of life and stirring about. Danica looked out of the bubbled window, and noticed the watcher had a look of bewilderment. Something was not right about this place that they had become a part of—pulled through a vortex of some type that towed them through the center of the planet, bringing them up on the other side of something that didn't quite look normal from anything ever experienced. Danica stood from where she was and opened the hatch of the hovercraft. She turned to face Renee, standing quickly behind the others.

"What do you see?" She asked Renee.

Renee still disoriented sensed the impossible had happened. Blinking to gather her thoughts from what flashed before her at that very moment, trying to find some reason that made any sense. Then Danica repeats herself. "Renee…what do you see?"

Renee's mind flashed of visions she'd never thought of before. "It's hard to explain. It doesn't look like anything I've ever experienced—well not of anything my mind could comprehend as being a normal world. This place is not of here, I mean it's not what's supposed to be here."

"You're not making any sense!" Danica said.

Then Amen stepped up to blurt out an answer. "This place has no history." He said, without showing any doubt about his statement. Everyone turned to look at their smallest of members.

Then Danica focus on Amen. "What do you mean squirt?"

"No one has ever lived here."

Their leader was curious why the half Aquerian, half human boy, would bring to words this misconception of reality. "So, what's that mean Amen?"

"Well, my sense of smell tells me others had passed through here as we have, but there gone now—I mean someone left vague imprints behind, but there not here anymore."

Argon spoke up. "Tell us something we don't already know Skippy."

Amen gave Argon a murky expression. "I don't hear anything coming from you meathead, so, if you don't like what I have to say you can take a walk—and by the way…good luck with the walk! We're in the middle of nowhere."

Argon stepped forward maybe to hit the little scoundrel yet big brother stepped up to the plate.

"Not so fast Juwantabe. He's half your size, and besides he's my brother." A flicker of anger crossed the boy's face.

"What's up with the name calling?" Danica said, while turning her attention back to the subject at hand. "What else could you tell about this place Amen?"

Amen reached up and scratched his top lip before answering. "Well, as you all know, I and my brother have other gifts that you inflexible meatheads don't know anything about. We see what the watchers see, but the watchers say that the younger minds are more perceptible at seeing what truly is—I mean through the trickeries of this place."

Danica moved closer to the seventh member to get a fix on his eyes. "And what are the trickeries of this place, Amen?"

"Well, it's meant to confuse—it's not real."

Argon shook his head. "Ha fewy…we're supposed to believe this mumbo-jumbo!"

Amen whipped his head back in Argon's direction while narrowing his eyes. "I don't care what you believe meat-head—you're too dumb to understand me, then just keep quiet and the others will explain when I'm done."

Argon's face turned hostile. "Watch it Skippy or I'll turn you into peanut-butter!"

Danica wrinkled her brow. "Shut-up Argon or I'll be the one doing the hitting—just let him talk, for God's sake!"

Amen looked up at their fearless leader with a smile and a new step in his rhythm that none of the others had. "Anyhow," Amen said, "since I was so rudely interrupted by mister trigger happy over here. This place is like what Dr. Zimmerman and our parents experienced—that place that changes."

Danica knew of this place. "You mean that place they called the Great-Gulf?"

Amen turned suddenly to her understanding and responded, "Yeah, that's the place." He said.

Danica wrinkled her brow with an expression of worry. "That false place where light doesn't dwell, where darkness rules the ones that live there."

Amen shook his head showing a hesitation of doubt in his eyes. "Yes, it's where the living aren't allowed to go…" Amen looked up without finishing.

"Why is it like that?" Danica asked.

"Well, every world has a place where the darkness lives. Light can't dwell here—I mean only the wandering dead live here because no light is in them. Their soul is given as payment. They live in a way not understood by the living. There's no going back once coming here."

Argon interrupts again, "And that means?"

"It's a place for the dead douphus—not peoples like us!"

Danica filled in the rest. "The Great-Gulf is for the future trespassers who don't go where the rest of us will go."

Argon got a grin and a sparkle in his eye. "Oh, so there's normal people like us involved."

Everyone turned suddenly toward the talkative boy. "Argon, shut-up!" Everyone said.

Argon lost the dimming sparkle and the grin. "So how do we get out of here without disturbing the dead?"

Danica's eyes fixed on the boy who couldn't hold his tongue. Tory stepped forward and gave of her opinion. "Look for clues," She said. "Everyone leaves footprints or some evidence that they were here— broken branches, trash left behind, or personal belongs now missing."

Argon interludes again, "And that's your answer of how to get out of here?"

Tory turned with a smug look on her face, "You have any brighter ideas. Then tell us. Otherwise keep your mouth shut. You shouldn't even be talking Argon." Amen reached up and flicked the back of Argon's ear. He felt the instant sting of pain and turned about. Amen pretends to look the other way, like he had no part in the flicker of pain. Argon narrowed his eyes.

"I know it was you Skippy…don't try to hide it."

Amen smiled before speaking in Tory's defense. "Try shooting your way-out lug-nut that's what you're good at."

"Not a bad idea Skippy. I might just do that."

Jacob spoke for the first time since starting this trip. "Argon, you're not helping things."

Argon's face turned hard. "And you are?"

"Stop it!!! All of you, we need to focus, and not point fingers at everyone!"

Danica starts barking orders. "Tory, go get your gear, and pull a map up on your screen, any map, Ismael, see if you can make sense out of what's in the watchers mind. Renee, try to find out where the other's went too, Argon no more talking, get the gear out below from the hovercraft, food, water, weapons, we're going to see what's in this place before we leave. Amen, you stay with me; you're the only one that's made any sense about this place so far."

Amen got a big kick out of Danica taking charge. "Yep, yep…my girl, you're making all the big boys' look like wieners!"

Argon cast a drab stare toward Amen.

Jacob interludes… "Enough of the chit-chat—there's got to be a way out of here, let's get a move on, before we become stuck here permanently!"

Ismael looked at Jacob with a halfhearted chuckle. "Amen brother, I hear ya!"

Little brother held an unsure look toward the older, "Not funny—ish."

Tory broke out her little satchel of pleasures. She had dusting powers, some type of gizmo for measure tremors. She had a beaker to measure salinity in water or sulfur for volcanoes, and an ambient tuning fork to measure depth and height. And something that measures pressure readings. Noting, all her instruments were in miniature form. Tory started looking for footprints and put a mask on that changed colors to see heat-prints or previous clues while using these night-vision goggles to assist her.

Remote by what they could tell, and full of trickeries as Amen had suggested, not visible to the human-eye when looking from their point of view. Danica signaled for everyone to get closer, as the Condorsorous and the watcher nudged their way in. She took each member through a door and came out fronting this towering mountain. Amen saw it as an allusion. The air was claustrophobic and stifling to breathe in. Confusion along with hesitation set in their stance brought anxiety to each member. Yet the watcher and Condorsorous were not fazed by the allusion of its draw. The warriors of this place understood from visions of an altered dimension would change with time and patients. The mountain was full of holes or cave like catacombs. From the middle of the mountain and up to the top where holes left to mystery. They looked like a way into Danica. Tory thought the same thing.

Renee grabbed at Danica's shoulder. "Don't go there…" while pulling their leader back.

Danica turned to view her disapproval. "Why not—the mountain is the way to the other side?"

Renee shook her head with a baffling stare. "We need to go around. It's a place of deceptions. There's no way out once you enter."

"How do you know that?" Danica asked.

Renee glanced up with widened eyes as fear began to show her a clearer path. "This place was meant to entrap those who come here. Something felt internally." She said.

Danica's eyes widened as she took another look. "We're going over it then."

Renee's face lit up, "What?"

"We're going over it!" Danica repeated.

Argon interrupts. "And how do you think we're to do that? We left the hovercraft back there behind us," as he looked back over his shoulder giving direction of the trail behind them.

Amen turned to meet Argon's glance from underneath his military cap. "We're hitchin a ride on Big-bird along with the one-eye watcher, lug-nut—how else!"

Argon raised an eyebrow. "Oh, I forgot about that smelling creature who came to assist."

Amen leaned in and whispered in his ear. "It's okay, that's why I'm here."

Danica's face grew a smile. "Okay guys, this is not a game of wits. Let's not delay any longer. We need to get a move on."

The Condorsorous took Danica's verbal sign dropped one wing for each member to climb aboard. Argon had a bit of hesitation in his eyes as he looked back at their leader before climbing up. It didn't have the appearance of being a comfortable ride, from his point of view, yet he followed after. Once being seated, Danica's mind began to wander of her years of youth. Reminiscing about these degenerates surrounding her, how she'd learn to find the beauty through the pain of training, gaining strength from her teachers and mentors from the many hours of testing. Everything surrounding her life had been hard fought to achieve on a physical level. This was a world of constant changes, in weather, in new developments, and the environment was never the same on any given day. Danger was always peaked around every corner, waiting to pull each member off guard. Change was something they all had to adjust too. She grew into a focused warrior, maneuvered by the best, leaving nothing to chance. She was a leader like no other, as she would learn to stand up for the others no matter the circumstance. She had a calm inviolability of what a good life was truly about, it involved these young members as a natural part of her everyday life. She had lived and breathed in air and reprimanded each member of her adamant crew, to draw them back on the right track of doing what they had to do. She felt free to love them, and took care of their misguided youthful thoughts, never feeling the loss of friendship or lacking in resources, because they were usually behind the walls of their little community. Yet closely guarded by an Aquerian fellowship. Now, they were learning of a world set apart from their own, disconnected from what they'd known to be a normal way of life, especially in this place of the dead. They were striking out on their own without permission from their Aquerian fellowship. Luxuries of comfort wouldn't always be there when expected, she'd come to realize they were gaining experience one day at a time. They could meet their end at any moment, as spoken of by her mentors. Danica sensed their life's were about to make a drastic turn, yet what direction that would be was still a mystery. Life was unpredictable. It was the everyday events that helped her find the joy in living each moment given that made the difference. The effort had to come from her desire to get up every morning and take part of each member's lives. She was the catalyst of changing their future. And noting, they were prepared by the best, had daily moments of sharing, while being committed to their little community. Danica, given so much already—now missing her parents for the last four weeks had taken its toll. It was time for her to give back. She looked back at the others, before smelling that winged beast take to flight in the air. She wondered what was ahead of them. She knew they had to stick together as a unit. They were like brothers and sisters bonded together by this unnatural setting. They were getting ready to be tested as she looked in route for the unnatural light from the sky.

The Condorsorous took to the air on wings of strength taking them higher. An unyielding presence seemed to surround them within seconds. They were sensing hesitation, wanting to pull back and go the other way, but somehow, they all knew that would never happen. They were a Circle of members clinging to their last bits of protection left behind of their community. And hanging on tight as this beast rose above the obscure mountains in front, taking them towards the other side. There were no visual references showing them where to go, no flashing of city lights to point the way, just their indomitable will, and this creature pressing them onward to unfamiliarity. A defused life of another time was Danica's reasoning to keep on moving, to find those answers needed for them to be free. Glancing at the leader of watchers, Danica noticed he appeared unconcerned of direction or what they might run in too. He stayed calm and collected, held together by years of experience, showed maybe as battle scars from other events, while taking in stride what would come next. He was embedded with character, not moved by the waves of difficult circumstances. The watcher was sitting tall on the back of this beast ready to face an enemy. From above, the air felt thick and musty, overpowering. The watcher showed an exoneration of skills ignoring what seemed to be just in front and concentrated on the mark that came after—finding parents, finding friends, and defending those that were vulnerable to the elements of a darkened world.

Amen blinked to draw focus of something ahead not seen by the others but sensed by what he could smell. Since sitting directly in front, he had a birds-eye view of what was ahead. Yet an internal gift of his signaled back that there was more than what the eye could see or understand. The expression on his face seemed to change with each passing moment. It looked like he was watching a Godzilla movie in 3D, each turn building on bigger moments to come, each burst of energy leading to the next. Renee could see this in her mind just seconds before. Amen points to a moving dark area just up ahead. The watcher understood this new direction with Amen's mental connection. The Condorsorous followed along the watcher's guiding nudge of mentality. Amen was paying attention on what was just in front, settling among moving colors prolific of form. It felt vague and unclear of making sense to a boy trusting of leaders in showing the right direction to go. Each member remained composed for the moment. They could see a massive lake blurred in roiling movement, lacking color, lacking a clear picture what might be beneath this void, lying to the east. Suddenly, standing in hidden shadows was an image slowly appearing of mass cloaked in roiling colors unaware of their presence until now, while moving in a direction of the water's edge. This image glided off the top of the water like a slow-moving fog. The mass was coming from the depths of churning water of graying colors causing confusion to the natural sight of human eyes. The shape swirled into existence from the void of the deep, completing something unexplained of a natural world. Light did not dwell in this place for darkness was its master to perform in the presence of others, to confuse, to disconnect those watching a performance of the deep while leaving each member exposed to this new experience. For what came from the deep was the master of deceptions soon to see. It was not recognized of being of their world or any other that made any sense. Each member had come to know light by its brilliance, yet the light of this place was unnatural. It was an illusion expressed without reason, for it was not of this earth or of a world that others would view to comprehend. Whatever it was Amen understood it as trickery. From words of a younger mind. A false representation of a physical world didn't make sense to a boy once lost when finding his way on this more than stranger particular day, not mentioned or jotted on anyone's eternal calendar for future reference. Yet Amen wasn't held to rules governing the deep. He was moved by skills held by a deeper meaning. None of them recognized this thing being of the human species or otherwise of a physical presence, as it was an ongoing mystery. It wore a noisome coat of mixing colors followed by smoke swirling behind. Amen reached up and covered his nose and mouth, because the smell was lucid. The coat was like the bodies of the dead sown together to complete it, covered by objects held in mystery. The eyes and face of a master could not be known in this coat that completed it. No hands or feet or eyes of a face could be registered of any life being a part of him or she or it. It was a product of the dead that completed its meaning. The Condorsorous pulled up short and landed just in front of this misleading lake and reared back when feeling the presence of something evil that couldn't be comprehended. The Condorsorous backed up to give way to space and respect for something that overwhelmed his senses. This was a place where the eyes of the living were deceived of a shapeless face for confusion was its draw. The presence was held to a greater esteem of this darker world held to a greater purpose beyond deception. It was a presence that involved dismemberment of the physical world, becoming eaters of souls appeared to be its purpose. Most of these young warriors had never faced the unexplained, for it was an apparition not connected to their world, but only a part of the dead that couldn't be explained with simple words from sight not of vision, because vision was only understood by the leaders of this world. They were bewildered in its company. They stood speechless while looking on.

Danica, being there leader, held her head high to keep her focus forward and mind not to wandering toward superstitions of the heart. The shadowy form moved forward by means to confront the others in defense, facing them with its back against the lake.

Danica spoke to this shadowy presence that stood before them. "Who are you, and what is your purpose here?"

The forming entity spoke with a voice not recognized as human, but a voice that would only be acknowledged by the inhabitable of such a place—it was a voice of liquidity that rolled and roiled like a disconnected song of the dead. No pitch was employed to perfect its meaning; a constant pushing of rhythm was set to explode. Each member looked wide eyed at each other and wanted to cover their ears from off key sounds, yet their leader stepped toward the darker image relaying this song of the dead to employ answers by this master of deception. He spoke.

"I am the master of this place, between the living and those that no longer exist. A place that sets a gulf between what was and what is and what will be. My purpose is to enlighten and give direction for those once lost can be found again beneath the waves," as he pointed towards the lake.

Danica looked confused by the answer received. She looked back at the others not knowing what to say. Amen turned to his brother to win his approval by a slight agitation of raised eyes. Ismael nodded his approval as if brothers of a deeper understanding would use their gifts.

"Don't listen to him!" Amen said. "His purpose is not what he says, his only purpose is to confuse."

"And who might you be little warrior?" The voice of the void asked.

Amen stood and removed his cap. He stood tall in attitude, even though the presence in front could quickly overwhelm them at any moment.

"I'm the seventh of seven of this Circle." He said. "I'm here to represent—for you know not the power of an all-powerful king, who dwells in a place not understood by your kind. So, you better stay cool Darth, or he'll sick his posse on you!"

Danica moved up on Amen and covered his mouth. Surprised, the seventh of seven jerked sideways from being startled.

"I've got it from here Amen. Good start though." She said showing a touch of nervous tension. Amen looked up at their leader and smiled, and then he raised his thumb.

Amen stepped back while big brother slapped hands as if words were the key to their dilemma. Danica's eyes drew focus on the entity representing many, as he took-up considerable space.

Danica broke in on revealing her purpose. "We're looking for others like us. They have left their prints in this place."

This creature of many appeared to see beyond the depths of normal sight.

"Why should we concern our affairs with you Oracles commissioned by a King?"

She was surprised that this creature of many spoke as if representing a legion and having knowledge beyond normal conditions of the human mind and heart.

Danica kept her poise and swallowed hard. "It's because of our King that I am commissioned to be here. My questions," she paused, "if answered truthfully…will bring such reward for this place…if answered correctly." She said it like to be in control.

"How can you say such words young human without the backing of a King?"

Danica looked with piercing eyes. "Don't be deceived old master from what the eye can see of sight is not weighed in that way alone, but also from vision. By the powers of heaven, we are commissioned to do the work of a king who sits in a seat of judgment. He holds the keys to this world and the next. We are commissioned by a greater calling that those of your world would never understand, for it is of this king that we breathe in air to do his work. He holds the fragile veil to all life of the living and those of before now of the dead."

This eerie presence remained silent to take in such words more deceiving than its own.

"If he's such a powerful King, why doesn't he present himself?"

Danica thought for minute before she answered, so that the few years of her experiences would expel her best representation. "My King is of such a great presence you could not endure the light or heat that radiates from his mere existence, for his sight alone would consume you and your host that represent this place. He uses his servants like what you see before you to do his work. In all humility, I wish not for him to use you as an example for what's to come. No mountain, no valley, no world orbiting a red-dwarf-star can contain the misery of what's to visit this place, if you disregard my words said so humbly."

The legion stood to pause another moment to consider her few words of wisdom. "And what would that be?" He asked.

Danica's eyes focused on this mass in front of her. She said slowly with emotion, trying not to draw their attention away. "I will give you the answers you seek, if you would do the same." She said. Suddenly, Danica thought of her uncle Randy. He had on several occasions used a term called 'a-ropa-dope,' hoping to elude this legion of lost souls in front. Randy had explained 'a-ropa-dope' to mean turning the tide on a difficult situation by letting it look like you held the more valuable information than those who appeared to hold the upper hand. After about two minutes the voice returned from the void, which seemed pressured to answer.

"Your father and his members are in a place where you have come to know in your heart young human. You and your group will be given passage to leave this place, if you give the answer to the question we seek."

Danica thought of asking another question, but she didn't want to turn the tides once again to this legion's advantage. She sensed more about their situation than first concurred, so she answered to what she thought to be the truth.

"What's coming is a greater force that the heavens above could ever hold. What's to come is as the sands of the sea in number. A force of brilliant light will take this place and bury inconceivable numbers of the dead, something never visualized by those of your kind. It will fill your void and suck the very life from this place. Your powers then will no longer be in control of this gulf between the living and the dead, but a king who sits in judgment will take this place and make it his own. He will make a new world of this place and destroy the one before."

The legion before her considered her statement briefly before returning an answer. "I will let you leave this place under one promise young oracle. Ask of your king to not let such a force come to this place, and I will always give aid to your service, from now, till the end of this place. I will look the other way when you pass by here again." The legion tossed something from under its coat that spiraled in the air and landed in Danica's hand. A golden coin with the markings of the dead would give her free passage from this place. "But others beware," said the voice of the void. "I will not be so lenient."

Danica looked into the face of the legion and only saw spiraling molten flames taking up space.

"I will promise to keep my word, and not let these creatures come here to take this place."

The legion pointed toward the West. "Then go and take your journey, and all will be well between us and this king who sits in judgment."

Danica turned and saw the hovercraft appear just behind them. Without saying another word, they loaded up the hovercraft as a group and left for the cryptic sky above them. The clouds in front opened up and prepared a path back to the living like this place was never here. Darkness and light mixed into tumultuous clouds that took them to the world of before. The watcher along with his Condorsorous followed behind. They spun forward into light and darkness would soon be left behind as two dissimilar worlds drifted apart. Fragments of a previous world faded and separated them to leave darkness behind while heading toward light. Twirling and twisting their way through the center of this magnetic hole of energy sparked with light. This tunnel swallowed them up and pulled them back through to the land of the living. Amen was turning a lighter color of green, which was usually not a good color for a half Aquerian boy to be. Usually this was a sign of discomfort while noting his normal color was blue. "I think I'm going to be sick!" Amen choked out. Danica tried to reach for him, but it was too late. Amen regurgitated what he had eaten from earlier, emptying out all over one of his closest member's. Argon looked at his acclaimed scuffle-buddy and yelled.

"Dude…you just yakked all over my new pants!"

Argon looked discussed, and then looked down at his brand-new pants and saw chunks of darker colors of something the boy ate earlier from a few hours back.

"What's that awful smell?" Argon belted out.

Amen looked up after great relief, "Well, I was going for cream-cheese, bagels, and chocolate," he said, showing a slight hesitation in his stance. Amen wiped his mouth with his sleeve and finished saying, "I was trying to make S'mores,' but I ran out of gram-crackers and marsh-mellow creme. I made a few substitutions. I don't think the onion creme cheese set so well on my stomach." Argon glanced up with a puzzled look as the hovercraft sat down on solid ground.

"You think so, Skippy! What am I supposed to do with my pants?"

Amen puzzled by the statement spit up more gruel. He had made a mess of the hover-craft floor.

"I don't know dude, maybe take them off?"

Like he was asking a question. Ismael looked for a rag to help clean up the mess. Danica's interest was drawn to where they had landed. They landed next to a beautiful lake of fresh water surrounded by rolling hills and timbering land. The air and colors turned normal and began to blend with this natural environment. There were birds of the air and white billowy clouds mounted high above in the sky. The land looked clean and new and fresh, as if the newness of this place was not yet known by the feet of man or beast or foul of the air, yet they were there to acknowledge this great wonder. The rolling hills were green and full of animals and insects, bumblebees were doing sorted chores of the day gathering their nectar. Accept these bumblebees were green in color, and much bigger than normal size bees that Danica had ever seen. She could feel freedom in the air once they departed the hovercraft. Above the brightening skies of the red-dwarf sun warmed her skin as it shone on her face, causing her to feel young and tender-of-heart as once thought reliving another day of past memories. Not too far, Danica could see what looked to be a country dirt road winding upside of a hill in front, trailing not too far while bringing back a similar day of memory. She was a little girl when she saw this same picture of previous days, but she wasn't quite sure if she'd ever been there for more than just of few minutes a time. Just enough to bring back the memory. It was more like something she dreamed when she was younger, now this same picture was returning to remind her of something of great importance, but at the moment she couldn't remember why she needed to be here. On her right shoulder, Argon was carrying a strange looking weapon that she'd never seen before, as all events of this day were strangely new and different. She wrinkled her forehead to draw focus. What was she actually seeing? And would there be consequences at the end of the day if she made the wrong choice or chose the wrong direction? Argon pointed the weapon toward a slowly moving mass of some type of animals grazing in a lower meadow. Yet they were still too far away to see what type of animals they were. And then, the land appeared as a richly uncharted world, except for the animals grazing in front. Jacob, standing on her left shoulder reached down and took Danica's hand. She felt his warm embrace but didn't pull from his grasp, because she knew for some reason, he felt what she had felt and didn't want her to face it alone. They looked down this unfamiliar road leading to who knows where. The road seemed to pull this Circle of members to a dissimilar way of thinking, like a beacon leading away to a better way of life. But was there a better life at the end of this road? Did it lead to a place of eternal rest? Would there be others like Jacob that would take her hand and welcome Danica to a promised land, maybe beyond the clouds into the heavens?

Then Jacob turned to glance at their leader. He smiled and squeezed her hand assuring her they were stronger together. "Are we going on?" He asked.

Danica squinted from the early morning sun trying to make out movement in the tops of the trees just beyond the first peak. She looked back quickly at Jacob.

"Yes, don't you think we should?" She said while feeling there to be dire circumstances to face if making the wrong choice.

"Well, yes, maybe?" Jacob responded.

"You can't be any clearer on your answer?" She asked.

Amen comes up quickly behind to draw her attention. "You sure there's no bugs on this search and rescue mission? I'm getting the feeling we shouldn't be here." Amen said. Everyone turned to look at him. Danica just realized that all of them were full of questions with no answers. This was a part of their journey, finding answers, making decisions that could possibly change their future. After stepping to the front of this present world they were in, she hesitated and looked back the way she had come. As Danica looked over her shoulder, the trail behind was one of darker colors and a world torn apart by years of wear and tear, and destruction of a battered life was left behind in memory. But she knew it wasn't her life she was seeing. It was someone else's. A world left behind was pictured in this young girl's heart, stirring her emotions. Danica couldn't make sense of what she was seeing. She was thrown off by the two dissimilar worlds, yet something else was missing from what she saw going both directions. Then it hit her. She had to use her heart to choose the right direction, not by sight, but intuition. Her sight wouldn't show them the right direction to go, she had to go off instincts, to find what was missing. Beauty on the outside of this dissimilar world was not what her king wanted them to see. He was leaving them to choose a path without considering their circumstances. It was a continued journeying, the changing of their surroundings was now facing them, not leaving anything to chance, or leaving anyone left out on their own. Then she turned her view back to the front. This place was very beautiful to the eye as she drew in breath to face what was ahead. It made her eyes flicker with a touch of doubt, pulling her toward this impossible altered world now facing her. Then Danica knew something was wrong with what she saw. This beautiful landscape in front was an illusion of what a better life should look like. She knew right away that the journey ahead didn't show a better way of living, it was only a deception like the great gulf had shown earlier. She had to wait to experience what was to come. She was moving beyond the borders of a comfortable world lived by the Aquerae. In their quaint little city of security, those protecting borders leading back to a healthier way of living. All remained silent in eagerness as Danica tried to figure out what to do next. Then Amen stepped up to the plate to view their leader, waiting like the rest, raising an eyebrow of anticipation.

"Oh…squirt…I think you might be right." Maybe that's why Amen took the lead in being so vocal. He spoke in innocence about what he had felt. Danica looked to the watcher for his point of view as he pulled up alongside. The Condorsorous squawked loudly and startled the rest. Amen turned and narrowed his eyes. Then the boy couldn't contain himself.

"Hey…can you keep big-bird on the down low…he's kind of distracting!" Condac looked down at the small irritation with blinking eye. Then he reached up and patted the over-sized beast and looked up at him. The Condorsorous squawked again throwing his head back in a fit of retrieval. Yet Condac remained held in reserve.

Suddenly, Renee saw flashes of something archaic passing through her mind. She was jerked off balance and was almost thrown to the ground. Jacob let go of Danica's hand and reached for Renee to keep her from falling. The watcher leaned over to assist. When Condac touched Renee's shoulder he saw what she had seen, yet Renee felt like it came from him. It brought anxiety of concern to his mind as it started to change their surroundings. The watcher blinked profusely, then pulled away from the top of the hill, knowing something was about to happen, yet not knowing where it would come from. He felt a disconnection of what Renee was experiencing. He turned suddenly to guide each member back toward the top of the hill, by placing his hands in front of them, to keep them from advancing. After touching Renee's shoulder, he looked at her. Unexpectedly, the visions became stronger, more vivid, an internal warning was making him aware of danger up ahead.

In a blink of an eye, no more than a glitch of a second, it seemed to be compressed together into a lifetime of memories. Renee looked up in wonder as the watcher caught her glance of worry, knowing her quickening thoughts. Stricken also, Condac backed away as if jolted. Renee tried to make sense of this confusing dilemma. She stood on top of this mountain, viewing the inordinate valley below. The world she was seeing appeared out of control. Not too far away and coming closer, was a burnt and decimated wave of chaos. It felt so unnatural to sight she wanted to scream, but when looking back all members were unmoved by what she saw, because they couldn't see any of her vision. Facing forward once again she could smell burnt flesh, and an acidic smoke rose in the air causing her to cough from a sense of burning. Chaos swept over her causing her to panic. A graphic description of the dead began to flash before her eyes. She could see through the eyes of the watcher. They were taking this visual journey together, bonded by this unnatural paradox. Something was off by what she could feel, and Renee was pressed to find an answer to this dilemma before giving in. Chaos stood in the limelight holding the leading edge against this physical world distorted from an altered way of thinking. What lay in front was a rolling wall of confusion. It was an apparition of what life used to be, turned into something malignant and revolting to the human senses. Condac was seeing what she saw and feeling the emotions that followed along. The sky, even though at daylight hours, turned dark and quickly clouded over. A billowing wave of blackness hurled foreword revealed thousands of bodies of the dead just in front with removed limbs illuminating of flesh torn off bones through mimicking the dead. This was a bad dream in the worst of forms. Renee stepped back and screamed like no other scream she'd ever felt. It was overwhelming. The vision was so real it brought tears to the back of her eyes. She could feel the Winds of Time blow across her face. The watcher felt the terror as he looked back to grab her hand. She turned a pale face of acknowledgment. Renee tried to shake the vision from her mind, but it was almost like her body was on some parallel existence, being controlled by something that lay beneath the surface. Something was controlling this event without them knowing from where or why? The watcher's memories from experience had taught him self-control and patience were a better way of solving problems misunderstood. Still advancing, this accumulated wave carried hot molten rock licking up the bones of the dead as it moved with strength and velocity. Faces formed of the once living shot passed her mind in a sporadic jolt of violence. It moved like a heated enigma with the veracity of having purpose. She turned to look and run but there was nowhere to go. They were trapped. Condac leaned in and held her up. The young seer's eyes were widened from viewing this incredulous apocalypse coming their way. It was death's face that she saw roiling along eating up the ground, adding dulled flavor to its insatiable appetite, leaving behind only destruction. Death had followed them between two worlds of another time. Standing in front, Renee saw a gentle fawn grazing in the green grasses of the meadow below unaware of the destruction shadowing from behind. An overwhelming darkness covered the light of day and turned this day into night. The fawn looked up suddenly without time to respond. Renee pointed toward the fawn as the others looked on. The wave consumed him in seconds. Chaos had a different face that day that showed no remorse or mercy on the weak or the innocent of life. It was a warning to Renee that they were soon to be its next victim. There was nowhere to run and nowhere to hide. They had to face what was coming with only seconds to respond.

* * *

Ismael, standing next to Renee, saw the fearful expression in her eyes. He appealed to her better nature. "Are you okay?" Yet Renee was still spellbound by the scene in front. Everyone turned to look at her.

"I'm not sure." She said, "The watcher has shown me visions… there getting stronger!" A quivering of emotion welled up in her.

They all looked concerned after hearing her scream. "What's wrong?" Danica persisted.

"Something is about to happen!" She said.

Danica reached for more information. "I don't understand?"

Renee continued her assessment of the area. "Death has followed us to this place. Something's wrong with this place?" Renee said. "It's unstable."

Danica looked surprised that such a place would be unstable when nothing in front looked out of place. The Condorsorous was getting anxious with movement. He squawked loudly and looked down while backing up. It looked like a giant shadow was getting ready to overtake them.

The sky turning dark from a normal azure color faded quickly, as the surrounding hills and valley's in the backdrop were undisturbed from any suspicious movement. It was a mirage of tranquility from a few minutes ago. It was the perfect distraction.

Suddenly the wind began to blow. All members looked up and saw the clouds come together, drawing air from below towards the sky. It pulled passed them as if a door had opened to another time. Danica turned to warn the others to get down. Any direction seemed impossible of saving them. They faced what was coming even though it brought fear to their minds. Argon waved his gun in several directions before realizing it was pointless. The watcher looked to Danica and sensed the panic in her eyes. Suddenly, to realize what to do she gathered everyone around and slipped through a door and took them to the top of the mountain just behind them, a good mile from where they had started from. Keeping distance between them and what was coming from the heavens. The wave of chaos mixed with bones and bodies of the dead took over the sky, headed at a speed incomprehensible of how quickly it moved. Renee could see the nightmare beginning to materialize. The leader of that other world left them to a fate not expected. It was coming from the heavens as a roiling black molten wave of fire, poured into a mix of confusion while consuming forest and wildlife. Renee's worst fear had come to life.

The oldest Circle member sensed the watcher's concern. Tory blinked and looked behind her, seeing the lake of glistening water reflected off the sky. She glanced in the direction of Condac. He blinked in understanding. The color from her face was flushed. None of them could believe what they were seeing. Tory glanced across in a parallel gaze of wonder.

"I need your help!" She said.

Danica looked at the surging mounting rolling black of fiery that was viewed to be only a few miles away.

"How can I help you?" Danica asked.

Suddenly, her mind went back to when she was a little girl. Her daddy used to hold her and tell her about important issues he'd experienced as a boy and realized all her dreams were built on her father's experiences, and not her own. She was too young to have had her own experiences. She was still a child in many ways. She felt incomplete. Then she'd been startled by Amen yelling.

"Danica, can't you send it back to where it came from?"

Danica turned around to notice the smallest of members. "What?" She said. Her face paled from the thought of losing her full crew.

"Send it back?" Amen said. By then Jacob got involved.

"Yes, open a doorway and send it back!"

Tory grabbed Danica's shoulder. "I'll help you with the water from the lake."

Ismael jumps in. "Me to…I can hold it back for a little while."

Amen with childlike faith. "We can do it, with all of us working together with our gifts." He said. "Danica send it back!" He repeated.

She couldn't believe how much this group of member's began to show a bit of courage when she thought there was none to be. There was no control in this world that they knew at the moment, as far as she could tell. Emotions brought to their minds and hearts of their dire situation. She wished she could see what the others could see in her, like her father. In many ways, she lived in an emotional bubble, protected from this outside world, protected from the tainted images left behind of memory. What was to become of them? Danica stood towards the top of the hill—her emotions still waving heedlessly in the wind. Then she yelled at the top of her lungs.

"Get back you monstrous beast, you have no right to be here!!!"

Danica's heart was pumping fervently as she yelled facing the sight of their coming retribution. She raised her sword toward the sky and pointed towards the heavens.

"Go you beast…go back where you belong…this is not your home!!!"

The wall of water and fire and chaos disappeared beyond of a different world…with everyone's help the wall of destruction left them through a quickening door…

"How'd you do that?" Amen asked. He lifted his cap from off his head.

Danica didn't answer Amen, because she was seeing a likely crowd on the next hill just in front. And an extra form stood in the midst not recognized of anyone she had seen before, but she recognized everyone else. Realizing her parents and other members of her family were now found. She focused to make sure. The extra person looked younger from the other members surrounding him. He was a little bit taller than most, and not bad looking from what she could tell by the silhouette. Amen reached over and pulled on Danica's arm.

"Hey you—are you going to answering me? I'm getting the feeling no one listens anymore."

Danica looked down to meet his doughty expression.

"Sorry squirt…I didn't see you there!"

Amen got this mad-dog expression of yeah, I bet…right.

"How could you miss me, I'm the little blue guy that stands out like that guy with the horn in the middle of his forehead. It's hard to miss our obvious differences. We're blue with gills in our neck…remember?"

"Yes, I'm sorry. There's just so much going on right now." She said. A flicker of emotion crossed Danica's eyes. "Besides that, Amen, you can go with me to meet the others."

Danica didn't wait for her team to respond. She took Amen's hand and went through a door to meet another destination. Suddenly, Danica and Amen were in front of the lost party of members. Too many weeks had gone by without seeing their respected crew of older members. The weight of water seemed heavy, building on the back of Danica's eyes. Quickly throwing her arms around her parents she kissed dad, and then reached over to take Anna's hand. Dad pulled her in towards the family of three. Amen looked up showing a silly inflection of misunderstanding.

"What about me! Anybody miss me?" Then Danica turned and looked down.

Amen was looking at his father from what she could tell. He had imagined, nothing looking different from what he had seen from before. The same imbued personality hung about his father's face like an alarm clock waiting to go off. Danica reached out and placed a hand on Amen's shoulder. Then his father caught sight of his youngest son.

"What are you doing here Skippy?" His father asked.

Amen rolled his eyes. "Oh brother, are you going to call me that dreadful name too? Do I actually look like peanut-butter? Maybe I could put a glob of myself on everyone's sandwich, and no one would be able to talk…hah!!" Amen said. "That would be the trick."

Everyone laughed. Tommy looked down at the unbalanced boy. "I don't know where that came from." Tommy said, and then he thought maybe it came from neglect. A hovering guilt glazed over on Tommy's face. He lowered his gaze when seeing his son. Then Amen looked up and saw his father's expression of guilt-ridden worry. A troubling glint crossed Amen's face.

Danica turned toward the youngest of their group and wondered of his thinking.

"Amen, come on. You haven't seen your dad for a month—don't you miss him?"

"Not really, he's kind of like peanut-butter, once you get a little on you it's hard to get off."

A raised eyebrow eluded Tommy. "I guess it's my fault he's like this," after turning a shade of red.

"Like what dad?" A pause in Tommy's stance before answering.

"I haven't been there for you all the time…have I?"

Amen's eyes showed a sparkle of light. "It's fine…you have important political issues to deal with that leaders do…and I have these goofballs to look after," as he turned his head to see his Circle of members walking toward them from behind, "and Danica lets me do a lot of training."

Tommy glanced at the youngest of leaders, holding a note of curiosity. She didn't quite understand Amen's jostling with his father but noticed him standing behind in the shadows of a father he adored. He was rather reserved but smiled gently when Danica looked his way. Amen broke off his stare when he noticed her looking back. Then the conversation changed directions.

"Dad," she said, "who's the new guy, and where did you find him?"

Drew looked over wondering why the sudden curiosity. And then he looked back at the taller silhouette from behind. His eyes hesitated before saying, "There was another star ship that landed about a year ago. It came from earth before the end." He said without completing his thinking. Their other party was only a few feet away heading towards them now and faces of a few weeks back began to make sense again. Danica continued her prodding.

"What's his name?"

Her eyes glanced towards this stranger's direction. She caught the color of his eyes being a bluish gray. Something felt a bit odd, but she wasn't saying.

Drew looked over and wondered of her questioning. A feigning expression crossed her face as she looked at her father when thinking. Her father reached over and took her hand.

"We were hoping you'd show up soon. We've been here too long already. It's time to go home." A touched line of uncertainty crossed his lips before finishing. "Torack advised us needing your help, and now it's hard to believe that you're actually here. Your crew showed up at just the right moment."

Anna leaned in to kiss her cheek. A few quiet moments of personal sharing gave in to support. Even, Argon put his weapon of choice down and hugged his father.

Drew shared what they had found from the last few weeks of searching. "There are others that live here. Their mostly the animals that roam this land, yet there are a few bands of Aquerae caught in small pockets of land, where there's protection from the storms that come here. But a few of his kind have been here the last few months." Drew looked back at their mystery guest who'd been quiet up to this point. "We didn't know there would be others. It's a place not guarded well from the sky, and not as fortified as our own city, and changes can be made to improve the area." He stretched out his arm and placed it on his daughter's shoulder. "Another two miles east is the coastline. It's different from our home, but not so extreme as once thought. The Aquerae say another fellowship once lived here, thousands of years ago. But their gone now. They left behind a language that the Aquerae have learned quite efficiently. The land here was once considered their inheritance. A future lost from compromise of their leaders. Something happened eons ago that changed their minds in living here. More to be explained once we get home." Drew said, "right now, we need to find a place of safety for the coming of a storm is moving in behind us." Drew pointed toward the sky. "If you look to the east," he said, "you can see the land supports several lakes and the mountains to the north have many rivers that never run dry. It used to be a place of peace and safety, yet now the land has lost its natural form. It's been turned inside out by massive earthquakes a few years back forming a rift lying south of our position."

"By the way" Drew said, "thanks for your help. We couldn't have done this without you." Danica considered their demise when confronting the chaos a few minutes ago. Argon reached up to give Jacob a high-five. Danica looked over at her father.

"I think we needed your help too." She said. "I'm glad it worked out and we found each other at the right moment."

Anna came closer an addressed their party of members as they stood around in small clusters to view. "Those of you who are younger have shown yourselves to be brave to come here. To stand-up against this enigma that had dropped from the sky. It took a lot of courage, took a lot of foresight, even though overwhelming from a visual sight and not losing control of emotions, you've found success in being here at the right place…during the right time. It has been the first of many tests that you will experience in your future to come." Pausing for a moment to view the younger members of membership. "We faced an enemy who'd shown us an altered world more than confusing, so revealing of deception in a mindset not of a world we are used to, as it tried to scatter each of our members when dealing with such a beast once released. But you've kept your heads, not losing focus of your real purpose here today. A time of learning for our enemies are many, hidden in places never considered as informal as the mist of the air, for we remain unaware of what comes next. We let our circumstances become our teacher. You've shown courage in character form. Don't forget what you've learned."

There was silence all around as their children stood waiting.

"I hope the lesson you've learned won't be taken lightly. Take it to heart there to be no other way to find the answers you seek. Keep your hearts and minds in-tune for the coming retribution doesn't come without a chance of folly. Let no mistake keep you from doing a king's work for he cannot accept anything less than your best representation."

Everyone caught the inflection of Anna's words. They knew she had their best interests at heart and would be there for emotional support. Both parties saw the three miles of damaged ground left in the wake. A four-hundred-foot-wide birth of ten feet in depth laid behind destruction. The markings of the dead, a reminder of burnt bones and bodies covering ground as an unnatural setting. The water from the lake had become their best plan on such a short notice. It was a miracle from Danica's point of view. She figured it a test.

With her new guest on her mind, she turned quickly to view him. Secrets not revealed would soon come her way. Staying silent out of courtesy, he finally makes an introduction.

"Glad to meet you, my name is Andrew." While holding out his hand…Danica stepped forward and shook hands. "My brother and I have been living here almost six months." He said, with quivering blink shown in his right eye. Danica wondered what that meant. "One other came with us." Andrew said. "He was an older man who was my mentor from another life. He's no longer with us..." Pausing for a moment to let that sink in. "Both my brother and I live southwest of the valley we're currently in." While turning his head to view her father. "Your father said we can go with you to the city above the sea—if that would be okay with the rest of your fellowship." Pausing again to win her approval. "I believe he called it... 'The City of the Aqua Rings'?"

Danica glanced at her father without answering. She couldn't quite understand how Andrew and only two others were able to flee the earth, without help by some other angelic force. It didn't make any sense to her. No other source on earth had left behind a spaceship of such capabilities, and only a few of his family had made it? Danica decided to put her trust in his words for the moment, until he'd proven himself unworthy. She would leave any doubt about his being here for another time, even though she felt him a fraud.

"I'll go with you to get your brother," she said, "if you don't mind?" Andrew looked across the space separating them and noticed a sparkle of light in her eyes.

"It would be a pleasure to have some company." He said, "We've only a few things of value to bring with us. I mean, if there is room aboard your hovercraft." A bit of nervous tension showed in his eyes while moving his hands in a misconstrued shakiness. Danica sensed misery in his words were more than deceptive, to be for sure, she was headed down a trail leading to further malaise. "We left earth in such a hurry." He said while trying to keep Danica's attention. "We hadn't enough time to take all our belongings. It took us almost a year to get here. That's when our other member left us on a day not so long ago. Our star ship crashed and sank in the water's below, a good twenty miles to the west of here. There was nothing we could do for him." He said with a pretentious stare. "He was injured from the crash. And now, it's just me and my brother."

Danica nodded her approval, even if it was temporary. "Well...I hope all is well between you and your brother. You're both in good company," while holding her stance in a cumbersome way. "How is it that you would find food in this part of the country?"

Andrew looked at her without answering. He saw the sparkle of undiscovered deception in her eyes, knowing she was reaching for answers. Then Danica took Amen's hand while looking back at their newest member. "Are you ready squirt?"

Amen expelled a glint of pleasure from the attention he was getting, "we're like peanut-butter and jelly!" He said. Danica's face lit up with a smile wondering about the boy's motives.

Andrew didn't understand his alien perspective. He raised an eyebrow of concern, wondering of lost words more than confusing.

Before leaving, Danica turned her view back toward her father sensing something a bit off.

"Dad, I'm going with Andrew to get his brother!" She said. "I'll be back as soon as I can."

A fatherly acknowledgment by the shake of his head, and she was off. Danger was not a part of his thinking from a father's perspective. He held faith in a well-trained daughter, chosen to be a warrior among an elite class of gifted students. No flaws in a character intelligently devised.

Danica turned to their newest of members, "which way are we going?" She insisted.

A puzzling glare shot from his eyes. Then quickly replying. "East about three miles. We live at the lower end of the hills…not too far from the coast. It's on a trail hidden in the forest, protected by the borders of the mountains going west." He looked back in her direction with the blue-boy of Aquerian decent clinging to her side. "It's only but an hour from here, if we hurry." He suggested, not knowing she had a quicker way of getting there.

Danica reached and took Andrew's hand as if the best of friends. He looked down in a state of confused acceptance. Amen held on to the other hand of her leading. Danica slipped through a door; in a flash they were there to this place he had mentioned. They were pulled along on a trail evading any darkness that was soon to come. She pointed the way with her gift. The wind blew through Andrew's hair as he felt an elevated heartbeat almost take his breath away.

When they came through the other side Andrew blinked and looked to his left, his mind weighing on the short end of where they had come from. "Just a little bit farther," he announced while shaking his head to clear where they had just come from. "It's only a few hundred feet to our left." Their place was behind a grove of trees that stood fronting a cave. Well covered and disguised from the watchful eyes of strangers. It was well hidden fronting a hill to the left, as understood as a deception more than inconspicuous. To the right lay a ravine fronting a cascading waterfall. Seeing mist shooting up spraying their faces. It woke up Danica's senses of seeing this place as what it truly was. "Turn left at the bend!" Andrew announced.

Amen looked up beneath the military cap. "Where is he taking us?" Amen paused before asking another question, "So, is he and his brother going to be our new friends?"

Andrew understood the gist of Amen's prodding and turned a smile from the corner of his mouth. A bit of worthy hesitation shown in his eyes when moving towards an entrance. Quickly noting Amen's insistence. "Well, Danica did help save us from that world of a hidden gulf for those who are eaters of souls." Saying it like he had experienced it. "Being a friend wouldn't be such an inconvenience, would it?" A flash of a darker meaning rose across his eyes.

Danica measured the statement more as a way to quiet young Amen than to give her any hope of future bonding. Who would know of any future between the two of them within the next couple of weeks, even if there would be time to learn of each other? She wanted to survive the next couple of minutes without something else going wrong.

At the bottom of the hill, facing the front of the entrance, she saw the cave of convenience, well hidden behind a grove of trees. Amen noticed an animal he'd never seen before with jetting spikes lining his back. This prehistoric creature in front was trying to pull the younger of two brothers from the cave. That's when he heard his brother yell. Danica reacted quickly by summer-salting, flipped to climb this creature from behind. With several attempts of jabbing her sword at an angle she found a stronghold in this creature's neck. Blood flowed to meet his end, as he whipped back and forth, trying to defy this warrior who'd fronted him. Danica jumped to run her sword across his neck before getting down. After reaching the ground she walked past Andrew and stood fronting the cave once again.

"Let's get this done before it gets any darker." She insisted.

The creature dropped behind her and hit the ground while a cloud of dust floated in the air. Andrew, somewhat surprised, by her bravery hesitated as she past his shoulder. She entered this place shadowed from the outside world. Amen quickly followed after.

"There's blood all over you!" Amen said. Danica flinched from his acknowledgment. Something else had thrown tension in the air. Amen looked at her a bit confused.

From behind, Andrew went straightway to a washing basin, poured water into it to his left-on top of a table made of left-over materials what looked like old Oak wood. He offered water to his guest to clean up with. From her point of view, she was lost in something else. What she was seeing wasn't something normal for a girl of moral standards at any length to be seen, not a very perceptive angle of seeing what needed to be seen.

Andrew's brother was standing just a few feet from her, when she realized he wasn't a normal looking twelve-year-old boy with geometric charm. His face was distorted by some oozing abnormality that made Danica pull back. She looked up and noticed that Andrew had this decaying smile. And had once a beautiful look of innocence now faded. Now his face began to show his true character. He reflected dulled gaps of skin that had been covered up by something unrecognizable. Danica grasped that she was on the inside of a bleak living quarters of something deceptive, hidden behind darker corners of the cave. She was waiting for the dead to come and greet them, from that other world between the living and the dead. She viewed a prognostic living arrangement of evil. Left behind were scattered bones of lying corpses from a previous meal. Then, this intense stagnation began to whiff in the air causing her eyes to water and throat to burn. Amen already covered his mouth thinking of regurgitating anything left in his stomach eaten from hours earlier. Danica sensed they were trapped, waiting for some vicious creature to come along and tear them a part. The unannounced festivities not mentioned began without Danica's approval. A creature misaligned, of a different world stepped in front of her. She contemplated their situation and placed her hand in front of Amen to push him back behind her. He looked up and gripped her hand as he felt the beating of her heart from behind. The two brothers of another kind began to show their true identity. Andrew's supposed little brother was covered in pocketed oozing sores, draining of something infested of liquefied abrasions. Danica remembered her father talking of those creatures called the Hellhound. Their sight was not of a redemptive nature, but one of blessed fiery and pain. His so-called brother was dying slowly of something never seen, something he'd caught while living here. The healing elements did something the opposite to these said creatures. A creature so gross it caused Amen to want to cut and run, but where would he go when trapped with his leader holding him back? The younger of brother's was changing since they'd come out from the side of the waterfall. His features were a disfigured body of malaise chaos, and what was that smell? The creature was not trying to elude its victim in the least but gave into the idea of bringing fear and utter panic to the both of them. Danica tried to stay composed while feeling Amen shaking beneath her hands. She wasn't falling of her rocker of confusion just yet. In a short amount of time, she adjusted to her situation, first, by quickly drawing her sword, and second, by backing away from a furthering corner of fading light. Danica knew just then why she'd felt an uncomfortable aura from the time when just meeting Andrew. She had a few cards to draw from but understood patience and being lined up to dish out punishment was closer than first understood. She wouldn't let her mind be confused by what was facing them. Traveling through one of many doors would uncover a darker world that once caused her to hesitate from before. She grabbed Amen by the coat and turned him around. Without saying any misleading words, she expelled to him there bleak situation, by turning his eyes toward a pathway to avoid these malignant creatures in front of them. Amen was a distraction as others had done so often of membership.

"Oh cool...I like those Halloween costumes!" He said, which confused these creatures fronting him. This was the perfect time for Danica to move through one of her infamous doors, taken by several somersault's as to drive home her sword into Andrew's little brother's chest. Younger brother's rhythm had quickly changed. Amen moved out of the way to stay on Danica's flank, not to be in the direct path of swinging sword. Sure, footed grace was both ah inspiring and swift. Andrew flared toward the opening. A set of blacken wings shot up from the back of his shoulders. Elongated shadows cast a line on the wall. Andrew lunged to drive a sword into Danica's heart. She had already taken the life of his so-called brother's form, deformed in a mutated heap of jittery nerves. Andrew moved with wings abreast and sword swinging to and frow. Agility in movements caught him to waver as she learned to duck and cover at the most opportune time.

Amen, stayed behind, out of harm's way, making jeering remarks under his breath.

With wings on full extension her foe was not of any ordinary dimensions, he was big, yet agile like the warrior in front of him. Danica made through a door to elude her enemy. Andrew, not knowing of her true intentions, took refuge by backing up. He solidified his frame before knowing of his foes direction. Danica, coming up behind drove home her point between his shoulder blades, catching him off guard.

High emotions were ten-fold. No time to comment on what just happened. Amen's eyes took in the violence all around. Danica looked down with a bit of extended confusion written in her eyes, wondering about the boy standing quiet— disconnected with a strange look in his eyes.

"Are you okay?"

"Well, I think so…I mean, I thought everything was fine, then all this…who could know?" Amen said, "and what was I thinking following these two impostor's who we barely knew, into a cave no less…and all this blood left behind! I think I'm going to hurl…" was his next thought as he leaned over to do just that.

Danica reached down and put a hand on his back. "Okay squirt… get it all out. You're just in shock." Just at the moment, a rush of air caught Danica to take notice of their company fronting the cave they were in. Drew and Anna, with the rest saw the two impostors and the remains of them. With Andrew laying just past the door.

Then suddenly Drew and his crew came through the doorway with bewildering stares. "What happened?"

Danica's breathing was sporadic holding an elevated heartbeat passed her ears. "They were spies, as my best guess...didn't really have time to and ask."

"You should of seen Danica...that girl really took it to them!" Amen shouted.

Even Amen couldn't believe he said what he did as everyone turned to look at him, even Tommy. Looking surprised at seeing the remainders of their so-called friends. Again. wondering of this girl so gifted, always finding a way to escape an enemy.

"How'd you know they were spies?" Her father asked.

"I didn't know...everything happened so quickly. I saw them changing once inside the cave." She placed her hands on her hips as she spun about walking back and forth in their company. She was still jacked up from the fight. They saw it in her movements. "What gave them away though was the pile of bones in the corner there." She said, "They were feeding off what they could catch as food. Most of their victims were predators from the fields or mountains by what I could tell. Look! There's a trail of blood there going east and one going north."

Everyone looked to the corners and witnessed the evidence by her words and knew. Drew wondered of his daughter's testing. Addressing the others as they came in closer to hear his words.

"I'm sorry... We had no idea that they were not what they had said they were. I guess I'm getting older and losing my grip on reality." He stated. "They couldn't have done this without having help." He paused while looking at the others. "Those of earth had come here before." Another pause blinking his eyes. "Remember, they were a race not understood by those of a human world. The memories are quite clear." Drew looked at his daughter with concern. "We should have suspected this."

A bit of reluctance was seen in Danica's eyes. "Maybe you're right! Our enemy has become creative in hunting us like animals. We can't be so trusting of anyone next time, needing to look further than what is seen by the eye."

Anna looked over, concerned by what she was hearing. She pushed back soft curls of brown hair behind her left ear. A softer expression glazed across her eyes.

"Young lady, I'm guessing you're ready for further adventuring?"

Drew's eyes widened at the thought of his daughter swinging a sword against old warriors of that other world. He spoke in defense of his daughter's future.

"Well, she might think she's ready, but that's something yet to be experienced by our little girl." He said, "Our own borders are the main concern before we go riding off into the sunset on the sails of that other world."

Anna displayed a soft glint of disapproval in her eyes. "And you're meaning?"

Drew's eyes were set in a daze-like-wonder. "It means she's not ready to give up her life at the drop of a hat. Besides, Thaliana and Gabriel knowingly, knew she needs this type of testing before being put into some future battle."

Anna cast a loaded stare at her husband. "Rightly so my dear husband, but besides our daughter, we can't just sit here and do nothing while they come after us. We need to have our own spies out there to know of their deceptions. This could bring some comfort back to our little community, with a little added security." She said, "Our borders are spread too thin. With a lack of planning, we could lose our way of living. We are but a few, and they have many."

"And your point is?" Randy asked.

"Don't be caught looking the other way when chasing after an invisible enemy. They cannot be broken by the swinging of sword, or the use of harsh language."

"And your parable means?" Randy continued.

"Well, try running in any direction without having a plan and see how far you get."

Randy looked back at Drew while shaking his head. "Does she always speak to the blind and deaf, who knows what's she actually saying, if holds any meaning."

Drew knew better than to answer such a question in front of everyone. He smiled when looking back at Randy. A flash of wisdom sparkled in his eyes, as he measured the statement and left it for another time. Anna knew that look alone and reached over to smack him in the chest. Drew flinched while taking the playful punishment.

All remained quiet outside the cave, then Amen gave of his opinion. "Oh brother…can't we all just get along?" Danica reached over to cover Amen's mouth. He tried to pull away as she held on tight. His eyes started to bulge so she started to laugh.

"Hey Goldie-locks…I can't breathe!" He barked out.

Everyone turned to see Amen turn a shade of paling blue. He removed her hand to voice his opinion. "Hey lizard-lips let go of me! Stop or I'll hock a loogy in your hair!"

Ismael thrown off by little brother's lack of gratitude. "Skippy… come on…everyone's listening!"

Amen looked back as everyone stood around. "What did I do wrong? I was only trying to breathe. I think I got dirt in my gills." He looked at Danica unwillingly. "Did you wash your hands after fighting those creatures?"

Even Tommy smiled while shaking his head. Amen made sounds in the back of his throat like he was gargling. He leaned over and spit on the ground. Everyone looked bewildered. "Hey, it's not funny man! I think she dented my windpipe and gave me germs! I could get spots on my skin from human germs."

"Where did you here that Skippy?" His brother asked.

"Mom said she got spots when dad licked her face."

"What the he…" Tommy started to say but stopped himself.

Amen turned to look up at their confused leader of seven. "I didn't do anything wrong?" She couldn't believe he was still complaining. "Are your hands clean?" Amen asked. "You were touching those creatures. They smell like daily bathing wasn't a part of their lives…you know, I could sue if I catch some dreaded disease!"

Danica opened her mouth in bafflement. "Ease up Skippy. I just saved your life!"

Even Danica started to smile. Tommy looked down at his abraded son, showing a quivering acknowledgment.

"It would figure…my own flesh and blood would copy my one weakness."

Bella stared in wonder of where that might have come from and glared at Tommy so willingly. "Sounds like something you'd say."

Everyone looked over and laughed. Tommy reached down and put his misguided hand on Amen's shoulder. He glanced down at him. Then smiled remembering some of his own troubling days that had gone missing. "Like a chip off the old block…"

Amen looked up at his father. "What's that supposed to mean?"

Tommy shook his head. "It means you said enough and it's time to end this day on a good note."

4

The Silo's Secrets

The trip home would be something they all looked forward too. If by some miraculous miracle they'd get home in one piece and nothing else would happen. The weirdest part was being far as they were, even though the youngest of members traveled only a few hours from where they had first started. The great gulf gaped between worlds was sending them beyond normal limits in lacking comfortable surroundings. The vortex pulled them across time and space, leaving them with blank expressions and silent words. Danica saw a different lay of the land, as others started to notice it too. Quickly, coming to land's end, a gulf between them and the direction they needed to go. Impeding their pathway of going home. A tethering discomfort weighed heavy on their hearts when looking out at this unsettling sea. Comparing them to a periling ship in the belly of a storm, drifting to deeper waters without knowing the consequences of their travels. A mystery of where it would take them was only a breath of air away. Danica knew they'd have to stay another night and wait out this coming storm. The sky was changing—as the weather mounted further protest of a raging sea, pointing them toward a detrimental end, fading of confidence, fading of strength.

"What should we do?" Danica asked.

"Do you see what's ahead?" Her father said.

Danica looked up from the screen to view these massive swells headed for the shore. "Yes, I see!

We should stay and wait out the storm!" She said, with a bit skepticism in her voice.

Drew didn't answer right away because the storm was making so much noise, blocking his words and distancing his frame of mind. And the sea brought something else carried on the waves of rolling thunder. Chaos moved from out of the deep past normal borders, it was as if mysteries of the darker waters were meant for those who had lost their way.

"Where should we go?" Danica asked.

"I don't know. We have to think this through. Let's stop and view a map away from the area below."

"Okay, we'll land over there…on the clearing where the mountains rise to the east."

"I'll be right behind you." Her father said.

Both hovercrafts settle down in a clearing to get a view of a place not registered on any map. Their ability to cross water without landing, verses having enough solar cubes to last across the sea wasn't something they were willing to gamble on. It was better to travel during the day. And thinking it was incomprehensible of two hovercrafts blazing through bad weather on the worst of days in the darkest of hours.

The day was done as the red-dwarf-star sunk below the horizon only leaving a dreary expectation. They'd find their way through this situation, but not until this weather cleared. Running out of time. They had to find shelter.

Anna, from a short distance of three feet, looked bewildered, thinking Drew left traveling back tonight was a chance he was willing to take. Danica had become aware of their dilemma, only after noticing the landscape had changed to the extreme. A battle of getting through the night was facing them. But where would they go? The two watchers accompanying them looked toward the group with concern. Condac got down off his Condorsorous and turned to look at the others while standing five hundred feet above the waves, at the cliffs edge. He glanced at the youngest of warriors, a girl at best in the prime of her youth, and then nudged Danica's coat as she looked at her parents. They were preoccupied by the storm fronting them when seeing the waves. Danica's father walked over.

Renee expelled a different point of view. An adherent expression of something new. "I know of a place…it can't be that far." She seen a place in a vision. She pointed toward a clearing over the top of the next ridge going northeast. The rolling hills were dark and wet and draining of washed rain all around. "It's on the other side of the valley in the next set of hills." She said. They were out of the direct pressure of the wind when at the lower level of the valley below, yet the wind would greet them over the top of the next ridge.

Danica moved her eyes in the direction of Renee feeling a bit of indecision. "You know of some place?" She asked, as if confused of their direction.

"Yes." Renee returned. "It can't be more than a few hundred feet going north. If we can just get to that place."

Danica looked over her shoulder after leaving the chaotic sea behind. The others were soon to catch up as Argon, one of the younger members took the lead. Danica was thinking of what was ahead when something started changing. She glanced over at a parallel vision to see Argon while Renee followed along. Their journey was taking the very breath from their lungs as they pushed passed the fear of losing their way, pushed past the last bit of energy spent on this faded day of building weather. Danica followed along, over the next ridge, the wind blew, and the rain came in at a slant, as the weather pushed them into the rage of a mounting storm.

The day was one they all wanted to forget. Danica pulled her coat collar closer around her neck. The darker part of the storm made it almost impossible to see. Up ahead, the path steepened, as the rugged terrain quickly changed their course of direction when trails of water pushed them to go around. Suddenly, the others were so far behind, Danica sensed her father only as her companion as the others drifted in memory towards the sea left behind. Their sight was impaired, and their journey uncertain, but they pushed on. The sun was no longer a factor in giving direction. They were unable to understand where they were headed. And Danica suddenly felt the pull of her father's hand. They moved in a rhythm away from the others, searching internally for a better place to be, going in a direction that didn't make sense. Past all lines of safety, pulling her confidence, depleting of energy at the very core. Nothing at the moment made any sense to the young leader. Danica felt led by an elusive dream taking control of her every movement. The Leading of a forceful hand by her father was the first impression of being controlled. Right away noticing a broken path of twisting foliage, enormous rocks mounded on the sides, and trees that seemed alive with movement. The land left a confusing feel all around, drifting from its draw of purpose. It felt to drain Danica's strength.

All of a sudden, she couldn't hardly stand because of the wind and rain beating against her body holding her back. Keeping her from seeing what she needed to see. Just in front, Danica saw a towering structure given of stamina of a time of many years hence. A giant silo was fronting her. Used by others from another time, used for agriculture from its form. Yet no signs of life were left of this place by what she could tell when viewing its mass. Her father stood to her right shoulder to take in what they were seeing, for only their eyes were the useful part of what needed to be seen. Danica noticed an opening, a door to the lower end of this place showing a possible secure way of comfort, out of the rain, out the wind, a place they could mend their way of thinking. She turned back around to get her father's approval, yet a strange expression was seen in his eyes. It made her feel uncomfortable. And a strange sense of awareness made a thick ashy smell rise into the air from a dream taking her where she didn't want to go. And rushing water all around at the foot of this place first considered safe, and now she didn't know. And her father at her side said nothing about this place of refuge. Danica looked to her left and felt compelled to run in any direction, away from this place of rushing water on the darkest of days, when picking up speed to get some distance. Almost right away she felt something behind her, as wings released of a father's prodding swooped down and took her off her feet. Knowing this creature, who had taken her was not her father to be. They moved without knowing direction, in and out of trees, battered by wind and rain, draining her further. She was bound by a greater power pushing her to get past this line of confusion, making no sense. Not knowing if imagined of a dream of any reality unrehearsed, her days felt stolen, unmarked of this darker world she was being lead through. Like a drug injected into her veins. Leaving family and friends behind, leaving her normal life from this trans-like-mist. A dream took her to the end of this place where she floated off to. She tried to muster any remaining strength but found none to be there.

This winged beast of the air, held her in its grasp, dove beneath water eluding the weather from above, represented by something not of a human world. Flowing through a canal like structure, took on the form of an old aqueduct, for watering of crops, from what she could tell. Yet now, leaving the remains of a ghost like structure in memories not of her own. It now lay dormant. Something scrapped off under fingernail of those creatures left behind had entered Danica's bloodstream, causing her to be pulled into a dream like sleep. It left her feeling alone and secluded. A test or a goal she did not know, misunderstanding it was a place she felt out of sync. She could sense every nerve in her body, every emotion kept her focused on this place beneath water, leaving her to feel vulnerable, disconnected from the life lived with family and friends. She was in a world not understood under a certain angle of perception. Geared for something greater than a dream. This wasn't real. Too far from a normal way of thinking. She was no ordinary girl lost out on her own, she was destined with certain gifts for a reason.

When Danica came too, she was still disoriented from being drugged. She was lying down inside a deep cemented pit surrounded by tall walls blocking out the weather from outside, but she could still hear the wind howling just beyond the walls of this place of refuge, reminding her of certain dangers they were still facing. She was wet and drained and felt a certain pain in her back, from memories of being pulled by a winged creature.

Suddenly, Danica jolted fully awake when a recognizable face stood tall in the shadows fronting her. Amen's blue face drew in with a grin to get her attention. His appearance elongated. His skin had been stretched over bones of something much bigger than the small boy's blue face with awkward dimensions, giving her his attention of this once unconscious girl. Yet he was more than just a boy, more than just a friend, he was one of the gifted standing tall although small as perceived by the others. He made a connection with the girl picked to be their leader. She blinked to clear the visual of this strange boy of annoying persistence. Trying to get a clearer picture of a youthful blue face with the trusting eyes, and a childlike acceptance of being best friends.

"Danica…are you alright…you passed out…some type of poison we're guessing!"

Amen, the little brother she never had, held her hand as if to never let go. He wasn't about to leave her care to the others by any means. It was his job to do was his thinking. Danica blinked…shook her head and leaned toward the movement of others. Amen, looking her way, looking to find a bit of hope in the eyes of a girl once disconnected. Showed a bit of hesitation in his stance when looking down at her. She had almost forgotten the dream that involved her father was just a moment behind her. The nightmare seemed so real, so vivid, so drawing of a time she didn't understand. Why the vision? Why something so bizarre? She gained her composure and slowly moved about, moving her hands, moving her eyes, reaching up to rub the blur from the vision, as her hands slightly shook as she took notice of everyone laying in this cemented enclosure of security. She tried to make sense of everything of before, but nothing seen of dreams made any sense to her. On her own at first, but now she was with others of her kind.

The night had already come, and both groups of the Circle were settled in a big circular addition, covered by something unfamiliar. The visions, the dreams, were all but confusing. She'd come to figure it held a deeper meaning. Something she would learn at another time was her thinking. Danica sat back against the cemented wall, in a supportive effort to hold up her frame, yet her mind kept wondering back to that place of entrapment. Torack walked over and placed his hand on her shoulder while looking concerned.

He turned to view the others. "She's had some type of hallucinogenic reaction to poison somehow injected into her." He said, with a worried expression, and a twitch in his stance as he considered the girl drawn to leadership. "It has to take its course." He said. "For some reason the healing-stones have no effect to cleanse her blood, of this thing she fights inside her. It's not of a world of healing elements."

Danica's father came closer to see her paling skin. She lay half in and out of what had happened to her. Anna brought a cloth filled with water and wiped her face and neck. Danica looked up beneath sweaty conditions and her heart beating strong, understood she was back in the comfort of family and friends. Amen was still knitted to her side with the acknowledged awkwardness of his gate. Tommy leaned in to push him away. Amen wondered what his father was up too and only stared. "She needs me dad…I'm not leaving her!"

Danica looked up briefly and fanned Tommy off. "It's okay…he can stay…" And then she was gone again beneath the veil that had taken her earlier.

The storm outside of this place of safety was heard making a thunderous stand against those of the gifted driven to hide. Sounds of rumbling were all around not giving a moment of peace in this chaotic storm. The wind whistled in and out of the small opening of the silo that they had all crawled into, snuggled together like school children holding on to each other in the comfort of finding safety among family, safety among friends. This was a place of a thousand years ago, carrying the memories of a previous life of members, now gone, left behind somewhere else in another memory. Their Aquerian leader stood in one corner surveying their situation. All of them, lying in wait at the bottom of the silo. Seen above, one hundred and fifty feet to the top of this cone shaped cemented home where crops of the fields were stored from another time, wrapped in the comfort of this place of giving them a bit of hope. A coat of armor all around.

Silence of this place was kind of eerie. Their forms of transportation were just outside the small opening. From across the room, of warmer conditions, of an open fire pit warming them, Argon and Amen, along with others of their kind, brought a few blankets along, left behind in closed and locked storage bins, found at a lower end of the hovercraft. Amen was wrapped up in one of the blankets with Danica. Their hearts filled with adrenaline were now gone of slow thrumming of comfort of a blue boy of smaller dimensions, showing his face in a soft glow of light, as he looked up at this aged monument from another time, which showed no signs of a previous life. A vivid reminder of another day of better conditions than the one they were facing now. They were being tested beyond all measure of this place of secrets, a place of refuge to rest weary bones. Looking to his left Amen blinked an eye open to notice Argon sleeping with his mouth hinged open to a line of drool rolled down his lip. Amen smiled when seeing this. He looked around this cemented room of security. Their team was all quiet in the surrounding of comfort, in the silent breathing of each member, as they wanted to forget where they were at the moment, and only rest. Amen, looked at each member, laying in the gentle snoring of quiet humans and those of an alien decent, resting from a difficult day now spent. Hopefully they'd get through this difficult day was Amen's thinking.

From atop the silo, looking down twenty feet above them, this substantial structure housed a specific system not understood by Amen with one eye open viewing top to bottom. His ancestors had landed on such a planet before his time. This was home to them. The structure cast a glimmer of hope in the eyes of a boy holding an awkward frame of mind. Amen was waiting for some internal signal to give him courage, to step up to the plate and be the leader he was meant to be, even though his size and frame of mind said otherwise. He was just glad not to be swept out to sea in the rage of a discomforting storm. Each set of eyes closed, movements of breathing, in the quiet flickers of light gave the boy a warm welcoming of friends and family. Ill-timed, on a darker day, but he knew there was reason for all of them being here, but why now? And why like this?

Anna, from across the cemented room, noticed his stare of a few feet away. A redeeming fact she knew Amen had his place of being here just like the rest. A test for sure, was her thinking, but something more made her stare a bit longer in Amen's direction. She knew of her own tests of youth, not feeling it to be so far away from years before, but like yesterday the memories were still there. A youthful hope where dreams come from are but a flicker away. Unparalleled of a youthful boy full of energy, full of fight to challenge the others on any day. This part made her smile. Amen was not one to submit so easily to others on any given day of the week. He was secure in his own way of thinking, of seeing life at an angle with a large amount of faith factored into every moment of living. Anna remembered making mistakes and finding answers to such questions were most revealing of facts not always holding answers understood, sometimes the right answers to so many questions went unsolved. Even though all possibilities would be raised and studied, all redeemable facts would be looked at with scrutiny, combing every hidden meaning. But life would always be filled with unanswered questions pertaining to why and how? Still waiting she wondered if they'd ever understand the true meaning of life how they seen it to be, as it quickly slipped through their fingers while breathing in air, from that perspective. Away from home, gave her a different angle of seeing the light of day, giving insight at a moment when all else seemed to fail. They stood tall against this force of nature that came to greet them, in a valley of misconceptions of a darker part of their world. Not trying to defy all sensitivity of gravity, or to lose their sense of conformity through humility, or losing direction showing a lack of affection of others around them. None of this had made any sense to them. The back of Anna's eyes watered a bit, thinking how much she had grown to love these apparent misguided youths in her company, and those of an older Circle of membership, keeping up to stride when rubbing shoulders with them. Sensing how small they seemed in the light of day, gaining more wisdom through time, through experiences. Each had hope, each held to the commitments of their fellowship, each had their part of a mockup world of different circumstances holding them suspended above normal everyday thinking, keeping them focused on the prize, to be experienced by everyday people standing at their side. This would be a special day of testing. She held hope for all of them. Then the first tear made its way down her cheek.

Trying to hide it, trying not to weep, she turned her face away from the others. Her emotions set on her shoulder for all to see. Amen looked up with an inquisitive stare. In his innocent gesture, given of his age and lack of moral upbringing.

"Are you okay?" He asked with a raised suspicion of curiosity.

Anna didn't see him looking up at her, but then she looked to her right, and he was there. Still stunned that he would pose such a question, she remained quiet, assuming she might ignore the gesture of surety and turn her head, yet Amen being the son of Tommy remained consistent.

"It's okay to cry...we all feel the creepiness of this place." He said.

All eyes quickly opened and turned to the small boy with the annoying tongue from glaring clarity, just like his father use to be. Each set of eyes found him in innocence with a speck of love conveyed with a few words of comfort. Anna gazed in his direction. She understood the dilemma they'd gotten themselves into. There was always a bit of hope when looking from an alternate angle of perception. Amen stood, and walked closely to Anna's side, of this despondent group and put his arms around her—that's all it took to send her emotions going in the other direction. The others looked over and understood. Amen reached to kiss Anna on the cheek.

"There now," he said, "no more crying. We have a world to save, and people to see!" Tommy looked at his son, and realized Amen understood the concept of courage went along ways from first impressions. Eyes of the many began to draw focus on the smallest of details from a boy as his imagination took them beyond the stars they could never reach on their own, passed the flickers of light in the galaxy, passed key moments of pain, and brought them back to reality.

After the kiss, the mood inside the silo began to brighten. Danica raised her head after missing the scene and said, "Where did Skippy run off too?"

"I'm over here...you want me to make you some S'mores?" He said with a crack in his voice.

Everyone looked past the fire of stirring flames and laughed. Argon looked at his little friend.

"Are you joking, or do I have to remind you of what you did to my pants!" Amen looked down at the chocolate blotches masqueraded across the front of Argon's pants that seeped up under his legs. Amen scratched his head and added a quirky smile to his face.

"Are you sure there chocolate stains?"

Argon looked up, realizing his embarrassing situation. Before he could respond everyone looked over at the boy who showed a mural of dotted blotches leaking between his legs. Amen pointed at Argon's dilemma with a crooked blue finger while smiling. Argon stood and tried to defend off the witty thought of the youngest.

"Oh this, it was an accident...I mean Skippy..." Then Amen had a thought.

"Mama has some soap that'll get those stains out, but don't hold me to it. I'm not quite sure she can pull off a miracle, beside you've been sitting in that stuff all day."

Even Anna put her hand over her mouth, as the others caught on, then laughed about Argon's dilemma. Tommy stood and looked at his son, who caused quite the rumble among the group of members.

"What am I to do with you?" His father said.

Amen showing a hesitant understanding. "Dad, you can do anything you want to me, just don't make me sit next to him," while pointing to Argon. "I don't think it's chocolate after all...he doesn't smell like his normal self!"

Everyone awake, laughed.

Amen rolling in the attention—Danica now fully awake, suddenly by the outburst of a half a dozen family members sat straight up. She looked across the room and raised her head. "What did I miss?"

Amen still drawing attention, looked at his favorite person of seven. "You didn't miss much, except that Argon couldn't hold it any longer!"

Most everyone covered their smiles and giggles while Argon looked hopelessly at the others. "You little brat, wait till we get home, and I get you alone!"

Drew stood for a brief moment to change the momentum of conversation. "Alright boys! That's enough. The joke is over...we have more important things to discover than poop pants."

Argon looked over at Uncle Drew somewhat surprised. "I didn't do what he said! Skippy threw-up on me!"

Tommy looked sternly at his son, Amen. "Sorry Argon...he goes over-board sometimes. Skippy, tell him you're sorry, or I'll..." Tommy didn't finish because of all the sudden confusion of what really took place.

To be a good-sport Amen got up and faced Argon, "Sorry guys... I'm just playing...I got sick and threw-up on Argon. It's not his fault."

Everyone settled down and started to focus on their current dilemma, for grace is operative in the darkest hours of new experiences. "Quote by Dr. David Jeremiah." Tommy got up and added more wood to the fire, as the night came in and surrounded the closely knitted family as sleep came to those whose eyelids weighed heavy on a certain day more than strange. Drew took the first watch. Argon handed him an oversized weapon known as the Element gun. With a slight grin without a smile, he thought to stay awhile and accompany their leader.

5

The Way of the Wind

Danica woke with the fury of wind whipping in and out of the silo's entrance. She noticed almost right away that a few of the men were missing. Tommy, Torack, and Drew were gone. This alarmed her enough to make her stand to her feet. Ismael blinked his eyes wide open, then noticed her looking his way. They both looked at each other. She moved fervidly toward the doorway staring at something just outside the door. For curiosities sake, Ismael got slowly to his feet and walked over to the opening too, when trying to rub sleepy out of his eyes. Being the older of two brothers, knowing something wasn't right about what he saw. Ismael earlier had slept in a coma like state, then rubbing his eyes when making the connection. What brought him to hesitate was an intense howling of the wind, blocking them from moving outside past the door. Danica stood frozen, as if petrified. She was in a trance like state with an intense view plastered on her face. She was seeing something strange that didn't quite make any sense either.

Ismael reached over and touched Danica on the shoulder, causing her to jolt backward. She turned to catch his glance. What both young Circle members saw was something told of visions by their parents.

Three Conquerites stood just outside the door. Standing sixty feet tall, of a grayish color, with wings abreast. They stood like statues in a frozen state.

From the sky above, the rain came down at an angle across their faces, and the wind tried to push them beyond limits, but nothing pertaining to the three moved them. The black of the night was soon to be gone, but current darkness still circled in around them. Unnoticed was a gaping hole from the sky that lead these creatures to land on the ground in front of them. A whirling of gray clouds circled in around, completing this area to be protected from another outside force. The wind howled, the clouds opened up, and the time that lapsed wasn't noticed because Danica was standing mesmerized. These giants stood in the rage of the storm without showing emotions or movement. Their colossal size, when landing, sucked every ounce of breathable air from the sky. These warriors were here for representation of a king from a world unnoticed from clouds of glory following them to this place of refuge. They were here to intimate, to set the record straight, there was no other form seen of vision greater in size or manner. Their feet were planted firmly, not moving a fraction of space, and effort to distract those of another world left behind in the rage of this day. To the left of these Conquerites, warriors of a crown, stood her father, along with the other two men that were missing. The monstrosity of Gothic creatures had them frozen, unmoved, and afraid of the fact of why they were even here? Danica tried to move through the doorway but was pushed back through its opening from the strength of the wind.

Suddenly, some of the others began to stir, waken by the noise, which seemed to escalate as time advanced. Danica turned and remembered the weapon her father awkwardly held that Argon had given to him the night before and thought of taking it, but then changing her mind, she walked back toward the sleepy boy who was in and out of a slumbering dream, with a bit of a dazzling smile plastered on his face. She wondered what he'd been dreaming about. Viewing weapons as playthings in his past, but he'd known better than to think in that way now. Danica had shaken him totally awake, and now that both boys were awake, she had their attention. They were suddenly pulled unaware by the girl chosen to be their leader, and suddenly, Ismael wondered where Amen had run off too. Argon blinked and looked down at his chocolate-stained pants, wondering if he'd ever replace them.

"What's goin on? What's that standing outside our door?" He asked.

He suddenly recognized that Amen wasn't in his usual place. Danica was standing to the side of Argon with an expression of concern. He could see the gentle lines that brought her beautiful eyes into perfect dilated form. Her usual locks of blonde curls were matted with dirt and water damage from the night before. She was a bit taller than Argon by two inches. He noticed, even in his still sleepy state, the deepening of her blue eyes were brilliant with color. It caused him to sit up and rub the blur from his eyes, while not wishing any demise of their leader. He stood up quickly then grabbed for the wall to catch his balance, as Danica reached over to sturdy him. "Danica, what's going on out there?" He whispered, in a line of closer resistance from moving in that direction. She pulled him to the side to answer his question, but the howl of the wind and darkness of the night had taken them to the end of their conversation. Shadows outside their door changed the mood she was feeling, as the sudden weather started to dissipate. She knew these giants of the realms were here for a reason, a reason she didn't know of at the time. They sat in the eye of the storm as it quickly grew still. Argon looked up at Danica confused.

"What's goin on?" He said, "You were looking at something?"

She gave a nod then said, "I'll have to figure out why they are here?" she said, "Go with me."

Argon nodded back his approval and followed after her.

She adjusted her angle of standing in the door to keep an ear bent in Argon's direction as she looked over her shoulder. Her watchful eyes darted back outside the door when seeing these monuments of another time. "Bring a weapon." Danica asked.

He reached down and picked up his Element gun then headed after her.

Danica looked back showing a sparkle of hesitation. An intelligent glint of wisdom overwhelmed her. Where was her little friend? Amen appeared to be missing, and the adults of this organization hadn't taken notice because they were asleep. Argon stiffened by the night's cold chill that moved through the air caused him to shudder. A moment of stress weighed heavy in Danica's frame when seeing these creatures standing all around the silo in a silent rank of stillness. It caused her to move quickly past the door. A trice circle of Conquerites through her off. She looked up skyward to notice their wings were still extended. This made her think that maybe it was a warning somehow, but without asking she didn't know. Danica was told they would protect those of the realms. Ready to do a kings bidding at a moment's notice in God-like-form. Her heart, felt to drop out of her chest when sensing their presence. Her hands began to shake, and she was at a loss at which way to go when walking around them. Danica gave a cold look of bewilderment shown in her stare. Why were they here? She thought. Argon fell back on his butt when looking up.

"What are those creatures?" Argon asked, as he thought to get up and move away in a direction he could run. He stood leaning against the silo while holding a blank stare. When his question wasn't answered he asked it again.

"Hey...I'm talking to you...why are they here?"

"Didn't know you were still talking to me." Danica said.

She left him standing ten feet away while trying to figure out what happened to Amen.

From an increase of voices others began to stir when the quiet of the storm still existed, but then it would return with a vengeance. Jacob woke the others when snoring quite efficiently. Amen was covered up by several blankets under the shoulder of another then hearing the snoring woke with annoyance. The tension in Danica's shoulders began to relax when seeing Amen poke his head up. She moved back to the entrance. He sat up and yawned. "Skippy, I didn't see you laying there. For a minute, I'd thought you'd gone outside."

He looked up curiously. "What...you mean out there?" Amen's curiosity perked from the direction of the door. Still rubbing his eyes, still disoriented and then blew something slimy out of his gills.

Argon looked over his shoulder and shuttered. "That's just not right Skippy...not polite to blow moco's out of your nose...get a Kleenex or something." Amen developed a widening smile and acted like he was going to wipe digestive remains on Argon's head.

"Get away from me you little ten turd before I tell your ding-bat dad what you're doing!" Amen looked offended by the remark, while following through with the obvious. Argon was beyond surprised and disgusted at the same time.

Amen shares of his uncouth manners and belligerent ways. "I wasn't going to put my boogers on you, until you took the verbal cheap shot at my dad. Maybe I'll find another and wipe it on your lip."

Argon stood and backed away from him, "You better not!" He reached for his head trying to locate the disgusting glob. Argon was appalled when he contacted sticky stuff between his fingers. "Dude...I owe you so bad...can't wait till you fall asleep. I'm going to trim a reverse-Mo-hock into that skull of yours!"

Amen's eyes narrowed while trying to find another slimy rendition of the same. He focused on a search, like he was exploring deep space. Danica whipped around and noticed the two boys taking their verbal cheap shots.

"Stop it...the both of you...so I can concentrate!" Danica said as she caught a glimpse of what they were doing. Argon found a rag and wiped the snot off his fingers.

"That's disgusting." Danica said. "Why are you picking your nose?"

Argon looked offended. "It's not my snot...it's his!"

Danica looked confused, "Okay, why are you picking his nose?"

Argon threw the snot-rag at Amen, "The little turd wiped it on me."

Amen glanced toward Danica with a touch of hesitation seen in his eyes. "Our trigger-finger fake over here was going to eat it. I'd tried to stop him." Amen said.

Argon's eyes flashed with anger. "I wasn't going to eat anything... he's lying...the little creep was picking his own nose, not me!"

Danica got a disgusting look on her face. "You two boys are gross. I've had it with little boys and their devious ways. I knew it was mistake, to bring you two!"

Argon raised his hands, backed away toward the wall and scowled at his little soon to be enemy. "I don't want anything to do with the little gross creep anymore, his disgusting, rude, a liar, and everyone always takes his side."

Danica's eyes narrowed in a fit of anger. "Just keep that personal vendetta stuff away! Do you hear me! Not everything is about you Argon!" She looked back at Amen. "He was probably just messing around to get your attention, and you take it as a personal jab, like he's out to get you."

Argon's eyes widened. "The boy wiped his own personal snot on my head...he's the one that's personal...not me!"

Anna stirred awake remarked. "Hey...that's enough...no more snot wiping, lugie-hockin, eye-ball pointing, heads a shaven, goings on...just stop!" Everyone that was awake laughed. Tommy walked in from finally being able to get back in from outside.

"What did I miss?" He said. Amen's face turned three shades of light green. Tommy saw the look in Argon's eyes, knowing Amen had to be involved.

"What did you do now, Amen?" Amen didn't want to look at his father.

"Nothing...we were just messing around." Argon stood to defend himself.

"The snot-monster thought it would be cool to wipe a booger in my hair!"

Tommy whipped his head in Amen's direction. "Dude, what, did I tell you about doing gross things like that...you're in trouble mister! Wait till I get you home!"

Little Amen's face drained of color. "I was just playing with him. The big idiot doesn't know when I'm playing or serious."

Tommy walked toward his son hurriedly like he was going to swat him across the head, and then Danica stepped between them.

"He's okay Uncle Tommy, I've got this. Besides while we're on this trip I'm responsible for him..." Danica looked over at the little troublemaker.

"Isn't that right Amen?" Amen perked up and looked at their fearless leader.

"Yeah...she is...I mean she's our leader and all. Sorry Argon, I was just messing around." He looked over at Argon with a bit of hesitation in his stance. "And I'll try to mind my own business from now on." Amen gestured by putting his two wrists together. "Put the handcuffs on me and haul me off to baby jail." He said a little shakily.

Argon had a dissatisfied look in his eyes. Then he looked up at his Uncle Tommy.

"Can I cuff his feet to his hands, like cowboys do to the calves in rodeos?" Tommy smiled and backed off with his flicker of anger. Shaking his head, and knowing well, there were more important issues at hand. Danica cautiously reached down to possibly take Amen's hand, maybe looking for a stray booger that got away from him.

"You should wash your hands Skippy before you infect us with germs." Amen developed a hurtful stare in his eyes, but then a slight smile graced his face.

"Look…see? No left-over boogers…believe me the trigger-nigger got all the snot in his hair…the snot-monster never misses." Tommy's eyes glazed toward his son again.

"What did you call him?"

Amen was a little hesitant about repeating the double meaning word. "Well, I mean he's a trigger-nigger…it's not what you think it means dad…honest, I even looked it up! I mean it's a derogatory statement, yes, but meaning something different than you think. The Google explanation of trigger-nigger means to be an African American equipped with a handheld firearm. It fits Argon to a tee. The meaning in third tense of the word means a person who goes on a crime spree of shooting up everyone that stands in the way. That's how the meathead is like. He shoots first and then asks questions later. I didn't mean it as it sounds, besides who's going to think I showed any prejudice way of seeing others, when I'm blue in color and have gills in my neck, and from a heart-felt warning it fits the description. And besides birdbrains over there, and everyone else calls me all kinds of names, and I never get hostile toward anyone. I don't mind being talked harshly too. Besides, my hide is a little thicker than that, and I have to make up for my lack of size with words."

Tommy looked over and couldn't believe what he was hearing. "Well, I'd prefer for you to not use the word in any contextual form because it's a reminder of what people had done before, and it doesn't sound very polite either."

"Euuhhh…careful dad that's a big word to use…contextual? I'm not supposed to know what it means just yet, but I do, and besides, if it wasn't for me, we wouldn't had made it this far. Ask Danica, she'll tell you."

Tommy looked across the room of cemented circles and caught the view of the youngest of leaders and blinked. Amen passed a disheartening look back at his father. "Well, it's not meant to bring comfort or joy to those hearing it dad. It's supposed to intimidate them, so they pay heed that I mean business. It's something smaller people do to get everyone's attention…and besides, Argon being the meathead that he is, needs to wake-up and pay attention now and then, and in his case, it appears to be working."

The day had started with the boys of misaligned partnerships. Drew walked past the entrance with Torack trailing behind. He looked up with a worried expression in his eyes, and his hair was misconstrued and flying about. Drew had a gentleness of character that followed him around each day, yet this day he was a bit slower in his actions. He'd grown shoulder length hair with a stubble shadowing his face, bringing out the older lines of starting to age. His face appeared set in a recent array of worry. All those that had followed him the last fifteen years sensed the difference in their leader's stride. The sun was not soon to come up as drizzle moved to rain within minutes. Anna, Bella, and the rest would follow along by getting up for the day pitching in to prepare the morning breakfast. What was more than strange, about this area was everything remained peaceful for the moment, even though a storm was soon to come back their way. And no birds of the air had followed along, no acknowledgments of a peaceful day was ready to break in of pre-dawn light. No insects scurrying about doing their morning productions, no animals were working their way toward fields of flowers in early morning sun. Danica wondered where her father had went. He was just missing from what she could tell. She noticed from before he had a lost look in his eyes when staring. The rest of her crew were just waking up.

From outside the silo, Tommy was the first to speak. "So why are they here?"

Drew's eyes fluttered with an altruistic stare. "I'm not sure what you mean?"

Tommy's eyes signaled toward the warriors standing before them, and then Drew understood. "Oh...that...well, I don't rightly have all the answers, even though you might think." Drew said with a raised sense of reluctance.

Tommy could hear a little agitation in his voice. So, he decided to leave Drew to his own thoughts, and got on with walking around them as antipathy filled his mind. Drew's hands were shaking, a bit edgy when cross-examining these creatures out in front.

From inside the silo, Danica knew confronting her father now wasn't in good timing to find answers she was seeking. In time, she'd find answers from personal experiences. Just then, little Amen came up behind Danica and whispered in her ear.

"Need my assistance?" His eyes were wide and unblinking in her line of thinking, which caused her to smile, as she dropped her eyes missing his glance. Danica quickly looked back down to catch him chomping on a piece of bacon. Mimicking the smallest of fisherman with the biggest catch. He was loaded like a smoking gun.

"Yeah...how'd you know?" She asked.

Amen smiled from the corner of one cheek. "I'm a good listener." He mimicked.

Ismael came over to get the meaning of the conversation. "What did you hear Skippy?"

Amen looked up. "She needs my help because I'm trustworthy." He said while rubbing two of four fingers against his shirt, in a mock procession of being smart. While Danica moved toward the door, Amen and his brother followed her from behind. Amen grabbed another strip of bacon on his way out. The wind began to pick up again as it whistled in and out of the opening of the silo. They had no idea of the conundrum soon to face them. Those warriors of heaven's elite had come quickly during the night without them knowing. Danica sensed something brewing currently escaping them. The Conquerites were on some type of mission. Danica wondered why they were here but left it to her father to barter of those thoughts to a king's way of thinking. Then noticing suddenly, two hundred feet ahead, how surreal the sky cracked thunder, a warning of returning violence was just up ahead. It was a distraction,

from her point of view as she looked on. Amen got closer than needed in
being, reached out and touched the foot of the first Conquerite he'd seen.
These angelic beasts weren't buying any temperamental dealings with
small boys of misaligned thinking. Ismael turned to see little brother in
some-kind of Trans. Held inherently cemented to this creature that had
taken him. He looked plugged into an electric socket, from Ismael's angle
of view, there was no way of releasing his grip. Concerned by the second,
seeing the smaller of brother's with fluttering eyes. Possessed by this beast
robbing his speech, Amen's body was shaking, with a blank stare in his
eyes. He was somewhere else. And his usual giddy self was incoherent of
anything else. Danica wondered what Ismael was staring at when turning
back around. Then she saw Amen.

"Hey…let him go!" She yelled.

Immediately Amen was thrown to the ground. He scrambled
backwards trying to distance himself from this beast that had him
trapped just seconds before. Speechless, Amen stared up baffled by what
he'd just experienced. Trying to make sense of endless glitches of what
he had seen. Some type of warning was all he could think. Definitely
nothing he wanted to experience ever again. Overwhelmed by the visions
he wet his pants. Now knowing what it was like to be trapped. With an
expression of panic in his eyes, and a line of drool off his lip. Within
another minute, Danica knew this was beyond what a boy of his age
would comprehend. The rest of the members were standing all around,
drawing in this picture of a detached boy holding on to something
strange. Amen's expression turned a paler color of blue. Nothing would
ever be the same. Danica tried to understand why Amen was speechless.
It appeared he was holding his breath. These elite warriors out in front,
standing tall from another side of experiences, created for a specific
reason. They were protectors of a crown, on a king's approval, not held
to rules and regulations of these human's limited excuses. Argon looked
down wondering where the boy had run off too. Caught in a trans-like-
wonder, not clear in his way of thinking, and hanging on the loose end
of denial. He looked overwhelmed from Argon's angle of perception, and
then he felt sorry for ever condemning him.

From a few years back, Argon had been electrocuted by one of
Torack's inventions, while not paying attention to what was around him.

He knew that Amen was traumatized from the experience by leaving no doubt. Argon reached in sympathy and put a hand on Amen's shoulder.

"Are you okay?"

Amen didn't take his eyes off the beast in front. Without words, he kept backing up by feet and hands as if there lay an image of unrevealing facts. Comprehending that he was back in the land of the living, and that's when it happened…

Amen let go of those dreams that, held him so vividly of another side of life, and began to cry. Not a cry like a child would cry from being uncomfortable from usual circumstances, but a cry reflecting an anguished fright. Danica leaned down to bring comfort, from being moved by Amen's heated emotions. They lay somewhere else of mixed-up vivid pictures. Tommy, and the rest of their members, came running out of the silo hearing the anguished screams. A wave of tense trills came from the back of his throat, like a dolphin would make warning others to stay away, not to face the fate he had felt that day. Tommy reached down and scooped up his son and ran, not knowing what to do in calming him. Quickly, moving toward the silo he took him undercover while trying to figure out what was wrong. How could others have missed this? Tommy thought, lacking adult understanding, not knowing the differences of playing around with these creatures out in front. They'd been educated to adjust involving unique circumstance, within controlled limits, usually not in a current no man's land out of control. What had gone wrong to cause his youngest to react so distractedly? To hold on to memories stripping the boy of self-awareness, like he'd been beaten or taken advantage of.

"What happened to him?" Tommy asked as he looked back at the two older boys.

Ismael's face turned a paler blue. He looked down, angled toward his father and the younger of brothers with bending knee. A look of confusion glazed in his eyes. Ismael caught the gist of his father stare and commented.

"I didn't do anything dad…he grabbed a hold of the Conquerite like it was some kind of joke…the creature wouldn't let go of him!" Tommy didn't quite understand.

"Wouldn't let him go…what…it did something to him?"

Renee stood in their midst and explained. "He saw something…the Conquerite showed him a different life than the one we are commissioned to live." Everyone turned to look at her.

Tommy glared at her. "What did it show him Renee?" Renee didn't know how to answer. She wasn't certain of the vision; not sure Amen had the same experience as her vision. He was connected to them like no one ever had been before, and sensing something stronger about his connection that brought fright to her sense of belonging. She could only assume he saw something similar. She knew what he felt was not meant for the eyes of a child. They were meant for a unique person of purpose involving those visions seen by those beasts of realms, and not so much a boy with an overactive imagination.

"The elite," she said, "those created to protect the borders of heaven aren't meant to understand the mind of a child. They are meant to rule with authority, given of a King who sits in judgment. They can only reveal what is commissioned for a warrior's mind, a mind of facts without fiction, for what he'd envision was past history. Whatever they showed Amen, it wasn't meant for the innocents of a boy so fragile." Yet something was missing from what Renee first concurred. Then she knew as quickly as she'd been interrupted.

Then Torack interrupted Renee. "It was a commissioning of a King for him to see what he saw, to make him stronger—ready for the next step for him to take with this Circle of members, who will take a quest to earth, to that other world left behind in memory will be his calling."

"And that means?" Tommy asked.

"I believe the young seer would be better in explaining what he saw."

Renee stood unblinking with a bewildering stare, as she swiped the back of her hand across her forehead. "He saw a past that a boy of his age shouldn't see. To be sure there was blood and dismemberment from the captivation of war would way heavy on the heart of such a boy so innocent. I'm sure he was shown a life commissioned with destruction all around. I'm sure he'll never forget." Everyone stared at Renee, puzzled by such prophesying.

Torack was normally the one who saw such things as this, had no idea how to explain the inexpiable. He was not of the human species, not understanding their way of thinking.

"Young seer, what is he to do?" Torack asked.

Renee shocked that she carried such authority. Torack considered it a reasonable question of the girl who mostly kept to herself.

"Show no fear of what the warrior reflected. We are all a part of this same membership of members." Renee felt a chill in the air as darker clouds began to roll in. A quivering of lips and eyes unblinking as she looked up.

"It took him somewhere. A place where the human mind cannot grasp. The dream's that start there never end." Renee paused so that she could select her words intelligently.

"Those beasts up there were created for the protection of the realms. They don't feel emotion or pain. Their meant for solving of differences. Evil of the former is not allowed to dwell there. It's not a place where evil is ever allowed to go. The Conquerite had given Amen a vivid picture of the other side of a disconnected life of those that go there. They are controlled by a different type of master than one so loving." She said. "Amen was allowed to get close to the visions he experienced, out on the edge of that other world where life ceases to exist."

Tommy stood and pointed at the older of brothers. "You should have been watching him!" Ismael through his hands in the air, totally unaware how to answer a father of unusual circumstances. Renee turned to view Tommy's gaze as she interrupted him.

"It was meant to make him stronger." She said. "It was supposed to happen this way."

Tommy wondered where she was going with her words. "Why?"

"He's meant to go with us. I mean back to earth. I saw it in the vision." Renee said, "And it's not our choice who should go back or who should fight. It's our commission of a King to not disturb our hands in this. It's been appointed by a Circle of members long before us."

"She's right." Anna said. "Amen was chosen for something not yet experienced. But he'll know of the time when it comes. He's connected to Danica in a way that connects us all. Something to do with his innocence." She said, "Amen is the one that keeps them motivated in going the right way." All of them turned to look at Anna. "I don't know how I know of such things, but I do." Anna said. "I know he is the key in connecting us to the end. We're only given what's needed today, and then tomorrow we'll learn of what we need next." She paused to look at Amen. "That's how it works. That's how it has worked since the beginning of time." Anna kept her gaze at the small bluish boy of shaky dimensions.

Everyone stood around Amen in silence. Torack looked over and wondered what was going on. He thought of the frightful visions. Amen's hands were still shaking when considering what came next. He wiped at his eyes and looked up. Fourteen sets of eyes caught him off guard.

"The Conquerite meant me no harm." Amen said. "There wasn't time to prepare for what he had to show me. The big flat-footed goon doesn't feel emotion like we do. He's different. He pulled me from that place where dreams are made of…before they could take me." Amen paused then looked up.

"They are Guardians like no other. Teachers have taught them of a realm, their way into that other world is by dreams given to them, but how they do it…I do not know?"

Renee looked down with a puzzling stare. "Amen, what did you experience?"

Amen's eyes lit up. "We have to go back. If we don't…nothing will be as it should."

Renee's eyes remained steady. Amen reached up and scratched his lip while showing a touch of worry. Something was different about him after coming back from that other world. He felt like he'd been gone for days in a fraction of time. His body shuddered from the experience as his complexion grew clammy. The Conquerite gave him a dose of reality, a reality never meant for those of earth. Now it was a part of him. His tongue felt swollen as his mouth went dry. Amen tried to clear his troubled mind while his heart rose up in his throat. The right side of his face gave a short shudder of uncertainty, as a bead of sweat graced his forehead. He was a paler blue than Ismael had ever seen. Anna interrupted Amen before he could get started.

"Let him rest for now…" Anna said. "He's not ready to explain."

Tommy agreed with a nod.

Amen took that as an indicator that he was off the hook for now. He took a deep breath and let it out slow…

Danica had enough of being pushed beyond limits. She stood and walked toward the door. Wanting to know what Amen had seen. She couldn't wait to understand the connection of the boy she felt drawn too. The Conquerites might show her just as well about the end was her thinking. When she got to the entrance an arm reached up and stopped her from clearing the door. Torack had grabbed her before she reached the opening to show his concerns. Danica turned to catch his inflection. "They won't show you what they showed the boy." A puzzling glance caused her to raise an eyebrow.

"Why wouldn't they?" She asked.

Torack paused for a second before answering. "His purpose in showing the boy has passed—he won't show the images again." Danica had developed an expression of anger. The color in her cheeks turned a darker shade of red and her lips tightened. She was drifting back in memory—something her father had told her from the past. Her father was sitting on the shoulder of a Conquerite watching him disembowel Dark-Angels in the dead-zone, like an extermination ritual—her eyes turned into a solemn stare of anger and confusion. She remembered three years before when Drew thought this lesson of war would be something Danica would remember for a life-time—well she had, and she did, but why was her stomach churning into knots? And why was she so confused about what was going on? The thought of blood and decapitation made a lump rise up in her throat. Danica had the unique ability to be able to see flashbacks of vivid pictures, but she was done with such creatures showing young minds what they shouldn't see. They had left more than a persuasive memory told by her father. It was more a spiritual delusion of facts. No emotions had been shown by these giants of heaven. The Circle wasn't given any path to take until needed. Almost like this was all a part of someone's masterplan, but it didn't included them into a planned out plot where each moment was prepared appropriately. But their journey was to be played out one sequence at a time, without any references to go by except clues at a moment's notice.

Danica reached for her mouth—just as the smell of bacon and canned beans hit her throat. She stood-up quickly grabbed her sword before throwing-up just passed the doorway. Without further consideration of who was around her, she ran out into open fields of darkness and rain headed for the forest, almost at a full sprint. Every second that ticked by every curve or bend in the pathway forced her to move faster, as if memories of her life chased after some past that she had clung too, memories that were laid up in the tightest part of her head, now with an empty heart and stomach eluding to the fact that a stressful day had finally gotten the best of her. This was the beginning of a long enduring day turned night. Streams of rain ran down her cheeks as she ran like the wind.

Back in the silo, Amen stood-up slowly, even in his precarious state and noticed Danica had disappeared from earlier. He slipped through the fingers of his father so quickly, shouting a passionate message, as he tried to choke out the words from his mouth, yet a dry mouth and swollen tongue held him from sharing any words. Amen's face showed a look of panic as he knew from internal instincts, Danica disappeared beneath covered feelings of leaving the scene. He knew she moved toward forest under stranger conditions. The heavy foliage all around had carried her toward an altered state, buried in the blackness of the storm. The boy of a broken heart looked up toward the sky. He yelled as if the devil himself had stolen love from his heart, through trickery and butchery in the sacrifice of blood. Connecting those dreams from another day of a girl detached from her usual self. He remembered those dreams so vibrantly. Amen belted out the words archaically. "Danica…stop…I'm sorry…please come back!!!" Amen looked to and frow of forest and saw nothing but continued to yell as the rain ran off his face and hands. "Danica…I'm sorry…I didn't know…please come back!!!" He was lost, a setting turmoil in his mind, slipping past reality of normalcy, started to burst up out of his heart. After several more shouts, Amen got down on his knees and cried feeling the interruption of a beating heart. An overwhelming injected pain weighed heavy on his mind as he thought of the worst. After surviving such vivid details, he couldn't face the fact that their young leader had left them all without giving answers of knowing why?

To make matters worse, the wind blew like hours hence of the night throughout, and the puddles of rain gave way to an earth of camouflaged reflection from the ground to the sky. They were living in a mirage of a different kind. The Circle, from behind, gathered a few items of survival and headed for finding their leader, as Amen was soon to catch-up. Drew and Anna were bewildered by their daughter's sudden emotional breakdown—now finding out she had left the safety of the silo now missing. She was set to get lost on her own, far from any of her kind, without a clue of knowing her direction. The most important concern of the moment was finding their daughter. They were among the worst of weather on the middle of another long storm. Tory, the next in line of leadership, looked up at Drew with a serious tone in her voice.

"Uncle Drew, we've got this…she's my responsibility when her heads not screwed on right, besides she's like a little sister to me." Drew's face had become puzzled by her insinuation of leadership. He stared into her eyes showing a sway of character of a gifted member of his kind, a young lady, grown into a woman, who'd been flown across the galaxy of her youth, from another day behind of 15 years of history. He knew this was their time. To experience difficult situations with only what they'd learned, and a bit of courage laid tucked in the back of their minds. Something to carry them to the next level. Drew didn't say a word. He knew she was right. Tory nodded toward Argon who developed a big smile.

"Let's go find our leader!" Argon shouted.

"I'm going with you!" Amen said.

Tommy reached over and grabbed him by the shoulders.

"Where do you think you're going?" Amen had a look of despondency fixed in his view.

"Dad, I'm going with them!"

"No, you're not!"

Argon stood up for Skippy for the second time ever. "Uncle Tommy, he's one of us. I'll watch him like he's my little brother." This caught Amen off guard. His eyes glazed over from hearing these words, and then he looked at his father.

"Dad…it's my fault that she left in the first place. I have to go! She needs me!"

Tommy's eyes showed a hint of emotion. Argon wrapped his arm around Amen. Ismael, from a distance, looked over and felt a touch of shameful reproach. They took off toward forest undercover of hovercraft in the fiery of the storm…

Danica was lost. She had been running so long, twisting and turning through forest without knowing which direction she was going turning her all around. Mixed up, spilling with emotion, not knowing which way to go, but something told her she had run for a reason, something was pointing her in a direction now pressed in the back of her mind. The elements of weather was her enemy at the moment. The rain blocked her vision and dulled her senses, but her mind kept steady even though she had given in to the confusion left behind. Her heart was pumping so hard her head felt to explode from the pounding. Her memories took her back to a time when she was thirteen. A certain book she'd been introduced to by her teacher. Pulled from Dr. Zimmerman's personal library, called 'Hearts of Atlantis' by Stephen King. The story was about a little boy at the age of eleven who had lost his way in life, when the only male-adult friend he ever trusted left him by the wayside, escaping to a world of confusion not understood by a boy so young, so innocent. Ted, his adult friend, was a neighbor who lived upstairs who had hired Bobby to read the newspaper to him almost every day for a few dollars a week, so he could buy a bicycle he'd wanted forever, as all small boy's dream of when first growing up. Through certain events in Bobby's life, they had become close, closer than a mother who had her own selfish desires ahead of her young impressionable son. A few months later, Bobby had moved with his mother into another town, another place far away from what he thought to be normal, from a neighborhood he grew-up in to find a new life with mom. Yet mom wasn't always there for him. He left friends behind, including a young girl who he had saved from three older boys who had beat her up and dislocated her shoulder—Carol, Bobby's young girlfriend kept a small seed of hope in young Bobby's life by writing to him time-to-time. What left the greatest impression on Danica, about the story, was the disconnected feelings the young boy began to harbor in his heart, and the acting out that showed later in life as each individual event took place had hardened him, as each experience began to play out that took his trust away. What touched Danica the most was that she remembered how in Bobby's innocence, he was like a book opened to the pages of revealed innocence, trusting so willingly, loving so innocently, as each moment played out in slowly stuttered increments. Opening his heart up to devious plans of others were soon to crush him beneath the weight of broken dreams of his mother, and the selfishness of his adult friend who'd deserted him. Danica dropped to the ground into the sobs of reality. She didn't want to feel like Bobby felt when he had nobody to turn too, lost, motionless in the pains of befriended reality. Danica grasped she was a leader of gifted young warriors, yet she herself was lost in the misconceptions of her personal struggle, lost in the impressions of having a complete experience of a good life. Her heart seemed from time-to-time, to find answers to the questions that pressed against her mind, but this day was different from other days that had recently crossed her path. Through this experience she was away from home like Bobby was, surrounded by an unfamiliar environment, out on her own, feeling she couldn't go back the way that she come. Suddenly, Danica looked up to notice the surrounding circle of a dozen silvery eyes…

6

The Search

Tory was flying the hovercraft with the lights at full volume. She pushed the craft to full power without thinking about the possibility of slamming into a tree. Even though the hovercraft was run directly by solar power from the Red-Dwarf-Star, it also had the option of running on the solar-cubes as back-up, like a battery charged car. Tory couldn't see really well because of the rain coming down in torrential slanted sheets changing the view from the surface of the windows. She was flying IFR, using only the instruments in front of her. The clouds of a darker impression of a storm rolled in and took away all visual sight. Not like storms of earth. It was something out of the ordinary so accurately named by the Aquerae as a Dark-Storm, yet the loss of sight wasn't the major problem. The problem was the wind, it was unyielding. The weather seemed to have its own special hands in the mix of a chaotic world changing their surroundings by every minute. As she veered in and out between trees in a mental blur of obscurity, she knew something was different from a normal storm felt back home. Being on the other side of the planet had left all of them a bit concerned. The right choices to make had come along and passed her by, given as a different meaning of this world facing them, and at the moment none of it made any sense, especially to a young woman geared for leadership. Glitches of another time crossed her mind and caused her to hesitate. What in the world had she been doing wrong? Who would back her up when her time came to make life changing decisions? This insane quest was leading them past the last line of defense, reminding her of how fragile her state of mine was compared to the storm now facing them.

Tory glanced around to make sure everyone was still present and accounted for. Everyone sitting buckled up and ready to give chase, while sensing and knowing their leader was detached from her usual predicaments. Noticed right away Amen staring outside toward chaos. A day turned night without warning. He was just a boy learning to lean in to bend and flex, with the rising tide of new experiences, he'd learn to find his way, on not any particular day of wasted moments or memories running full speed in his little alien head. It was time to shine. Tory was somewhat stalled before turning front. She suddenly avoided a tree she almost hit. Then her mind began to wander back to an earlier time of learning as young girls do from altering experiences. Thinking, they appeared to be normal teens. An occasional internal scuffle between them, but nothing that couldn't be fixed with a nudge of reality. Everyone had stresses of growing-up, without family and friends, but weren't these degenerates her friends and family? Tory viewed her life apart of this giant puzzle missing pieces, not everything fit together like it should be. But wasn't that normal when growing up without a mom from her past and a father who'd died when she was very young? Each flash of memory left little moments of unclear thinking in the back of her mind, from a time now gone of that other world, living on dreams and teachings from adopting parents. She'd hope times of courage would come in handy when pushed to her limits. Needing only time to sort out all the changes, too find that center of control. Resourceful lessons of history to learn from, guiding hands of parents and teachings from Dr. Zimmerman. Tory inquired the gift of being able to move water. No one else was suited for such a gift. She didn't understand the circumstances behind why their parents and Dr. Zimmerman made ready for returning to earth, to face those creature once again. But knowing she was equipped with such a gift for good reasoning, she'd have her moments of success—with patience and insight from their leaders and friends. Still not understood or determined of purpose by the younger Circle members of this fellowship, yet one day it would begin to make sense, and when it did, it would make for a better day of tomorrow in the end. She'd learn to treasure adopting parents with a bit of hope taking in the little girl she knew so well. She looked in the front console mirror before looking away again. Then thinking leaving so quickly, without a second notice, leaping out into space beyond any normal conditions. These children were destined for a different type of life than the ones lived by their parents. Then she thought of Danica, she had to find her. She's in trouble, I can feel it. Then she stirred back to reality when bouncing the hovercraft off several trees, turning it sideways before slamming it into a third tree. It bounced several times through soggy terrain with mud and muck and drifting wind. All covered in mud and damaged and dented before coming to a complete stop. Luckily most of them were strapped in their seats with seat belts. At Amen's angle he could see his brother was not moving. He noticed a trickle of blood coursing down his brother's face. He shot up out of his seat. The usual mental connection with his brother now gone. And from outside the hovercraft, they skidded close to a sheer drop-off implicit of a darker place below. A deep gorge dropped into an abyss of an unlikely form. Renee envisioned this from a dangerous angle of perception. She unstrapped her belt and slid to the lower end of the floor. "Sit still!" She barked out as everyone turned to look at her. Well, everyone but Ismael.

"Where at the edge of something not recognized...don't move...we could slip off..." She said with a certain amount of uncertainty.

Amen being the boisterous one of the bunch looked over at his brother. "Something's wrong with Ismael." Argon was sitting to his right and noticed the trickle of blood too. Being concerned as much as Amen, he decided to reach over and take his pulse. After finding the injured member had a pulse, he looked back at Amen.

"He's alive...but his breathing is kind of shallow."

Amen turned around and made an announcement. "Did anyone bring a healing-stone?" Everyone looked back through the wondering eyes of little brother. He was on a mission to try and save the day by helping out one of the injured, yet no one gave a positive response. Tory reached into her jacket-pocket, within a few seconds she pulled out a packet of peppermint lifesavers, a Bobby-pin, a couple of computer chips, and some type of stone—but it didn't look like any healing-stone that she'd ever seen. It was gold in color, and seemed heavier, but smaller in size than a normal stone that held any meaning. She held it in her hand with a blank expression. Renee looked over and saw the stone and wondered. Surprised that it went unmentioned. Yet thinking of their present predicament of being at the edge of their possible doom she'd consider first, leaving the hovercraft behind was of a greater importance, then next, Ismael's condition. As all was being weighed in the balance of her pretty little head, she would get on stable ground before making any further decisions. Renee then looked up and gave an announcement of her own.

"We need to leave before something happens."

Tory reached from behind and handed over the stone to the smallest of members, as a sparkle of gold lit up his face. Then he looked back at Tory with a hesitant grin.

"What kind of stone is this?"

"It's just a rock I found." Tory said without over exemplifying her finding.

Little Amen developed a puzzled expression. "What's it for?"

Tory had a look of doubt when looking back at him. "I don't know…maybe for killing birds." Amen glanced back at Tory like she was speaking a language he hadn't learned yet. Tory rolled her eyes. "I found it on the ground inside the silo."

Amen wrapped up the stone and slipped it in a pocket to use for another time, and then he improvised about the small gift from their present leader. "Well, I don't plan on knocking any little birds out of trees with it, but maybe it'll work on my brother?" Argon looked over at Amen with a puzzled expression.

"What—you're going to throw a rock at your brother?" Amen glanced back at Argon like he was one of those kids that wares a yellow helmet with the long hot-pink flag on the back of his bike. "Dude—don't make me say something and call you names—we're in a fix right now, and I don't have time to argue!" Argon looked a little uncertain about what Amen meant, but left it unsaid for their thoughts of troubles headed their way was more immediate at the moment. He reached up with the blunt end of his gun breaking a large piece of glass out of the upper part of the hovercraft. A shower of glass splattered a sudden burst of emancipation catching them all off guard. The group of teens comprehending the weather's wind and rain suddenly slashing across their faces. Amen tried to cover his brother's face from shattering glass fragments.

"Dude really, come on…a warning would be nice!" Amen yelled. Argon looked down and noticed everyone taking a stance of duck and cover.

"Oh…sorry guys…I wasn't thinking!" Amen had a bemused stare in his eyes and thought the lug-head deserved a comeback.

"So, when God was handing out brains, you thought he said trains and took yours?"

Argon looked a little confused. "What's that supposed to mean?"

Amen added the punchline. "It means your Chew…Chew runs down-hill only."

Tory looked over with a scowl on her face. "Alright you two…there's no time for this…we've got a mission to accomplish!"

Once getting out, the hovercraft looked to be in sad shape from behind them. While creaking it wobbled slightly to the edge of the rift. The hovercraft seemed not to recover from its bout with the trees, and the gorge below left them all feeling a little uneasy. Argon, being the one with muscles, besides Jacob, looked to pick up Ismael, yet assuming he was severely injured, not wanting to bring further injury. He couldn't help but smile when he thought how Amen would always argue with his older brother. Renee touched the young man that remained unconscious.

"He'll be okay, but we need to get him out of the rain, and in a better place so I can take a look at him." As a look of worry graced her face. Ismael had a paling blue ailment surrounding him, and Amen didn't look happy about his brother's color either. He cast a concerned stare back as Ismael's condition loomed over him. No one knew how bad he was injured.

Slowly and confidently, Danica reached for her sword without standing, angled with the search of hoary eyes all around. The water she stood in had a stagnated odor, as if a crop of dead animals had been washed down beneath the run-off of rainwater and gathered below her feet. Being well trained and up to par with her present gifts, Danica began to sense an eerie presence overtake the wet irritant odor lingering around her. Flashes of vivid pictures ran through her mind about being close to the den of vicious hunters of the four-legged kind, an animal she hadn't seen yet by her limited travel of space. The view of a dozen silvery eyes gleamed in the darkness of glistening rain. She had remembered the teachings of the Aquerae, whose idea of survival was totally different than the human perspective of making an impression. They had believed the eyes were easily tricked by what was visually displayed. Danica had to think as the wolf, keen with the ears, and up to par with the scents in the air. She cleared her mind to home in on other senses to take careful control of her next move. Danica was standing in a lower indentation of land surrounded by trees; branches laid waste across the ground, as fern and forest hid dangers undercover. She stood in three feet of water flowing from the small inclines, gushing rivers of rain. She remembered a passage of poetry she once read that fit her situation. She couldn't recall the artist, but she did see the words flash through her mind like a blink of redemption.

The heart of pain that sufferings caught, that fills the gaps of redemption bought. Slip or gloat between the dreams with unrealized moments of distant schemes. The memories left that time forgot, is the place where lives the flesh that rots. The heart is the place to keep the dreams, close to the eyes not what it seems, close to the eyes not what it seems...

Danica slowly slipped beneath water like a chameleon blending to its environment. The eyes that had captivated her descent assumed she had taken refuge beneath water's hidden reality...

Argon quickly pulled Ismael's unconscious form from the hovercraft and laid him beneath a large tree out of the rain. The older boy's lips had turned a darker blue from a normal scene of a healthy specimen. The air was thick with moisture making most members feel they couldn't catch their breath. The day looked as if night had taken precedence of rights becoming a violent interpretation of change. The sun disappeared above as clouds rolled in of an ancient passing. To keep from breathing in too much water, Argon made everyone put on safety masks like a fireman would wear. He reached down and put a mask on Ismael. Amen looked over at the muscle-bound boy with liquidated space between his ears.

"What are you doing?" Argon looked a little puzzled by Amen's questioning.

"The rain...I don't really want him to drown." Argon informed the little sergeant.

Amen shook his head and hardened his eyes. "The Aquerian species can breathe under water douphus...that mask is not going to do anything for him except fog up!" Amen at his wits end pulled the mask off his brother. "Let me worry about him—you worry about our safety."

Argon, embarrassed, gave a half salute receiving the gist of Amen's message. The hovercraft from behind, slid off the edge and skidded into the abyss. Amen had a bewildered look in his eyes, as the group of young Circle members turn to look at each other with baffled glares, knowing they had escaped a near death experience. Amen reached into his jacket pocket and pulled out the stone. Looking down a glint of gold lit up his face.

"What do you think it's used for?" He looked up at Tory. She shook her head.

"I told you I found it! Something that Torack dropped, I think. I mean...I meant to give it back, but then everything started happening... you screamed...everyone ran outside..."

They all looked down to view what was in Amen's hand. Six young people stood in the pouring rain with the tempered wind trying to find out for a second time why, they were in a quagmire of chaos bending into the wind? Renee looked up after seeing a sparkle of light.

"It won't work on your brother." She reached up to try and clear the rain off her mask.

"How do you know?" Amen asked.

Renee stared back at Amen unblinking. "I'm a seer—it's my job to know!" She shouted above the storm.

In innocence, Amen tried to find a fraction of hope in a use for the stone. But the stone was left still like a cold rock that it was. "You could be wrong," Amen said, "it's worth looking in too."

Renee put her hand down and shook her head. Amen looking over unrelenting.

"Then what's it for—I mean Torack would have a purpose or a reason for having…"

Then Renee interrupted him when remembering. "It's a courage-stone." She said.

Everyone turned to look at her.

There was a bit of confusion in Amen's eyes. "A what?"

"It's a courage-stone." She repeated. "I don't know why he's never mentioned having one, but I can tell you what I do know." She said. Everyone stared in her direction while waiting for her response. Amen impatient for an answer pressed her to keep talking.

"Renee…what's the purpose of the stone?"

Renee looked back trying to find the right words to say. "It was meant for this Circle" She said. "You don't put it on anyone's forehead. It's sort of like a good-luck charm. The Aquerae say it has even a deeper meaning, but I don't know how to explain it." She said.

Amen looked down as it started to glow. "Why would Torack carry such a stone for good-luck?"

"I don't know the answer to that Skippy." Renee said.

"Hey guys, we're getting a little off the subject." Tory advised. "We need to find our leader before we get washed away with everything else!"

As a group, they were running out of solid ground, as rivers of water poured toward this abated hole behind them. Two substantial gates of earthly once stable masses of land, built up on two sides gave a soggy rendition of cohesiveness. It was crumbling before them. The view below appeared to be without form, as the bottom couldn't be seen from the top of the straggled ridges. Foliage of fallen trees and stratified rocks with dirt loomed together by fragile soils misplaced of solid ground. In its own personal way, life was given to this earth as it appeared to change without notification of those who shared its borders. An incredible source of water once flowed through this monstrous valley of what used to be, yet as seen from how the land was cut; a massive earthquake had scourged this place of another time yet held to a fragile state of existence. The wind blew, the clouds rolled in, and the rain came down, as a fading light showed clumps of mud moved on downward inclines of drifting descents.

The mountains behind and front laid gaped by considerable distance, catching all of them inattentive. Renee's feet suddenly slipped out from under her. Argon, with gentle agility reached for Renee quicker than anticipated and broke her fall. Tory flipped on a light that was on the top of her visor, comparable to a minor's headlamp. The ground below them was moving like slow cancerous mounds of earth. They were gradually being forced toward the edge of this apocalyptic rift in the earth. Even the trees in the distance were pulled by the rivers flowing towards them. Tory had to do something before their circumstances got any worse. She immediately began drawing water from the earth. Arching waves rose up before her, on both sides of an upward pathway. Like Moses parting the Red sea. The water mounted a central path cutting toward higher ground—moving away from the acoustic gap below, as tons of water poured into the blackness behind them. Their group of members had taken a higher road. Argon draped Ismael over his shoulder like a bag of dogfood from a local supermarket. Tory used her gift to continue cutting a path toward an uphill climb. A road leading towards the forest. Amen shrugged his shoulders and slipped his fingers into Tory's hand, like a small boy with a clairvoyant focus of survival. Tory gripped his hand with coldly frigid fingers sliding between the comforts of human warmth. Amen let out a breath of air as he looked up. His mind and heart set in sequential rhythms of purpose, beating with adrenaline and trust. Tory, a tall and slender young woman, showing long ringlets of red hair plastered against her face, molded in this environment from failing circumstances, water glided off her arms, as beading droplets shimmered from partial light. Her clothes clung to her body resembling an altered experience of extreme weather. She being a well-balanced warrior trained by the best. A woman who would passed each test given, practiced and implemented through sacrifice by being consistent in daily living. Her life was shadowed by a reflection of personified perfection, bending in service towards six members of a youthful heart. Their lives were but those that were gifted, chosen by a King of realms, cutting a trail through this rugged country, brought on by an altruistic gathering of a functioning unit.

A dozen silvery eyes leap toward the lower incline of land that had faced their leader. Danica slipped through a door and came up behind a pack of wolves of thickly woven coats of fur. She swung her sword in a silent calm of clarity. The spreading of blood and fleece thrown into the mix of mud, rain, and growls progressively played out as a quicker version of things not seen but experienced. Then her mind reversed in slow motion what had been seen by this girl turned warrior. Danica had seen each movement of pain, planned out each moment provisioning sword to swing in finesse as a female of strength could learn to be. Her movements were as if a heavenly host of an immortal-kind tread on sodden soil beneath silent feet knowing direction before making hast. The wolf-pack lunged toward air, water, and forgotten bones of obscurity. Surprised to feel that she was not there quickly disappearing from thin air. Three wolves gone beneath sword and confusion—outsmarted by a leader of gifted warriors, talents tested to the max while hanging on to the loose end of intelligence. Danica flipped and turned with an accuracy of redundancy. She stood on a trail straight from hell, dripping of blood and confusion. Standing firm in the confidence of her training, fervently poised of over exposed unfriendliness, dressed up in her usual wares of giddiness, leaning towards better conditions than what had been seen from previous. Positioned with heavy breath—gazing into the eyes of instinct and scents in the air, with moistened rational in commitment, from chaos coming from the silence of sporadic confusion and forgetfulness. The larger-than-life wolf rumbled a growl at his pack showing teeth and tail toward his latest rival. His face set to focus on the fight, not giving in, not turning away from misunderstandings of flight. Danica gave a stare of unwavering anticipation. She whipped her sword from side-to-side, lost in the concentration of this strange situation. The pack turned back giving them room to roam back and forth. The Alpha leap high while Danica swept low. The rain kept pouring over them into the fierceness of adrenaline. Both went with the lead of intelligence, swishing sword with claws and teeth and spits of rage. The wolf fought fiercely through the storm as energy spent of incremental details. Rage and instinct in beastly fashion informed the Alpha of fleeting character. Yet he laid no hurt-on Danica. She avoided teeth and claws with duck and cover, swishing past her adversary. Heaving high her sword, thrusting toward the sky. The Alpha's eyes lost in the wonder of his demise. He could not see what the eyes should see with confusion all around him. Danica wrapped him up within unshaken hands she made connection with his chest. The cry of unguarded pain wailed in air of fleeting life. The Alpha lay in a heap of slow rhythms of a soon to be end, as his blood scattered in puddles of rain. The rest of the pack disappeared through bogs and trees and sudden endings.

From a distance, the water rose higher as it rushed left and right. Tory used her gift to move the water in the direction of an escarpment as it rushed toward the rift. The depth and weight of water moved as if alive in the surge of push and power. The gap in the land resembled an eerie plunge into a bottomless pit. Once on higher land, the Circle noticed they had a view crossing this great valley to the other side. Amen looked up with a childlike stare.

"Where is she?" Amen asked. Tory turned her view toward the seer of the group.

"Maybe she can answer that question a little better than I squirt?" Renee caught between Amen and Tory looked back at a boy detached. He was full of many questions and misinterpretations.

"Do you know how to find our leader?" Amen asked.

She looked back hesitantly, rolling her eyes, looked past trees while standing in a clearing on the side of a little hill. Suddenly Ismael stirred awake flapped his arms to get free from his entrapment. Being deliberately thrown over Argon's shoulder had caused several limbs to fall asleep. His head bobbled in-doll-like fashion flitting back and forth under duration of being thrown about.

"Let me down numb-nuts, you've bruised my body beyond recognition!"

Argon was so surprised by the announcement from the dead of limber limbs almost dropped him. Ismael was livid from the sudden splash of cold water kicked up by Argon's heels. Argon suddenly stunned by Ismael's awakening, knew further complaining was soon to follow.

"Dude...I'm not a football! Be careful with the merchandise! It's not like I have parts to replace me!"

Argon tripped over a root beneath the water losing his grip and dropped Ismael about a foot off the ground. Ismael hit the puddle of water just in front. Looking down they could only see the whites of his eyes. Ismael was covered head to toe with mud. Amen looked over and smiled.

"Hey dude…you scared the crap out of me." Amen said. Then a vivid thought of the 'Ghost-Busters' movie ran through his head. "I ain't afraid of no ghost!" Amen mimicked a close rendition scene he'd remembered, all bug-eyed with his bottom lip sticking out. Everyone laughed at Amen's little recital of ghost like features. Ismael didn't find it funny. And Argon reached down to help Ismael up off the ground.

Looking offended Ismael remarked, "Go-ahead…laugh at the guy with the bump on the head and mud in his eye." Amen covered up a smile.

"We are…but don't be so offended." Amen said. "Argon pulled you out of the wreckage, and the rest of the hovercraft fell off the edge—it's gone!" Amen pointed back behind them. Ismael looked up in all the confusion. Reaching to scrape mud out of his eyes, blinking back a muddy scowl, then noticed their recent ride had departed off a cliff.

"I knew there was something wrong. What happened?" Ismael asked.

Amen wondered about his brother's frame of mind. "Look around you numb-skull, it's raining cats and canaries, and were walking in a foot of mud. It's not like a bus is coming your way. We're all mucky, or did you miss that part?" Ismael looked around suddenly realizing little brother was right, they all stood in mud half-way up to their knees.

"Oh, sorry guys, I didn't understand where we were headed." Argon patted Ismael on the back and helped him to his feet. Tory pulled a rag out of her back pocket and offered to wipe mud off his face. Ismael took the rag and relieved his eyes and face of muck and mud. He dipped the rag in rushing water and rung out the excess. Ismael's face looked like he was wearing a thin layer of brownish make-up. Tory stared for a moment from the sudden change of color.

"I like the new look." She said. "You look better that way than the usual blue."

Ismael's bottom lip trembled with a bit of misguided interpolation. He wasn't sure of the latest complement, soon to lose interest he batted his eyes and shakily walked up the hill fronting them.

"Does anyone know where we're going?" Ismael asked, as he quickly looked back.

Tory pulled out her compass to get a clearer picture of direction. Jacob tired from carrying Argon's over-zealous element-gun handed it back.

"Here, you take it now...too heavy to lug around...besides I'm tired and need a break."

The other members had their own backpacks pulled from the wreckage before it slipped off the edge. Then Ismael noticed his backpack missing.

"Hey...where's my back-pack?" He belted out.

Amen gave him a sheepish look. "I couldn't carry everything...its gone...you should of stayed awake." Amen informed him.

Ismael pushed little brother lightly wondering about personal stuff missing.

"So, where's my stuff?"

"Lighting-up big brother, it's in my backpack. I couldn't carry two packs, so I improvised." Ismael looked over noticing little brother's backpack was plumper than usual. Amen pulled his arms through and set it on top of a rock.

"Did you get everything?" Ismael asked.

Amen couldn't believe what he was hearing. "Hold-up...ish...we crash landed and we're still alive, and you're wondering if I got all your stuff? You better think again big brother!"

Ismael retained what little stuff was saved by little brother and wrapped it up in his jacket. He wondered about the little scoundrel losing his things. By then they had reached the top of a hill just passed a clump of trees where the area had opened up to a bare spot of land portraying a different set of circumstances. The sky was a darker gray as the rain came down blocking most of their vision, yet something slightly beyond the cliffs on the other side of this rift looked a bit strange.

Danica suddenly realized the pack of wolfs were giving her room of respect for killing their leader. But she knew they'd be back within minutes to make another stand against a smaller foe. She leaned forward to catch her breath, then shook the water from her hair and tied it in a ponytail. She wiped her sword off while adrenaline coursed through her body like a freight train. The aches in her shoulders and pains in her back reminded her of being human. Her heart felt like it was up in her throat, and her hands started to shake when realizing she just bested a pack of wolves. It caused her to feel alive. This was crazy. Danica knew certain answers to certain questions wouldn't always be so clear. But at the moment she knew without thinking she'd escaped a sure death. The sudden realization caused her heart to pound and her ears to burn from blood running to her head. This lesson of survival would teach her of strengths and weaknesses. It was a time of learning, to pull from resources she never knew she had. She had come to know the fact that only through her best efforts would everything begin to make sense. A girl of eighteen yet already a warrior. Today was the beginning of a new life showing her a magnitude of living she wasn't sure she could live up to. Knowing this was the type of living she'd come to know, while living on the edge of her father's success and experiences, she would find her own way leading back home. Henceforth, by looking up, lost in waning dark shadows of the storm. With a calm clarity set in her eyes her surroundings would soon begin to make sense.

Within minutes, Danica started walking again mostly northwest. The darkness filled in like incremental cracks dug out in this Mesozoic world absorbing everything in its path, as the rain and wind beat against her face and forced her to move in an impossible direction yet standing tall, she pushed on. From her view, going back didn't look the same as coming. First, because it was getting darker from the violence of this storm pointing her back to where she had come from, and second, she couldn't remember walking this far uphill, because now she had been doing just the opposite, she'd been walking downhill. Ten minutes later, Danica came to the edge of a deep and widening rift, pointing her toward what looked to be a bottomless pit, as water rushed before obscurity in all directions. Yet her problem remembered was being on the other side separating her from where she was at present. She was gaped across a deep and fathomless canyon going north and south as she walked along the edge, trying to find a way down or a bridge or any other way of crossing, but at her present position she appeared to be on the wrong side of this incredible gap of land. She tried to recall any spaces of time to even be tenuously close to any such gap in the land, but nothing came to her—just a mystery of this great valley keeping her from moving on in the world of where she needed to be. Danica reached in her jacket pocket, forgetting what it was she had put there from two days earlier. She found the pouch and opened the top and noticed right away the healing-stones glittering at the bottom. She didn't know why she was drawn to them, but it was her luck taking them along. The stones were all she had that made any sense at the moment, and her sword strapped to her side had kept her alive, but an unnatural feeling reached into her gut pointing her into a different direction. Then suddenly she saw the smaller than usual stone on a golden chain of soft, precious metal at the bottom, glinting on its own without making a connection. Taking it gently in her hands while brushing back the rain off her face, it caused her to smile for a brief moment of realization of having a purpose. She didn't wait, she took out the necklace holding the stone and hung it about her neck, hoping to be signaled by something beyond the stars, as she looked up towards the heavens. Maybe the stone would shine past the atmosphere giving her a way to get back to the others. She hadn't bothered or remembered to bring her back-pack or anything of the ordinary to save lives like food, water, or dry matches to start a fire to keep her warm. She left without thinking straight, being emotionally separated, unbalanced in taking the right path. Now she knew she'd gotten herself in quite the mess. That's what happens when young girls leave in a fit of emotion, traipsing off into the unknown world into places they've never been. Wow…what was I thinking…if at all? Danica made a mistake, taking off without giving notice to anyone else. Knowing they would stop doing what was considered most important and chase after her. She knew this had to be the dumbest stunt she's ever pulled. In her eighteen years of life, nothing had been left behind for others to figure out quite like this. She was surrounded by chaos at every turn with no way out, nowhere to go, nothing around looked familiar of being home. The pressure of not knowing what she would face around the next corner, the next test that would take her past the limits of a girl like her out on her own. She was sitting on the doorstep of a crossroad in her life, waiting for this place around her to make any type of sense. But when had anything in her life ever made sense…until looking up and seeing an enormous shadow lurking towards the sky.

And then the thought hit her, maybe that's all I needed was a good spin through the forest facing some unnatural beast that was there to test her. Pumping her blood up to an abnormal level was her own personal cure of insanity. But then she began to feel stupid for getting lost and losing her head. This self-destructive behavior was getting her nowhere down a road by herself, without including her friends. Who would even approve of such behavior in her state of mind? She was supposed to set an example for every one of her little group of members, yet today, of all days, she lost control out on her own disconnected from the rest.

On further notice, Danica couldn't get passed this apparent barrier from one side to the other, and the gap below was something she couldn't comprehend. It was farther than she could imagine jumping or flying or taking a bus or train. It looked impossible. Her powers were somewhat limited to her vision, and being the drop was much more than an endless fall, she became hesitant about moving through a familiar door, for the fear of death was blocking her sight. Momentarily, she thought of slipping through a door, but where would it lead to? Maybe another life covered in darkness like what she was facing, she had to do something. She stood stationary for a moment to clear her way of thinking, then reached up to wipe the rain off her face as a chill went through her. Not knowing why, she felt so alone, but she did, and it started to get to her. No light from above had given her reference points of north or south, and the wind pressing her wasn't helping either. She sensed her timing had to be perfect, with the slightest drift of the wind could alter her direction or change the way she made her decisions, considering her previous acquaintances were probably soon to come back her way. A warrior girl in deafening chaos stood still for a moment in the darkness of the storm. She stood and listened to the storm around her, took in the scents of the air and the beasts of previous that roamed there. Then suddenly, a gentle breeze of cleverness overcame her. A heartbeat within gave rhythm of this world she was in, as it tried to reach for the enter parts of her very soul. An indistinguishable emotion began to surround Danica. She abruptly became connected to it—but to explain that to a person familiar to her wouldn't make any sense. Not being of ordinary boys or girls she had learned to live with it, like the constant changing of her circumstances would eventually set her to do the right thing. Her mind had been racing before like a freight-train. Set to explode on impact, similar to an eight-year-old waking up to unfamiliar surroundings, while missing family and missing friends. She had to regain her focus. Find a place to rest for a few minutes to get a better view from the top of a hill or a tree or something she could reach, before being hauled off to a better way of living, not on a darker road leading farther away from what was considered normal—if there was such a thing. If making a mistake it could be the end of her life.

Up ahead, not too far, maybe a hundred feet along the edge of this apocalyptic crack in the earth. She could see a giant tree stretched out across a good portion of this unimaginable rift. She thought it a bit strange that such a tree could remotely begin a journey across this forbidden gulf, yet as she got closer, she almost sensed it to be an invitation—this physical specimen of a tree like no other was inviting her to take refuge among its branches. Once Danica got within arms-reach of this mammoth exhibit of growth beyond measure, it almost made her smile. The tree was not any ordinary tree by any means—oh no, it was a tree, yes, but something seemed different about it. From first impression, it was over-sized...bigger than most, comparable to finding the tallest man in the universe standing in the midst of midgets, it was enormous. The tree, if stood straight-up, would be at least four-hundred feet tall—no less, and had mammoth branches reaching out like arms of comfort to a helpless girl of ordinary dimensions. Danica stood staring and developed a lump like knot rising up in her throat, with her mouth open from surprise not seeing what had approached her so willingly, she swallowed a big bumblebee, and the darn thing didn't know to head north or south—but to her it just stayed right smack in the middle, which caused an alarming condition of wanting to choke it up. Worried about the bee or the tree, or the long arms of branches that seemed to enthrall her, she hadn't known what to do. The nagging bee feeling stuck in her throat, and the massive tree calling out to her, in a way she had never felt, became like an unsettling truth choking the very life from her to decide, to move forward, to do something extra-ordinary that on first impression she would never do—but would she? Danica reached for the first set of branches, which seemed more impressive on that first touch. Something was good about this tree that stood silent before her, almost similar to an aged professor, who had given his all to bring or shed a little light on a few choice students, whoever they were to be, all precious in the eyes of the creator, but was anyone even watching? Did someone actually care?

Danica coughed up that bee like a golf-ball with legs and wings set to flight. Away across the sky in the shadows of air beyond the calling of a girl up to her neck in troubles of a rumbling storm. Funny how feelings are, you know, she thought, they get the best of us, that's when she began to cry… Danica's tears weren't about, poor-me I've really done it now.

Danica was crying because she saw this massive tree as something giving comfort, like a sail to a sailboat, or a bridge that leads across to a continued journey, or just a place one finds rest. She imagined this massive tree that swished its arms in the rage of the storm were in a way, a type of portal—a bridge in a troubled sea of non-conformance. A place she could possibly gather her thoughts, to make sense out of what had happen to her, comparable to her father, who had been caught behind unfamiliar lines of the dead-zone. Then suddenly, she looked-up and saw that bee coming back, Oh no, you don't—not letting you back into my life, she thought, I've had enough of your troubles.

Danica had forcibly been climbing this tree of her own free-will, and her legs and arms seemed too reach quickly as if time was of essence, trusting each branch as she moved forward, leaning in close to the smoothness of each curve or perpendicular likeness of conformity, like the coziness of a mother cradling her young, adjusting her positions for her baby's comfort. The higher she got in the massive tree, the more the leaves and branches engulfed her, like arms of security. Only a tree, but it was enough to let her know there seemed to be always a branch of hope, or a wrapped strong-arm of relief just ahead, as if she had to trust this tree in her way to get any further on in her life, and why a tree of all things? She remembered climbing trees when she was a little girl, but never like this, not in this way, almost like it was supposed to be there, and nothing else at this time in her life mattered more than her successfully climbing to the top. By then the rain was coming down so hard, yet it seemed to go unnoticed because Danica was so mesmerized by her upward movement that she began to lose sight of the cold, the rain, the darkness, and the wind, her mind was focused on what was at the end of this short journey, and wouldn't you know it, it would take this huge comforting tree to change this young girl's focus. It was no longer on her drab situation, or the possibility she might not make it. Her focus was on this massive tree that had reached its branches out to her in comfort, maybe not completely covering everything in her life, but still having an effect of, don't worry...I have more branches, just a little bit further... and somehow giving Danica an ounce of courage, or a drop more of faith in herself, but bygollygeeyourrightfrank I'm going to get there.

At the top of the tree, Danica noticed the branches had broken out above the clouds, even as the turmoil below, blew and hissed, and showered, it remained peaceful on top, almost like she had front row seat of watching the 20-year veteran Colby Bryant going down-town with a massive dunk on Stephen Curry in the seventh game of the NBA finals. Wouldn't that be a blessing? Just a tree...Danica thought...but was it?

Amen had his mouth open so wide, because he was looking up and noticed this wall of water coming toward them. Renee screamed, and Tory who was master at moving water had not even the remotest inkling of trying to move all this that was in front of her. She seemed just as surprised as Renee. Before Amen closed his mouth a big bee flew in and hit the back of his throat. The bee hit so hard that it knocked the crazy thing unconscious, and Amen swallowed it.

Suddenly, the alien-boy who was irreverently called Skippy, started hacking and sputtering from swallowing the biggest insect of legs and wings he could have ever imagined. Like it or not, Amen had downed this big bee, and despite everything to choke it back up, it wasn't happening. Argon being his usual ornery self, noticed the bug when first entering Amen's mouth. With a well-timed grin, Argon asked the question "was it tasty?" Amen looked offended at first, but then grew a smile.

"No, but filling...sucker had to weigh half a pound!"

A disgusting look on Argon's face was noticed by an upturned nose pushed towards the heavens, and his lips pushed as far south as they would go, before rubbing it into the little troublemaker.

"How was that for your dinner?"

Amen kept a straight face, and slowly rolled his tongue to and frow, and adhered a brighter idea when thinking. "Tasted like a honeybee with horsefly wings." Everyone's face expelled an expression of repulsion.

Renee pretended to act out by throwing up in her own mouth. Amen tried to milk this for all it was worth. "At least I won't have to worry about dinner—filled me up about as much as a two-pound Octus steak!"

Tory whipped her head around in disgust. "You're gross Skippy."

Amen continued his little barrage of pleasure. "He would have tasted better on potato bread with a touch of mayonnaise and pickles."

Renee got an expression of motion sickness going really good by now. She had just pictured getting one of the Bumble-Bee's wings caught in her teeth. "Amen, stop it before I throw-up!" She said.

Amen made it worse by burping real loud then breathing in her ear. She started throwing up almost right away. Ismael reached over and grabbed his little brother by the collar.

"Not cool Skippy!" Amen had a confused look about him.

"You're not the one who had to eat a bug…don't be haten?"

Tory raised her hands and circumvented the water around them like the children of Israel walking on dry land. After the water had passed, along the downhill for a ways, before spilling out into the giant rift they left behind them. Standing on top of this mesa about two hundred feet higher than the rest of the ground below, they gave notice of being about a hundred yards from the depth of the darkness below. It followed a winding curve bending along the edge of this great valley, forged from water years ago going north and south, not knowing where it would end up. Amen saw it first before anyone else, and at the same time the strangest thing came to his mind.

It was a slight sparkle of light reminding him of the courage-stone. Amen reached for it and pulled it out of his jacket pocket. Quickly looking down he noticed it began to glow. It shined a brighter brilliance than any stone he'd ever seen. This caused him to perk from the sight of light. Looking beyond the valley, standing on his tippy toes, just ever so slightly, to get a better view of what he'd seen from the other side. Past the deep gorge, a glimmer of light drew his attention, forming in the top of a massive tree standing alone, sitting on the edge of the cliffs, branching over to the other side of this endless rift. The funny thing about the tree, was that it was probably the biggest tree he'd ever seen, more than four times the size of any normal looking trees, but what was normal had never entered into Amen's mind. What entered his mind was finding Danica at any cost. Curious, he pointed to the other side of grayer conditions without missing a beat. "Look everyone...see that sparkle of light in that tree...watch!" He raised the courage-stone in his hand and held it high for everyone to see as it lit up.

Tory then made the connection and remembered giving the stone to Amen, from suddenly realizing she had no use for it at the moment, but now something made her hesitate. She saw the connection and put two and two together, which started to make sense, when thinking it had come from Torack. It had to be, was her reasoning. The night before, Tory, being sleepy, incoherent from the previous day, had been spent to the max before realizing there was a connection she had missed. Anna had mentioned something touching a chord in her—if she could only remember what it was. Renee looked at her a bit confused by the hesitation seen in her eyes. She wondered when the girl would make details known or atone for something redeeming of an already miserable day. And then Tory suddenly remembered.

"Torack...he didn't lose the stone." She said, as everyone turned to look at her.

"What do you mean?" Amen asked.

"Torack left it for me to find...it wasn't by accident that we have it with us now, it was supposed to be with us on this little journey."

Then they were looking at the stone still blazing like a smart little light pointing the way, but the way to what they didn't know, for the light was just discovered recently. Amen got excited by the light because it suddenly was connecting him to something else that others had missed. The light still twinkled in the softening rain. Amen finally blurted out what he could see was so obvious. "It's Danica...she's in that tree over there!"

Tory developed a curious look on her face. "What do you mean Danica's in that tree?"

Amen turned his excited body to glance back her way. "She's calling me, that's why the stone's lighting up and..." Amen couldn't finish because he thought to sound foolish, and only pointed while jumping up and down. Argon looked over wondering if Amen had a bump on his head too.

"Now just hold on Skippy! Don't get yourself all worked up over nothing!"

"But it's her, I know for sure!"

Everyone turned wondering if all this excitement was causing him to hallucinate from being over stressed from an already hard bout with the Conquerite a few hours back. Amen was dancing like he had to pee, while Argon tries to stamp out any of Amen's show of courage.

"Dude…you're losin it! There's no way you can see that far, and Danica didn't even go that direction in the first place." Amen got this big scruffy looking frown as if wanting to punch something and looking toward Argon like he'd be a likely candidate.

"Shut-up lug-nut…you don't know…she's there…I just know it!"

Argon got aggravated by Amen showing a big attitude. "Okay smarty pants…how do you know?" Amen looked offended that Argon didn't believe a word of it, and he looked like he wanted to kick him… you know where…in the lug-nuts.

Amen didn't hesitate he just said it. "The Bumble-Bee told me…I don't know how, but he did!"

Argon had his mouth open, and then he started shaking his head. "Dude…I told you to stay out of the field of drug-weed, and your dad is probably going to blame me, and then I'll get in trouble!"

Tory interrupts the two boys when noticing the light across the way too. "Amen's right…the Bumble-Bee told him!"

Argon pulled away from Tory like they were loosen it. He wondered if she'd been bitten by the same bug that flew down Amen's throat. "Come on! The Bumblebee told him? Next thing you're going to tell me is that Chris Kringle has a brother named Fred." Everyone looked bewildered by the statement.

"Shut-up Argon…let Amen talk for once!" Renee belted out. Amen got a big smile showing alien teeth of a bluish tint. He was stoked that the girls were taking his side. Jacob stayed neutral because he wanted to hear the story about the Bumblebee and its connection with the stone.

"Anna told us last night that Amen is connected to Danica somehow, which connects us all. So, you're the key?" Tory said.

Argon ignores her while Amen concentrated on the two lights glowing in unison. "The Bumble-Bee knows her!" He belted out.

Argon started laughing, and then mocks Skippy. "The Bumble-Bee knows her...the Bumble-Bee knows her...heeee...the Bumble-Bee knows her!"

Tory reached over and smacked Argon in the back of the head like his mom showed up to keep him in line. His face turned to a hurtful stare when looking back, but there was nothing he could do. Amen broke out with a smile and tried to cover stuttering giggles. The stone lit up so bright that it shot a beam of light toward the sky. Amen sucked in air while a line of drool slipped off his lip. The rain had calmed to a slow drizzle while a narrow line of light shown on the only tree of the other side of the rift.

"Look...the stone is signaling her!"

Danica sat in the very top of the tree and took notice of the stone held in the precious metal around her neck as it started to glow like nobody's business. In the valley, across this vast gulf she saw this golden color of light shoot up toward the heavens. She drew in breath suddenly, from being so spell-bound by its sudden arch of light. Her eyes perked from the sight to the point she had to catch herself from falling. With a quick glance toward the ground, she had hurriedly noticed below her that this large tree was more than holding her up, comparable to a friend or family member who never looked back at your short comings.

This made her think about a book that her teacher, Dr. Zimmerman had forced her to read. It had stuck with her for the last couple of years. Pertaining to the subject of real love, you know that hooey gooey feeling that makes you stand on your toes to reach for kisses, as your arms prickle with goosebumps. Danica smiled knowing fairy tales about fairy princesses from dream like states were just an illusion of the mind. But then where did real love come from? What she recalled from a book that Dr. Zimmerman had given to her with a show of resistance. It was an attempted warning of his. He pushed the book towards the edge of his desk. From her point of view, it wasn't a story she had ever envisioned about love or conquering the great passions of life, or about knights in shining armor, riding off into the sunset on a great white horse. It was a story about this family that seemed the most awkward from anything she considered normal, because this band of degenerates usually did what was anything but the norm, and halfway through the book she wanted to put it back on the corner of his desk, and forget she ever started reading it in the first place. She remembered Dr. Zimmerman being like an old Kirby-Vacuum cleaner salesman, with this big silly imaginable perkiness adhered on his face and hosting an unusual countenance of knowledge. She had remembered staring at him like, what the heck—you're going to actually make me read this old book, what for? And why are you being so pushy?

Dr. Zimmerman had only chuckled at her lack of sparkle about reading such a book that had already shown evidence of extreme wearing, and the pages had all turned a dingy yellow color that had her thinking of someone's great-grandmother, who she'd seen in pictures. Her skin was wrinkled like prunes, with an extremely pale observance, kind of like that book he was pushing towards her. It didn't look like any book willing to teach her about the pangs she was experiencing just recently, and certainly not something she would slide up on her bookshelf for a trophy to be remembered by. Danica remembered staring down at the book for a long time, before she decided to pick it up and skip on down the hall like she couldn't wait to open its pages. It was her punishment for not finishing her studies in a timely manner that had been set-up for her, and she had felt almost mad, but then she began to stare at this book on the corner of her nightstand. It appeared to exude some type of hidden message to teach her. Who would even guess that this old book, with the binder starting to lose its elasticity and colors were fading, would turn this young girl's heart around to picture love as something that you had to work for, and how did that old woman she pictured so vividly have anything to do with an ugly old book? What had caused so much wear and tear on that old face, which caused her beauty to fade, and why were those lines in her face so defining to the point that she looked so broken, so old, so used up like that book she was about to read? Then she remembered reading it in one afternoon, from cover to cover. When she was done, she closed the cover of this tainted covering of aged cleverness and held it close to her face. By then, Danica had both arms wrapped around this book like a security blanket, and then kissed the cover while tears rolled down her face. Why did her old teacher know so much about how she would feel, and why this book? She sat this reading material down on the corner of her nightstand and stared at its cover...she didn't know why it had affected her so, but she wasn't going to think that way ever again, it was time to move on, and she got up off her bed, brushed the wrinkles out of clothes, went over to a small desk in the corner of her room, and wrote a note to her teacher.

Being only twelve at the time, and still held the innocence of youth, yet in so many ways she grew-up that day realizing love was not about getting your way, or about being talked to a certain way, or being swept off your feet and twirled in the air. It was about a personal commitment in the bond of being together. Bonded together by some special magic that didn't come from the imagination of frilly moments of kisses and giggles. Loving others was hard work, because you had to over-look all the short comings that each individual carries along with them in life like baggage. Maybe I don't talk just right, or maybe I have a goofy walk like a duck, or maybe I'm flat-footed and my teeth are green, but I still have this deep desire to love, but maybe my love is not the right kind of love that will last forever. Maybe what I see isn't about me feeling loved, but about giving it, and maybe that rainbow on closer view isn't as pretty when close up. Love...who was I kidding? Danica thought...what was I thinking? I didn't know that life at times really sucks, but the nasty habit of loving someone else could still be there at your side, poking you in your ribs saying...come on, you're not done loving me yet...there's more journeying ahead! Tears flowed down Danica's face in the mammoth tree, which hugged her tight like her father did when she was small. Funny, this thing called love...you don't even need to talk, you just sit there and soak it all up like a sponge holding to water, comparable to that first time reading that worn-out book, or climbing that mammoth tree, leaving your heart to drop right out from under you. Danica missed her crew of young degenerates, even though they argued and didn't see everything on first impression. She missed being with them, and her father, and mother, and the rest of her family of friends. Somehow, she had to get out of this mess and find her way back to a place of security. Realizing love shown to others wasn't always going to stand out, yet somehow it would always be there hovering around the next corner of experience or buried at times somewhere beneath all the other feelings that completed her. So, love has its secrets. Sometimes love is everything around, encircling you like the arms of that massive tree hugging you gently in strong arms of support, or like that worn-out book with the yellow pages holding a deeper meaning. Who would have thought that a tree and a bee with a book from her youth with a storm by a deep separating gulf would help a young girl find love?

Amen held the stone up as high as his arms could stretch. A golden brilliance of light lit up the sky just in front, causing him to widen his eyes and suck in air. A beam of light expelled a bit of hope experienced through bliss beyond a boy of smattering knowledge. He knew Danica would see it if seated in the top of the tree. If only the others could believe like he thought, they could believe. He couldn't help but think Danica would feel the same awe of wonder, something yet to experience. Everyone could see it, near or far or possibly beyond the thinking of all others that breathed with life, and then it dawned on Amen. Maybe it wouldn't be so wise to let a world of cosmic light shine so vividly. It was meant only for a girl in a tree just beyond the valley. Having the ability to attract an enemy lying close to discovery, yet not to close, but then he didn't care. Amen wanted everyone to experience what he was feeling. The stone meant for courage was showing Amen the way to their leader. Why couldn't the others see what he could see? Out on a dreary morning of a raging storm, a moment revealing of a better path of finding her way back to those who loved her. First, from a misaligned girl searching for answers, and now a boy pointing a concerning stare toward a flicker of light with a bit of courage. Coming from a heart full of faith and a strange adherence of brilliance shining bright from a quickly fading night.

Isn't it funny, Amen thought, just in time for our leader to see...I know she's over there in that tree, and I know she knows that I know that's she is in that tree too... Then he blinked twice trying to get a hold of what that really meant. Knowing how it is with little boy's trying to get their points across, it doesn't always come out like it should, using only the words available to them. Suddenly a giant shadow gently floated over this group of Circle members with wings stretched out beyond comprehension, on the top of this insignificant hill looking across the valley. A Condorsorous of enormous size stayed hovered overhead casting a shadow that overwhelmed—

Amen points to the sky, "Look…Condac and big-bird must have seen the light!"

Suddenly, a hovercraft, above slides in close to the Condorsorous over the group of young Circle members, who were standing tall in a moment of being redeemed. Still looking ahead of the giant rift being gaped between them while both lights glowed in unison. Drew saw the sparkle of light from the short distance of a few hundred feet away. This tree, standing by itself, across this enormous valley stood stoically in a flickering of light, just enough to bring it to his attention. Amen pointed the courage-stone in that general direction. Looking up, letting his uncle know of Danica's position. Sure enough, Uncle Drew headed for the enormous tree. Everyone clapped and shouted and whistled knowing that their precious leader was waiting patiently, waiting to get rescued. All could see that Danica's father lit up the top of the tree with flood lights, illuminating everything around. She was quickly lifted up into the warm comfort of the hovercraft.

"I told you she was their! The Bumblebee told me. I only had to listen." Amen said.

A learned lesson from a boy of innocence showing a moment of courage when needed.

Danica rode in front as the others sat behind. Water was still dripping off the back of Danica's hair. Amen's lips were a deeper blue than normal, and his brother was noticed with a good size goose-egg on the top of his head. Amen grinned at big brother and asked, "Does it still hurt?" Ismael appalled at his little brother's question returned an answer with a bit of sarcasm.

"Let me put a knot on the top of your head, and ask you when you wake up, if it still hurts Skippy."

Amen's eyes narrowed, "You don't have to get hostile I was only trying to make conversation…yet deep down I know it still hurts, numb-nuts…well it's supposed to still hurt, that's why you have that egg on top of your head." It was quiet for about five seconds before Skippy finished his thought, "Besides…I like eggs…their great on turkey burgers or egg salad sandwiches, but my favorite…" Skippy couldn't finish his sentence because big brother reached over and walloped him a good one right on top of his head with a heavy book his found underneath his seat. It hurt so bad Skippy saw stars…and he lost his train of thought because big brother just knocked the snot out of him. Amen's eyes got all teary-eyed, "How much do you like your eggs now, since you got one of your own?"

Amen was so surprised by the unannounced retribution he bit his tongue. Now bleeding, sitting there with a grimace of pain trying not to show any emotion. Danica turned suddenly catching the gist of their little scuffle.

"Why did you do that?" Danica asked.

Ismael had a look of indifference. "The little turd thinks everything about pain is funny…especially things that happen to other people not involving himself. Maybe now he won't be so prone to spout off with some smart-ass comment when feeling the same vulnerability." A couple of tears leaked out of Amen's eyes. He didn't have the heart to look back at his brother. Danica got out of her seat and got two inches from Ismael's face.

"Try putting a couple of knots on my head…it would figure you would do this to someone half your size." Danica tries to intimate Ismael, "come on! Put some knots on my head! Try picking on someone that can defend themselves!" Silence could be heard in the cabin of the hovercraft. Ismael glared at their leader, yet deep inside he knew what he did was wrong—and there would be payment from dad for seeking revenge on little brother. Big brother wasn't playing the right role, and Danica was there to set him straight. After that altercation, Amen didn't speak to his big brother for over three weeks, before he recognized him again as being one of them. The egg on Amen's head actually got a little bigger than his brothers, but in the end, this made Amen feel bad that he made fun of others so frequently.

Days later, on a warm afternoon, in the quiet part of the day, Danica had seen Ismael actually helping little brother do homework, and after that Amen never, ever, ever, made fun of big brother ever again.

1

To the eyes it's not what it seems

A month had gone by since that incident on the other side of the planet. Those new Circle members were set to take a journey of a lifetime across the galactic plain, a journey beyond the stars spread throughout the universe. Danica was training her crew to stay in the best of shape. Ismael was standing on the high beam, a good twenty feet up off the ground, trying to keep his body balanced as he walked across the beam barefooted. Little brother kept his mouth shut, making faces when appropriate, showing a nervous twitch about big brother floating so high in the air. This was part of their training, to pass the course and onto the next level. The arts were something taught of an Aquerian fellowship, something deemed as necessary. When Ismael finely made it to the other side, Amen stuck his fingers in his mouth and whistled loudly. Then Danica turned and looked at the youngest.

"It's your turn squirt—everyone has to walk the plank." Amen's eyes got as big as saucers.

"What…why me…I'm not very good at this?"

Danica reached over and put a hand on his shoulder. Amen grew two inches since the last time he tried the balance-beam. Remembering all too well when big brother had to stop him from falling by using telekinesis. It was a close call almost hitting his head. The visual came back to him quickly, restraining his usual spirits of emotion. Hesitating before climbing the rope, not looking down he put hand over hand like Danica had shown him from before and looped his feet and legs at the lower end. This would take some of the weight off his hands and shoulders, like a well-trained trapeze artist inching their way to the top. It was a bit easier than last time he had done this. His arms were stronger, and Amen still hesitated just the same, taking a deep breath then letting it out slow. He didn't like being up so high without some type of physical support. Trying not to visualize falling like before. Big brother reached up and handed him the ten-foot-long bamboo pole that was used as a balance beam, yet still wondering about making it across without losing his nerve.

"You'll be okay Skippy. Piece of cake!" Big brother said.

Amen looked down as he reached for the pole almost losing his balance with a shuddering step before gaining control, then suddenly it dawned on their leader. She looked up quickly to give him something she had around her neck. Amen understood what it was right away. The courage-stone was like the one he left back at home. Forgetting all about it in a tucked away sock drawer. Walking back to where the rope was on the corner, hanging down from the bottom branch of a large Ogonia tree, waiting for Danica to meet him half-way. Placing the precious metal around his neck and smiled down at her. Almost right away feeling an unequivocal type of energy. A strange sense of help was on its way, equal to cough-syrup to a cold or a Band-Aid for a cut, yet this was only an omen of a mental nudge of confidence. Quickly to catch his balance, making his way across the high beam without dropping the pole. Looking down before making it to the end. Everyone whistled and clapped. Showing a giddy acknowledgment by his usual funny facial features, reaching for the rope at the other end of the beam. Responding to his own surprise, quickly caught off guard by wiping a hand across his face.

"Piece of cake...like you said...ish...not too shabby." Amen dropped the pole without looking down. Then looking into the eyes of their leader, after getting down and handed her the necklace back. Danica, somewhat surprised, placed the cherished gift back into a side pocket in its usual pouch. Amen looked up with a bit of uncertainty in his eyes.

"What's next Captain Nemo?"

Danica wondered about the sudden confidence. "Why the name calling squirt?"

"Sorry Danica…it's just you're going to be flying that contraption of a ship, and I was just thinking about the old program you have on your computer…you know that program that Dr. Zimmerman got a kick out of. The lost city of Atlantis…something about well-suited gentlemen fighting the known evils of the world." Jacob walked up behind Amen and flanked him without a whisper or sound. Picking him up around his chest and pulled back, before Amen could respond his body was jerked off the ground so hard that Danica heard Amen's back crack halfway up his spine. Suddenly responding after being sat down.

"Well, okay J, I was meaning to get an adjustment, my back is soar. After all the war games and training. You got the kink out of my shoulders." Jacob surprised by the announcement, was only trying to hoard in on the smaller boy to get a closer view of their leader. Showing a distasteful stare toward the boy named Jacob while rolling her eyes. Danica wondered of Jacob's true intentions.

"So, what's going on in your head?" She asked. He was expecting a complement but got the opposite. Danica surprised him and grabbed Jacobs's shoulders, and flipped him like a pancake in a skillet, slamming him hard to the ground. Jacob was overwhelmed with shock. First the wind had been totally knocked out of him, and he couldn't get the words out. She had a look of indifference in her eyes.

"Look…I only ask one thing of you bigger boys. Leave Skippy be! You're really going to feel bad if one of you injures him, and I'm not risking it on my watch. The next boy to touch him in a physical way will have to deal with me!" Danica knew she had over-reacted. She slammed Jacob so hard he let go of his urine. She looked down and knew she over did it and fighting violence with violence wasn't the answer either. She reached down and tried to help Jacob up, yet he was so embarrassed and hurt that their leader would take such action he pushed her hand aside. He looked up into her eyes, and she knew.

"I'm sorry…I didn't mean to hurt you if I did…"

Jacob slowly pulled himself up off the ground with a look of apathy in his eyes, saying more indicating he was done with her taking advantage and walked away.

"Jacob…I didn't mean to hurt you!" She said. "It's just everyone wants to pick on Amen and being a warrior is more than just fighting! Its caring about the ones you live with!" Jacob, dismantled, turned to face their leader, showing an onerous look in his eyes.

"You don't think we know that?" Jacob contentiously looked unblinking. "We're trying to toughen him up for what's to come. I wasn't trying to hurt him like you think."

"Look I'm sorry." Danica said. "You can hit me back…okay, don't go…Jacob…I said don't go!" Jacob turned suddenly realizing he sensed a quivering pain in Danica's character. He stood there for a second, waiting to see if their leader had the guts to go after him. Danica hesitated at first, but then she'd remembered the lesson of love, and her mouth moved with a bit of emotion, for a fleeting moment. Jacob could see an evinced character crumbling before him. He walked back to meet Danica's glance. Only inches from her face he reached and gently touched her cheek with his fingers. He could feel Danica pull in air to hold her breath. The other boys stood back waiting and watching.

Amen showed signs of life. "Wow…Jacob, what's up with that?" Amen gives himself a hug with faking fish lips and mocking kisses all wide eyed. The other two boys hold back a smile. This brought Danica's eyes to sparkle. As the group of Circle members walked arm-and-arm in the evening twilight. Amen shows a goofy character in his gait. The wayward actions of clambering boys walked with their leader down a road of familiarity. Ismael pushed smaller brother's head while pulling him close. Jacob shows forgiveness by placing an arm around their leader's neck and kicks her lightly from behind. They were all tired and ready to get something to eat.

This was one of those nights where each member would get together once a week and have a grant supper in an unusual looking club house. Dr. Zimmerman had started this tradition, and no one over the course of fifteen and a half years ever thought of breaking it. The night was a cool evening. A fall night, with a brilliant sky of darkening colors started to turn a reddish sky to move close to the end of another day. Drew was sitting next to Dr. Zimmerman, who'd just celebrated his ninetieth birthday. They were all around in a complete circle of friendship. Amen looked up at Dr. Zimmerman like he was the ghost of Christmas past and considered all personal flagellation to expel dust from a lower end of him, imagining memories of old-aged-cheese that sat in his shoes to long. Amen blurted out a laugh when he made the connection. Danica looked over from across the way wondering about Amen's frame of mind. Dr. Zimmerman only raised an eyebrow to contemplate the boy with challenging circumstances, noting an overactive imagination, expecting his youth as one of less personal control. He saw the children as empty shells needing to be filled with reliable intelligence, skimming along in life without any logic to their humor. Somehow the professor found a smidgen of value in their existence. They were kids that needed direction and leadership, and love, along with patience was the key.

The banquet room was built a few years back, adding to the central part of the room. This specific place would become a neutral zone to share and laugh and talk about life and friendship, while rubbing shoulders with their children. The club house was a good forty-five hundred square feet, housing an enormous dining area and kitchen with a cozy central fireplace in the background, surrounded by couches and chairs and Octus skin rugs, with bathrooms toward the back end down a hall. A gymnasium was off to the right side of the building facing the kitchen, where they could play basketball or run around an indoor track, something created from Drew's mind when thinking of earth from earlier traditions. The ladies would pitch in and help clean up while the men would get together out on the patio and smoke their cigars and talk about conquering the universe. And eventually they would all somehow end up around the fireplace on the closing of another day, to talk about the latest of inventions or just about everyday life. All snuggled around the burning amber's of fire set to glow, pulling them toward dreams of tomorrow. Telling stories like no other could do, Dr. Zimmerman. The children would listen emphatically about dreams or travels beyond the stars as only could be imagined by those to experience. This was Danica's favorite time of sharing while growing up, from when she could barely talk, to now being a teenager headed toward adulthood. This is where she'd establish her roots of value, her enter character was attached to all the moments of this place, added up to something never imagined from such a girl of her age. That night was not much different than any other as Dr. Zimmerman was moved by some great story, he was engrossed in. The children were all spell-bound hearing the gruff voice of aging wisdom telling such tells. No sounds were heard except flickering of flames and the voice of emotion plotting it along. No other lights were on—just the fire reflecting faces held in interest from the rhythms of the story told. Amen had got up out of his bean-bag chair and slid in close between Danica and Anna. He wanted a clearer picture of this great storyteller in front of him and knew this would be the top-notch place to be. Danica had her right arm draped over the back of Amen's shoulder and started playing with the back of his hair. She didn't know why she was drawn to the boy, who had been so willing to take the lead in most activities before thinking of their conditions. Knowing and being by his side was more important than any other thing she could accomplish at the present. She was focused on being his protector. Tommy glanced over and noticed the connection between the two, caught off guard by her hyper-real, yet it made him smile by her over protectiveness. Tommy was sitting at the back in a metal chair trying to dislodge something from his nose. Not thinking anyone of normal intelligence would catch him of recent entertainment of finger fishing into the darker reaches of the human nose. Ismael caught dad reaching and couldn't believe what he was seeing. If caught, it would be quite embarrassing. Ismael showed a wrinkling recognition looked around to make sure no one else had saw the drama. Quickly to overwhelm him to the point he thought Tommy was a specialized surgeon doing surgery, to go deeper than no ordinary man has ever gone. Ismael chucked a pillow in Tommy's direction, of a darker spot two rows behind, held only to a flicker of flame of casting shadows.

Tommy jerked suddenly from being attacked so forcefully, then thinking to have stabbed his brain from over reacting reflexes. Once noticed, to have been caught, he withdrew the bloodied stump on a quickened remission. Then the thought went through Ismael's head, what's up with flagellating rednecks picking their nose and sharing with friends. Why would he have to be my kin? And who on this earth would choose him to be so smart? Someone pulled the wrong number from a hat and dad accidentally got tripped up and had crossed the line. And who were they fooling to find claim to such a man? Tommy looked at the bloody stump and wondered what direction to go. Then looking up tried to figure out which direction the pillow came from. Bella had seen him too, but only covered her mouth and dropped her eyes.

This had been a good year for all of them, when it came to their studies, but what on earth was appropriate about catching Tommy doing this? They were better off traipsing back through the Winds of Time on a mission better suited for them from heaven. Even though the past was gone, finding a better way through a good life would lead through a door of new experiences. Anna, a row back, on Dr. Zimmerman's left, wasn't paying attention to the story told so vividly. She was lost in a distant stare set in her eyes. Bella was sitting in a loveseat with her husband. She noticed Anna's shiftless gaze too, staring off into a place she'd never been. Probably leaving the last of her remains behind while the rest of her goes off floating in a land before time ever existed, to new journeying, was her thought, and of course, not including any of them. Bella remembered competing with the estranged woman when she was trying to win Drew's heart. Those mixed-up feelings were gone now, left behind from memories healed from a young girl's heart. She moved on to a better way of thinking or not thinking at all when dealing with the past, as she'd learned this was the best thing to do, to find sanity back into her life, now attached to an older girls way of thinking. Then Bella thought of her new love Toby, at first, like a friend she'd never had, but now bonded together by marriage and memories of growing up together, facing the tides of life as children, now again as a couple. Once losing all hope of ever being loved by Drew, she'd finally given in to Toby's constant prodding. Only winning her heart after never giving up. Somehow, he brought with him a deeper healing in Bella's life, never envisioned by a girl so incoherent. In the end it worked out. Bella looked back to her left noticing right away the tampon hanging out of Tommy's nose. She guessed from bleeding, and covered her mouth, when she saw the string dangling from the end. She barked out a laugh while holding back more giggles, then everyone turned to look at her. Tommy sitting across the ways was left in the dark about the recent chatter, he not realizing to be the center of attention. Amen turned around and saw dad…his eyes lit up like Roman candles. All of a sudden, another pillow sailed across the room hitting Tommy squarely in the head. He had no idea that his first-aid choice held a different purpose. Someone had left it behind in the first aid kit. Then Bella couldn't help getting the thought in her head, and he's one of the brightest, set to conquer the world on a blaze of showmanship. Boy is we in trouble. Then she couldn't hold back, she started to laugh. Dr. Zimmerman came to a complete halt and looked at her, wondering why the rude interruption. Then Amen, without a filter spoke up. "Dad, why do you have a tampon hanging out the end of your nose?" Everyone turned to look at the severed redneck, who was lost in a distant state of wonder. It was a picture worth a thousand words. Everyone laughed. Tommy had no idea what was so funny.

"Sorry grandpa for interrupting," Amen said. "My dad's having a brain meltdown."

Then quite quickly the story had ended…

Amen was in his bedroom lying across his bed, playing with a model star ship, similar in characteristics as the star ship beneath the dead-zone, except this one looked to have complicated sides. Oblong in shape from the top, but different underneath. It was built similar to an oil tanker, to hold something valuable was Amen's thinking. Suddenly hearing a knock on the front door, and a familiar voice heard in the background. He skidded off his bed, with a quickening stand, and headed in the direction of the front door. His ears perked to hear some significant happening was about to take place. Standing at the beginning of the hallway, he waited to see Danica's familiar face.

The ears of the Aquerian species were more sensitive to sounds and vibration, since having the ability to travel underwater. Having gills in his neck had its pluses too. From afar, sensing a little tension from Danica's voice. Being separated by only one wall from the front door he could make out her voice at almost fifty feet. His dad let her pass without considering her reasons of being here, even though it was already passed ten PM. There were no set curfews for young boys having guests, but this felt a little different so late at night. Wondering if she had something private to say, without others around to hear her words. Amen was game at the drop of a hat. He saw the female contours of her silhouette. She was wearing her favorite jeans and boots with the golden hair and eyes of blue, bringing out her highlights. She was full of good reasoning by what Amen could tell, shown by a flicker of intelligence seen in her eyes. He noticed her arms were held loosely at her side, and a slight hesitation was viewed from her posture. And knowing what she had to say in passing of a twelve-year old's ears wasn't just meant with him in mind, but an entire group when being picked to be their leader.

Ismael met her out in the hall, along with his brother. Danica met their anticipating glances. A sullen expression that both boys had seen. She was here for something they'd all been waiting for, something of importance long overdue.

Ismael was the first to speak. "What's up?"

Danica's eyes were set in a grimace of worry. "Dr. Zimmerman said it's time to go."

"Go where?" Ismael said.

Danica turned around to see if Uncle Tommy was listening. "He said we have to leave tomorrow—there's no more time."

Amen's eyes perked from hearing the news. "Do I get to go?"

Danica looked over with a disheartening glare while running her fingers through her hair. "Yes—the professor said you have to go, or we wouldn't be complete."

Amen started jumping up and down. Danica, seeing him, compared to a particular breed of mangy mutt on steroids. Then he did a little jig while shaking his booty.

A smile broke out on Danica's face. "It's not going to be all fun and games—and of course, you're not fighting—you're staying attached to my side, no disappearing acts—got it?"

Amen's smile turned to a frown, "How come I'm not allowed any weapons?"

Ismael answered for her. "Because we're not going to fight, we're going for a different reason."

Amen scratched the back of his head. "Then why are we going at all, if not to fight?"

"Because we're playing taxi for a bunch of left behind people, and we're taking others along for the ride needing their assistance.'" Amen developed a pasty look in his eyes.

"Yuck… we're taking those smelling creatures with us…aren't we? It's going to smell really bad in the back of the star ship for the whole trip." Amen said, "So when to do we leave?"

Danica placed her hand on Amen's shoulder. "Tomorrow morning, so get some sleep and don't stay up late watching old reruns of Battle Star Galactica."

Amen's face lit up like blue bulbs on a Christmas tree. "Oh, don't worry. I've seen enough of that. I'm ready for the real thing." He said, "You can count me in."

Danica reached for a hug. Then both the boy's said their good nights. She quickly made her way back to the front door. Tommy closed the door behind without saying a word and turned out the lights. Amen and Ismael looked at each other. A smile broke out on their faces. They knew an adventure was waiting for them around the next corner. Earth bound in the morning was their thinking. They turned around and went back to bed.

8

The Blue Planet

The sun had just come up over the horizon. It was a beautiful day, peaceful, serene—full of promise for a group of the gifted in finding their way. Danica had rolled out of bed early that morning and was jogging with dad on a short brisk five-mile jaunt. Two and half miles out and back of conversant ground, closer on the inside track of their inner city. The air was crisp, clean, filled with the fragrances like earth after rain, a dampened chill of early morning moisture tickled their faces. Drew was in his late thirties, still training to keep in shape, with seventeen years gone he'd aged quite efficiently. His daughter could hold with his pace after hitting her teens. She looked over to catch his glance. His focus was on the run, yet a sense of worry was seen in his eyes. After two miles, sweat began to bead on their backs and legs. They were in step with each beat of their heart. Together they had a gift unfamiliar to the rest, of sliding in and out of doors but something else of gifts together gave a new twist to power. When touching hands their thoughts of mind and body became of a metaphysical world. Their gift was stronger than just an invisibility or moving through doors. They could travel in a non-physical world, between worlds—altered states that carried them across dimensions of a different form. Nothing could touch or harm them when together of mind and spirit. They were left between doorways, suspended between gaps held of memories past or futures not yet revealed. A world showing them the past and parts of a future to come.

Suddenly, shadows cast overhead reminded them of the Condorsorouses given of flight fallen from the heavens in the very front of them. This beast of dragon-like-fashion skid a good hundred feet before coming to a complete stop. Drew noticed Condac above moved slowly to dismount. From a sparkle of light, they ran over to help those in need of this other world. These vivid scenes were only of a future not yet recorded in memory. They couldn't touch what they could see. They wondered of Condac sitting atop of a travel companion that moved quickly to the ground was injured. Drew's eyes filled with pain when noticing blood coming from Condac's mouth. Danica couldn't imagine what had happened to them, and why the sudden vision of vulnerability...

"Dad...he needs the healing-stones..." Danica said as if they were really there. Drew stood looking in the direction of the Condorsorous. This was a scene from the future, a future set unless they changed it from the present. Blood flowed from his side, and shallow breathing gave him a sense of his end.

"Yes...I can see that." Drew said. He was stunned by their appearance—something had happened escaping the others. He wanted to reach for him but couldn't. He felt a gentle appeal in a comforting way. Flashes so graphic of images surreal and competing to the point of overwhelming. Drew's eyes squinted in a bewildered stare.

An obscure mass of darkened winged creatures broke through the ranks of the land west of the dead-zone. In the vision, Drew thought something ill-timed of a beautiful day now gone wrong. He could see they were taking flight to get out of the area. An evil that had overtaken the land east of their city was heading their way. Then the vision of the future left them...

* * *

A few hours later, Bella sat up in bed with the strangest feeling of being summoned by their leader. She had the strongest urge to seek those of the gifted. She'd understood from earlier years a sense of remembered past, something of importance was prodding her heart, something redeeming of a better life faced their future, but Bella didn't know at the moment what that was. She knew Drew was reaching for her from a mental perspective. From across the street, Tommy, Jake, along with Angela and Anna, were gathered for a meeting waiting for their teacher. Dr. Zimmerman, henceforth to meet their company. Quickly to share about their dilemma of being overtaken by an enemy who'd left them from years of their past. Their little community, set of a natural state, had been dismantled by those creatures of that other world out of control. He had the same visions. He'd seen Torack summoning an army of soldiers headed for the gathering of the gifted in a place hidden from the rest. They had to protect their borders at all cost was the visions message. The Aquerian leader had no time to plan any type of battle strategy. Only his years of training in wisdom from other experiences would have an effect on his decision. Time was of essence, as time stopped for no soldier's appeal of readiness. Dr. Zimmerman looked his direction trustingly, within towing affections, out of friendship and respect.

"There's been an attack." He said while shaking his head, "some sort of invasion from those creatures of earth." He paused and looked deeply at his friend. "We have to gather our forces against them and make ready for a battle that's soon to come." Toby walked in from an open door dressed in battle attire, of shield and armor for protecting his own. A sword molded from an Aquerian craftsmanship draped at his side. A bone knife gripped in hand glazed in earlier morning sun cut from the bones of Octus were hints of a war at their door. He lanced the painted colors of the forest on his face and body to hide him from an enemy geared to trick and deceive. He was wearing shin-guards of a metallic color laced in green and shoulder pads that gave an appeal of a soldier held to a different meaning. Bella followed closely behind wondering of the deception of gear. She was reluctant to dress in such a way, she was more into exploiting the misgivings of the misguided in the untruthfulness of an enemy overspent. Tommy looked over and smiled, knowing they were warriors of the same type of thinking. He saw the expression and knew, Toby was gearing up for a fight not of a world ever seen before, for they were in their own land of acceptance and friendship, geared for greatness, geared for getting it on, molded as the gifted, focused on a fight they thought they could win. Tommy knew he had to do the same as they made ready, for the day of the dying was ready to begin. Three Conquerites stood silently among their ranks, surrounding their family and friends, working as a team. Quickly they moved without being summoned of elite warriors, created specifically for days like this of judgment and dismemberment. Like automatons woken from the dead, once idle and out of service but now on a mission of revenge. Danica moved in quickly touching the first fronting her. The vision detailed was of darker clouds gathering all around them, breaking through the barrier above. She turned concerned to view her father.

"We need to go!" she said, "My Circle of member's need to follow after those of a willing heart. We have a war to win out on the edge of that other world where we haven't been." A quivering of lips and a disdaining sparkle of pride was seen in her eyes.

He knew her meaning even though the words were but few. They would move through another door toward that other world, expecting to change their future. A mission for the younger members of membership for sure.

Suddenly, Drew awoke as the dream left him…

Drew was standing over the top of Ismael jerked awake, seeing their leader's shadow overtake him. Ismael rubbed his eyes to find clarity of his response. "Why are you here…what's going on?"

Drew's face took on a serious note. "Wake your brother…it's time to go…your leader waits for you." Ismael jumped to his feet, and Drew disappeared into thin air. He was then standing over Jacob, who, on short notice was rubbing his eyes trying to figure out why Uncle Drew was in his bedroom. Once Jacob focused, Drew tells him the same as he told the others.

Jacob, sleepy eyed, with his hair sticking out from the side of his head jumped to his feet.

"You are summoned by your leader." Drew said. Jacobs's eyes were set afire. "The time is now for your Circle to go." Then Drew pulled through another door, as Danica had done the same to the girls. The boys from both homes, and the girls from theirs, were dressed and ready to go. Danica, and her crew, made it in full uniform. Drew looked from a parallel vision of his only daughter with perplexity set in his eyes. "Take your Circle and go with the watchers back to earth…history is about to change."

Danica knew this day was coming, yet hesitated, surprised that this day was finally here. She reached and hugged her father, then held him at arm's length. Anna was standing at his side. Drew saw the look in her eyes, without wasting another minute he said, "Go…before it's too late!"

Danica turned quickly, knowing they had a mission to accomplish needing strength from the healing elements of this place. Her crew was standing and awaiting for her to decide. She turned and didn't look back. Danica took their hands and led them through a door…

Suddenly, they opened their eyes facing the entry of the star ship. Torack had it prepped and ready to go. His team of Aquerian officers were entering coordinates into the star ships computer. Amen reached for Danica's hand.

"Are we really going?" He asked, like there might be other choices.

She looked down on the seventh of members. "Yes…it's our destiny."

Amen didn't know what to say next. He imagined taking flight toward the heavens of that other world was before just a dream, but now it was a reality facing them. Looking to Renee, their seer, he'd envision a host of watchers coming along for the ride, on dragon-like-steeds, fit for a ride in tightly fitted quarters, blazing across the sky, set to change history. And then thinking, the smell wouldn't be too pleasant taking them along, when drifting odors would float by in from an open ventilation shaft or door. "Do we have to take them along?" Amen said, while looking at their leader. Amen could see them being loaded in chambers below on a computer screen, like entering an Ark.

"Yes, we wouldn't make it very far without taking them along." Danica said. "A full legion at best for our protection, and the ones we intend to pick up."

Amen covered his nose when noting the odor, wanting to stuff odor-eaters into every crack of the main deck. Seeing them rolling along on a computer screen in a rumbling procession. The smell caused a natural gag reflex when thinking of them. An alien fellowship of watchers sitting buckled-up for safeties sake, waiting to make an impression at best. The view in front lit up the sky as the star ship from their world was bound for bonding of those creatures bound for earth. Forward in time they went. Taking flight in daylight turned night, while moving towards that other world, with a handful of the gifted buckled up and ready for changing the future...

Three weeks went by before seeing the blue-planet of fading light on a day not too far from hence. The earth looked silent of a penumbral existence. Danica was nervous as were the rest of her crew of the gifted. The control deck showed signs of life from moving about, from the captain and his crew. Only a few lights pointed the way to that previous life of years that had faded. Danica had no known experiences of the world before of just minutes in front. She'd only remembered stories told by Dr. Zimmerman in his study, and many a story told of her father. This was a new path chosen of a king watching and waiting, an unimaginable destiny was part of a future quickly to come. Her position was in giving direction to the few youths of membership. What would come next, she wasn't quite sure. Slipping through the perfect door, at the right time, would take them back two months before the end. What happened earlier of here could happen on their planet on days to come, taking away their way of life as shown of dreams only a few weeks past. They were in a paradox of uncertainty. Inserted into a crevice between the past and future. Placed at the right juncture of history, to teach them of other journeys slated for those of a higher calling. A mission they weren't sure they could live up too. The past and the present were held to the gentle control of a hand which made and formed the universe. Danica reached over and took Jacob's hand. Amen held the other. The Circle spun forward into another existence, only seconds were measured. They took notice of change viewed from this new experience. It took them on the tail of the wind in this magnificent ship filled with creatures of war and a handful of the gifted. Tory could see what was ahead. Time of past and present spun all around them. A future not seen by this Circle of membership was about to unfold. She opened her eyes to envision color like never imagined. A sidereal gleaming of stars shot out headed in all directions. Each member realizing a portal had been breached as they zipped through the constellation without realizing their speed.

Tory and Danica were the only ones traveled of a past before these fragile worlds ever existed, except Torack and a few of his crewmembers. Her companions held on to the assured hope that they would find the correct path leading them towards a better way of life. Amen opened his eyes to see a blur of a world never imagined as time reversed course to another dimension. It moved in quickening glitches overwhelming the senses. Amen blinked to clear a blurred comprehension. A trip leading to the edge of life. Danica saw Amen's confused expression. "It's okay…" she shouted. "We have to make the door before it changes!"

They were moving at an unknown speed, as light and darkness mixed together as a altered world spun into existence. Sliding in a gap of incremental details. No physical bodies of the living were seen of the moment, nothing of a dream as Amen would have thought from his bout with a Conquerite. Held in the protection of a star ships confinement. And those called the ancient ones were standing close by trying to comprehend their next move. Stars and planets gave way to the bending of light as it took them to new experiences. They were in a future headed towards a past that no longer existed. It showed them a world beyond the borders of this place they had been. Danica could feel the draw like her father had explained to her. Tory was looking for the gate that so far had eluded them. She turned to catch Danica's glance. Disorientation set in Danica's eyes, "hold-on…we're close!" She yelled.

The star ship turned and creaked like being pushed by the wind. Tory yelled at the others. "Hold on! It's taking us!" The Circle moved to the groove of light showing them the correct path to take. Tory, looking for the gate, led with mind and emotion as the gate took them to another end. Danica opened the door and pushed them through. Tory closed the gate behind. They spun forward into perpetuating light through the Winds of Time…

Back home, Drew stood over the Condorsorous, a beast of mighty proportions, bulging with muscle and attitude, and that awful smell. The sky was filled with an elusive blackness from behind him, yet something else was coming quickly like a bolt of lightning shedding a trail of light overwhelming them. The Circle-of-old held on to each other as the sky dropped this host in front of them. A presence of opened wings caused Drew to turn and stare with wondering eyes. He focused from a short distance of a hundred feet away, just comprehending the figure was Gabriel, followed by his captains of the guard, standing in organized ranks of leadership. The heavens above had delivered a host of angels from the other side of existence. A good dozen Conquerites stood behind waiting to be led by these leaders of the realms. The voice that once shook this place so many years ago was suddenly brought back to memory. The mountains and valleys lay in the background of a troubling time, a gathering of those that were gifted, worked to a higher purpose and held to a greater esteem.

"Your time has come young warrior. Those fallen of a kingdom not yet experienced are here to try and take this place. My King has other plans which include this Circle of membership, and your children that have come after you will be given free passage of the world before."

Drew stood in a parallel gaze as Anna pulled close to his side, under sheltering shoulder and arms of security. Gabriel understood this young lady he had met so many years ago, on a better day than this, for they understood this to be close to an end of those creatures or possibly them. This was something they were not ready for. Anna remembered him from years of her youth, now older and wiser facing this warrior of the heavens. He smiled as she understood the gist of his thinking.

"I see you have made a good life for yourselves here," Gabriel said, "but if you aim to keep this place you will have to fight and stand up for those that live here."

Anna's eyes reflected a bit of uncertainty. "So, what do we do, leader of realms?"

Gabriel looked back up from where he'd come from. The heavens were a bidding place for those of character and wisdom. He viewed Anna, knowing she was one with wisdom and integrity. "We have no time for plans but need only ride on the shoulders of these Conquerites, toward those fields left of blood and dismemberment. It's your destiny to ride on the wings of these beasts." Gabriel said. "Find those secrets left in darker places of the universe. I will make a way to this place held to secrets. But you must find your own way back home, for it's your destiny to find a better way leading far away from what you consider home."

The couple didn't quite understand a place in the dark he was talking about. They were chosen for an altered path than the other ones of their kind would take. The first Circle of members took to the sky on giant winged beasts. Heavens elite was waging war in the backdrop of an early morning sun. Anna and Drew both sat on the shoulder of a Conquerite of their own. Angela and Jake rested on the shoulder of the next, and Randy and Janet shared a ride on the back of a beast familiar to them. Toby and Bella had taken up the rear with their own creature sitting on the shoulder of a similar beast, heading into the building of a storm. The atmosphere was filled with blackened winged creatures fallen of heaven as the red-dwarf-star lit up the sky from behind. Anna saw them circling below looking for victims. A billowing of clouds starting a funnel from the beginning of a storm forced of wind, and water, and elements of this world fronting chaos. Looking like a stream of hornets giving chase to their latest victims. Something unnatural of an obscured sky with officious placement was set to confuse. Anna could feel an impetuous heat yielding forth like sweat running off steer in a stampede, caught in the aftermath of rumbling thunder. The vision gave Anna an esoteric view of redoubt, while sitting up high on the comfort and safety of heaven's elite. Drew looked over and saw the transcendent movement of her eyes. "What should we do?" Drew asked. Anna's mind went back when she was a little girl. She remembered when she were fleeing a storm that hit the coast. Her family and others were forced to evacuate their homes. She saw something similar of this storm. It had stolen life away from what she'd remembered. As she looked down, she noticed the funnel doing the same, trying to steal away life like the storm did when she was a little girl.

"We shouldn't head toward this storm." She said, "We should head away from it." Drew looked over deciding her words as sound advice. He touched the mind of the beast they were sitting on. Within seconds the Conquerites moved in a different direction. Suddenly, pulling back from the chaos of the funnel. Anna remembered learning about this place from her husband, lying in wait to give of the dead, resting in confusion, only to be buried in the ground by those creatures of the sky, after tearing flesh off bones that ached from the cold, and caused hesitation seen in her eyes. She knew it was just a draw—to entice them to another way of meeting their end. "It's a trap…there's no way out, once we're inside… that's when they'll take us!" She yelled as her face and hands began to heat up, feeling the rage of what was above them.

"Those creatures have made a deal with the devil!"

"So—what's your point?" Drew asked.

"The point is—we need to protect what we have back in our city. It's up to our children if they find a way to stop these creatures of the air. The fallen's only motivation is to destroy everything here." Anna suddenly sat up in bed with a cold sweat when realizing the vision but a dream…

Danica opened her eyes and saw lights flashing before her. Unexpectedly, Amen was standing over the top of her waving his hand. "Hey, are you okay?" She hadn't remembered passing out when her head started to spin. From a closer view, Amen's face looked elongated with bigger-than-normal size blue eyes staring down at her. She blocked the air with a wave of her hand. She sensed a foul odor lingering in the air. He saw the look and knew.

"Sorry Danica…must have been those sardines I had for breakfast." Danica moved her hands in a wave of revulsion. When she looked up, she knew they were in a barren land without life.

"Have we been here before?" Danica asked.

Amen looked around in three different directions. "I don't think so," Amen said, "unless you've been here in your dreams."

She sat up and looked from side-to-side to take notice that they were just outside a cabin that looked familiar from a time before, an Alaskan frontier of a future not ever seen by this circle of members. Jacob reached down and helped Danica to her feet. Her head was pounding on the back of her skull. She braced herself to get her balance as they made it toward the entrance. The cabin was exposed to the elements passed a missing door. Noticing Ismael with a flashlight looking in closets with a loft overhead. Worn from time and seeming to have layers of dust cropped along the floor and along edges of furniture. There was a bedroom on the other side of the central room off to the right, with a wood burning fireplace in the central part of the great room, yet the missing door remained a mystery. Tory had already lit a fire to warm up the place. From what Danica could tell, it was twilight, and everyone was breaking out food from backpacks and water from their animal skins. Argon was in the corner looking down at the floor, staring at something that looked like a trap door.

"Hey guys, what do you thinks down there?" Everyone turned to see the opening. Renee saw flashes of a fight of flailing swords tearing flesh from bone.

"Don't go there?" She said. "Something's not right by what was left there."

Argon moved his head to view their seer. "Why, what's wrong with this place?"

"They were here," Renee said, "I mean, there was a battle that took place here many years ago." She said somewhat apprehensively. "We were destined to come back to recognize this place, experienced by our parents." She moved her eyes from left to right before completing her thought. "We are to move on though. There's another place after this." Everyone looked at her. She was trying to instill some type of intelligence in this incipient place of a past they didn't understand. She paused for a minute before looking up. "They fled…those that came before us got the best of them."

Danica turned to view Renee's stare. "How much time do we have before this place changes?"

"Only a few hours." Renee said.

Danica wondered about the look in Renee's eyes. It made her worry.

Danica moved in the direction of the front porch. When she reached the open field, her crew met her twenty yards past the steps. Torack stood at a distance in close communication with the watcher. Condac wasn't impressed by the mountains and the area where once stood glaciers of blue, but they were gone now, held only to an empty background of rifts and dark colors of a life now dead from changing circumstances. The mountains lay bare of trees and wildlife, and the sun above look paled from battle days left behind as a reminder of a war showing the end of this place. He stared looking up, wondering what went wrong in a world once so beautiful. This place reminded him how good they had it with their lives back home. Condac understood and blinked his only eye, viewing stratified layers of soil in tomb like form. Then Danica's paralleled gaze viewed Torack's pondering plan of redemption. "Our fight is not here." Torack reported. "We're here to learn of the others, protected by a crown, in a hidden place of refuge."

Danica looked over wishing the conversation was a bit more revealing than it was, but a wish was all it could be for now. She wanted their time here to go smooth and easy, but knowing how the world was at the moment, it couldn't be a normal place where a girl could get along with others. It was torn apart from those creatures who didn't belong here. She doubted if her crew of members would have an effect on such a big world stopped spinning from neglect. Still looking at their leader as if to pull rabbits out of a hat. "We can only help if we find them." Torack said. "We can't be anywhere near this place when the chaos starts." While looking at the others, he shook his head and dropped his eyes left of mystery. "You can't change the future if caught being here." He paused and looked around before saying, "Let's leave this place, before they come again."

"Where are we headed?" Danica asked, with a strange sense of knowing he was right about what he had said.

"We'll go to the edge of this earth—if we have too. No people of this planet are left on its surface. We'll be seen if here too long." He paused to look back. "The fallen can't know why we're here."

Danica acknowledged with a nod and a slight dip of her shoulder.

Torack, from a distance, looked uncertain of this place they had landed of the past. His vision kept them moving to a new beat, a place of another time was on his mind. "You'll know what to do when the time comes." He said. "Be ready, for time will not be on your side when the dying starts to number the dead."

Danica didn't like the words said of the dying and the dead, it was a bit alarming from a young girl's perspective. She headed back toward the star ship, held at the very edge of what used to be fields and forest. The sounds of night circled in around them, but where trees once stood tall in the green wonder of a time not experienced of a girl from another world was not written in any script for others to read, it was lived and toiled each hour of breathless living, in a time of failure, it floated thick in the air and on the ground all around. It was the end of all endless days that held meaning, it was years of toil left behind of heartless ambitions and senseless living. She thought of the stories told by her father, of mighty warriors of heaven making a stand against this enemy that, gave no reason in their selfish endeavors. Then thinking something strange was about to happen. They had to prepare. She looked at the youngest asking of his assistance.

"So, what do you think Amen, where should we go?" Amen's expression was one of excitement. He was more than happy to assist, as the others were left in the dark. He felt the connection. Danica felt it too. He looked up and smiled as she smiled back.

"Michael is coming with us." Danica turned her head in the darker shadows of a soon to be finished day.

"And who is Michael?" she asked.

Amen looked up and pointed toward the heavens above them. Seeing the cloud-cover, then looking back at her.

"A brother said he was coming from a place beyond the clouds," then pointing up. "One of the realms." Amen said.

Danica wondered if Amen's thinking was even clear.

Wiping a bead of sweat off his face then looking up into Danica's eyes. "His name is Michael…well I think that's his name…yeah… Michael…that's it!" Amen looked a little uncertain but remembered what the Conquerite had shown him from before and it seemed to frighten him again, but then names were last on his list for remembering. Danica saw the look and let it ride for what it was worth. Unexpectedly, the wind blew, the clouds moved in, and change was coming to the atmosphere. Then it started to rain.

Danica wondered about Amen's connection with the Conquerite. So, she just asked. "Amen…what did you see when the Conquerite had you?" He turned to look at her when boarding the star ship and taking the seat to her left. Still skittish about saying too much. Then he heard some of the Condorsorouses in the background. Realizing any new information wouldn't be easy to swallow after the experiences he'd already been through, —no experiences yet to compare them too. He wanted to tell her what he saw a few months back—yet held out at the last second. Raising his eyes in a flutter of forgetfulness and left it for another time. Amen turned to look away from other sets of eyes. He'd been frightened so badly from the experiences of that other world. Wanting to forget ever being there. Wanting to move on. His voice failed him miserably as his lips moved in a quivering motion of nerves and holding a lump of emotion in the back of his throat. Just a boy in his innocence, not knowing what answers would be correct. Wondering if being tested, facing growth, facing fear. He wanted to wait for a better day.

"Their real..." Amen said. "The dreams are really supposed to happen...we can't stop them...there not meant for us to stop. We shouldn't have come here in the first place." He moved his eyes away from them to the outside window to his left. "It's a learning place...that's all I know."

"Why...shouldn't we have come here in the first place, Amen?" Danica asked. Ismael looked over wondering what he'd missed also.

"We're not supposed to be here?" Amen said.

"Why Skippy?" Amen looked over and then lowered his eyes, as the star ship sat there idling. Torack came over to find out what was holding them up.

"What's going on?" He asked.

Danica looked back at Amen's wavering silence while Torack stood to the side to listen in on the conversation. "Michael was the one that pulled me away from the dream." Amen said.

Torack yelled to the front to one of his captains. "We need to leave!"

Amen's eyes hardened. "No...not yet...she needs to know before we go!"

"Know what Amen, what do I need to know?" Danica asked.

"You need to know our world will be the same if we don't find a way to stop them." He said. The watchers were loading up with weapons in the back of the star ship, getting ready for another fight with those creatures of the sky. They were preparing. They didn't understand the surroundings of this present world. A world less familiar than the planet they were from. The younger group of Circle members sat tightly bonded together, from the inside of this magnificent ship, among the comfort of friends. The rain broke through darker clouds showing the flow of the terrain, from only a small area of a darker spot through sleeted rain. It took the very breath from them when looking at its hidden message. They were facing death of a planet. Amen knew he couldn't get this out any other way, but now, this way...out in the middle of nowhere, on the edge of a world once spinning out of control, now sat lifeless. Suddenly pushing out a difficult breath of air.

"It will be different than how it is now." Amen said.

Danica wondered where he was going with his train of thought. "How is it different Amen?"

"We'll be better prepared," he said with a quivering emotion seen in his eyes, "we can't move on without changing history, for this place is different from the world we live in."

"And the purpose of all this?" Danica asked.

"That warrior from heaven is waiting for us." Amen informed them. "He has the gifted where no one will look."

Danica didn't understand. "Has who Amen...who does he have safe?" She asked.

"The ones we came for...their not here now...their here of the past, but not now."

Danica tried to piece together what Amen was saying.

Renee reached up and touched Danica on the shoulder. "He's right...we're not meant to be here yet...this will cause a paradox if we find ourselves in this place...it's time to go." Renee said.

"And where do we go?" Danica asked.

"You already know..." Amen said, while having a connection with what Renee was speaking about.

"No, I don't know...so what do you feel I already know?"

Ignoring the question Amen finished by saying, "The end...it's coming, we have to go there...we have to make amends..." He said. Amen's eyes filled with reluctance. The darker clouds of before started to roll away leaving the star ship standing in a patch of light. Amen sat staring at their leader without blinking. It felt as if death had been here earlier and now was gone, only to reveal itself at the proper time. The land looked like it was scourged by fire and flame from a few years back. Mountains and valleys were free of trees and birds flying in the air. There was no signs of life in this world left behind of days or years of an earlier phase of living. They were too late to fix this world of the future. Amen understood they were shown this world first for a reason, a reason they'd all face as being the death of this place once called earth. Life had ceased to exist without them changing history.

"The earth has stopped orbiting the sun," Amen said, "No more seasons...that's why the changes of weather and temperatures. That's why most of the water on the surface is gone. It's been used up or hidden somewhere." A breath of air from the star ship parted Danica's golden hair.

"It isn't quite the end..." Torack informed them. Everyone viewed the Aquerian leader to their left.

"Why has their king allowed all this?" Renee asked.

Torack shook his head, "I don't know young lady, but our reasons of being here will soon be revealed." Danica looked bewildered in trying to make sense of everything around. Her emotions began to weigh heavy on her mind. She was at a loss of what to do next...

9

Stopped Spinning

Once off the ground, the star ship headed above the atmosphere whirling towards another time. They had begun to prepare for a jolt of reality, hoping a better day of tomorrow would be there to greet them with better circumstances. Their group sat there waiting patiently. Without notice, everything began to spin backwards. Danica and the rest sensed them moving at a speed not comprehended. The star ship had left the ground in another dimension heading back in time, giving them no time to prepare for what was ahead. Danica's concern was in doing the right thing, without fear. She viewed Amen from a parallel gaze, wondering what the boy had experienced from days past so vividly. He sat next to her left with a pasty pale look in his eyes, tense to the max, feeling overrun by something out passed a window. She couldn't help feeling for the boy so overwhelmed from that experience with the Conquerite. Maybe that's what he was seeing. She felt the connection of the half human, half Aquerae with a greater respect. An Aquerian frame of mind was quite different than human. They could sense effects before they happened. Amen, from her point of view was only a child, innocent of an adult world that would lead him away from what was pure of a boy not experienced yet of character. She knew she had to protect him when the time came as they continued to drift towards the rift—or was it him who would have to protect her? —which one she didn't know at the present time. At the moment, she couldn't understand why he was the one that stood out, but somehow, she knew, in the back of her mind, they held to a faint connection, not including the others that had come along for the ride. Her heart told her he was the key to everything.

Staring out beyond the star ship's view, they'd face an intangible image of a world torn apart from the inside out. They were moving near an earth recorded of before, a time now only a part of past history. From their prospective, it was a place foreign of any home close to the comforts of life of any better way of living. Even Tory, barely remembered earth when their planet started to change, started showing signs of the end. Danica looked outside the star ship window, an empty feeling of loss had filled her mind and affected her heart to beat congruently. Her life, her mission, and her love, for others was connected to these young adults that had filled her with every moment of life.

It felt like a heavy burden pricking at her heart, as a heavy weight holding her back from doing what she had to do. The earth expelled a fading history, trying to take away value of what used to be. Danica was done not feeling for people of before, who'd died by the thousands on a once beautiful shore. She was done scraping by with only a few humans left of earth in the past they were headed too. She wanted something more out of life that stood out like the courage-stone did in that giant tree experienced in the rage of a storm of memory. Now feeling like castaways headed to the edge of oblivion. They were on the edge of discontented space, looking for signs of life where no life left felt to exist. Danica knew they were hanging on to the last bit of hope when courage was needed. She clung emotionally to the boy who showed a sparkle of energy in his form, directed on the road to a clearer path of perceptiveness. Amen was game. An amazed flickering of light shot above the clouds, then it dawned on Danica. Her help would come from the clouds…

Anything she understood as solid ground wasn't so clear, she had built up hope, on the people that had surrounded her life and showed her a way to love—showed her how to get through all the remedial barriers that seemed to block her way. Danica remembered Anna telling her once that a king found hope in the hopeless, found strength in those who had no strength to give. She had remembered when her father would take her hand and walk her through the gardens and show her personally about beauty, about things that stood out as blessings in her life. She knew from a father's love that this was their time to shine, to stand out like the Tommy's who yelled in the distance to find Jake, about the Drew's who stood in defiance of a wheelchair and didn't give in to defeat. The Renee's who stood up to hope when hope couldn't be seen, but only lived and experienced from dreams like no other could do. Danica wiped at a tear moving down her face. She turned back around and looked into Amen's eyes. "So—Amen what do you think is the key for our success?"

Amen showed a sparkle of light. "Never stop believing." He said, "Didn't you get that—weren't you listening to that small voice in your heart? You know, like the courage-stone showed us back home." Danica reached over and gave Amen a hug and kissed him on the top of the head. He turned a darker blue than his brother had ever seen. The other boys looked on as Amen's bottom lip moved with a quivering emotion. "Wow—she kind of likes me." He said.

Jacob looked over with a ting of jealousy. Danica smiled and stared at her crew of once misguided youths. She put an arm on Amen's shoulder then looked out into space of a glimmering light and saw colors of green and blue quickly light up the sky…

Amen looked a little apprehensive about chasing after dreams from schemes he didn't understand. But were they dreams and were they schemes really put in his path? "The earth is about to end in this place it took me—can you see it?" He said, while looking up at her. Amen held in her gaze but didn't say anything about the dreams he experienced. Fear kept him from saying those words. It was easier to relay a message he couldn't voice through metaphors explained telepathically. Renee understood the boy showing their leader in this way.

Suddenly, the sky turned to darker colors eluding to change coming quickly. The rain and wind of another time brought them to a place once stopped spinning. Danica saw the opportunity of an elusive door and took them through it. The star ship drifted towards a rift of colors, dropping them to the lower end of this changed world, as time stopped spinning backward and sat them on earth eight years behind. They sat waiting for their leader to lead them to a world of the past. What they thought existed of the Great-Gulf couldn't compare. They were all duped speechless. Once outside the star ship, after sitting feet on solid ground, a lingering odor drifted in the air. Amen and the rest looked all around, trying to figure out where they had landed. Each member felt closer to the victims of this physical world than the one before. Laying low in this apocalyptic time to complete them. The staggering of light crossed their faces, illuminating direction of where they've never been. The land was dead and burnt and an acrid smoke circled the sky from previous of obvious dimensions that had been passed by. The unwavering smell pulled at their stomachs. Jacob was first to touch the ground of smoking cinders. Powdery bones blew by their faces as the wind headed north. They thought this to have been caused by weapons of mass destruction. Danica started looking for any evidence of life left from where they stood, nothing close by drifting from the East made any sense. Maybe a field or glade of trees were near by pointing to a better way of direction, but nothing could be seen. No vegetation of any type, no skeletons of another way of life, yet nothing left behind to remember them by of history, barren of color, empty land lacking water and signs of movement. The mountains were scorched beyond recognition, and the fields were no less than dried up mud and sand and debris of powdery bones, lying dormant, lying dead, no place of safety to rest one's head. Danica walked around the star ship calling out like she was looking for family or lost friends. The idea of walking to find life was beyond the thinking of a girl looking for a better way to save any humans left of earth, on any shore, in any crevice of safety, hidden from those devils of the sky. Amen followed behind her in a quiet procession of getting along, looking for children, looking for a mother, or a father, maybe a brother left behind on any other better day gone missing, until now, before giving up and casting in their chips. Amen looked up to notice Tory's eyes, and remembered her guidance when their leader was lost, looking to find her way home. "Where is everyone—there's nothing here?" Amen said.

Danica had remembered running through the forest as a little girl and finding peace and joy among her people. At the moment she'd felt they were alone in this world of emptiness. It was a place of retribution of the innocent in their dying, it was a place of faded resistance, a place unrecognizable of any type of home. She turned to look at Amen. "Maybe we're looking in the wrong place?"

Renee felt something strong pulling them toward the south. According to the electronic map, they were about seventy miles from San Diego County. Then suddenly, Danica remembered having grandparents from San Diego when looking down at the hand-held computer. This once beautiful city that lay by the sea was a vacation capitol of the world, yet now everything in their view was burnt to the ground—turned under from smoldering heaps of coals, relying on bones of bodies not recognized of another life, while the ash of the dead floated by of other memories. The smell of death lingered in the air making them quite aware their time was coming. They had to wear masks for fresh oxygen not quite breathable. This world of their parent's was almost unbelievable. The atmosphere didn't feel right. Something was left behind as a reminder that this planet was counted as lost. Shadows of the night began to slowly creep in all around them. It left a chill in the air. A mirage of dreams gently touched Danica's heart as she heard cries of the night from those who had suffered of another time. The world of before floated in and out, in telepathic form. Bodies and bones of the once living were dead and gone of that other life. The night to come began to defuse their way of thinking. Nothing was there except the memories of ash from the violence of war left in the wake of days too hard to forget.

The group of members sat down to take a break on rocks two hundred yards away from their star ship. Torack had flown one of ten hovercraft's out of the star ship since back on earth. A few of the Aquerae soldiers were left behind to guard their ship. Condac and his fleet of watchers and dragon-like-steeds, took to the air to survey the area. Argon was carrying a big gun close to his chest. They were all armed to the teeth, except Amen. He stood close by Danica's side. The air was warm, but the earth was cold like a once warm body losing heat before giving up her ghost. The planet was no longer blue and full of life, a stench that followed them that day moved with the wind in mountains and valleys of a once remembered place, before reminding them of those still missing.

They had to head in the direction of a place called San Diego County. Danica turned her eyes in Renee's general direction.

"Do you sense anything?" She asked.

Renee was trying to figure out why she felt vibration. Yet it wasn't coming from the ground.

"Do you feel that?" Renee asked.

"Yes, I do, but where is it coming from?" Danica said.

A look of surprise was seen in Amen's eyes. "I feel it too!"

Each member turned to look up behind them. A milky matter of quickly moving clouds was moving towards them as the wind blew the clouds from the north. Condac and his trusty band of watcher's turned around in the sky to face whatever was coming their way. Whatever it was didn't look friendly and coming at a speed not comprehended. Danica yelled for them to get back to the star ship, but it was too late.

"Hold on!" Danica said to Amen. "Get us above the clouds!" She yelled in Condac's direction. Danica took two members at a time and placed each one on the back of these dragon-like-steeds, controlled and powered by watchers taking them higher. She led with Condac in front and Amen behind. Each riding on the backs of the Condorsorouses. The air was thick with the spreading of moisture as it overwhelmed them within minutes. Tory had strung her bow and Danica had her sword ready. Argon's Element-gun was locked and loaded as he warmed it up with the glowing of light as it hummed in a rhythm for the dead. The sky was filled with chaos. The black that covered the day turned quickly night, shadowing them, soon to take over the atmosphere. The Condorsorouses, in angelic like form, were fire-breathing-dragons setting the pace for those of another world would be duped of their quick arrival. A vengeful stare graced each set of eyes willing to perform harmonic vengeance, as the Fallen swarmed above them in anticipation of a fight. Danica turned to look at Amen. "Hang on and stay close!" She shouted. "I have to float in and out above them…I'll be back in a minute!" Danica floated in one door and out another. She landed on the back of Argon's beast of dragon-like-fashion and whispered in his ear while pointing straight ahead.

"Cut a path down the middle while I follow along from behind!" She spoke. "The rest of you follow me!"

Renee nodded her approval while Ismael raised his right hand. Argon opened up like Gatling-gun retribution, firing his Element gun in a pattern of short burst, blasting across the sky as the Dark-Angels veered left and right. They tried to move out of the direct path of the boy's focused aim. There were too many to make any dent in bringing them down. Argon cut through their numbers as they fell from the sky. Killing and spilling of blood in gifted like fashion. Ash spilled from the sky like tears draining of emotion from so many all around, it floated in the air and covered their bodies, leaving a hidden meaning causing confusion in these devils of the sky. Danica used her crew as a suspending bridge jumping from one to the other. Having vengeful sword in the fight swishing to and frow of where to go in warrior-like-form. She used her skills to cut through their ranks resembling a master at her craft. Preparing each step taken, sliding between the gaps of safety, homed into a spiritual awakening of the dead. The legion of Condorsorouses formed a giant circle braced up against this enemy. A thousand steeds-of-the-air dared them to cross the line. The sky turned black, the wind blew, and an endless number of the dead circled in around to take advantage of their lack of numbers.

Fear overwhelmed the members of membership, yet they tried to hold the enemy back. Danica swished back and forth taking her sword through bones and bodies of the decrepit enemy. Five would fall and ten would take their place. The fire breathing Condorsorouses shot out flames all around hoping to scourge this enemy. Argon shot through a half dozen only finding them to be quickly replaced by brothers of the same. Sweat beaded on his face and back as they began to smother beneath the weight of these blackened winged beasts. Danica twisted and turned beneath the ranks of fists held up in fury in the determination of trying to find hope and victory when fighting side-by-side. In the aftermath of a severed world giving up the dead, in the pounding of retribution troubling the sky without waged warning of purpose, pushing past sword and flame and weapons amassed destruction. Danica felt the pounding of their bodies, well-tuned, geared for getting it on. They were standing strong in the fervor of the fight, not giving up to these petty humans even though gifted of another world. She felt to be the smallest of warriors trying to find a moment of courage without giving in to the fear. Danica felt the loss of adrenaline, the loss of courage to push on in the fight. She had to save her brothers and sisters if only a few. Then realizing the existence of confusion drifted all around them. Their enemy was without form and numbers. Danica saw her other members staring in bewilderment. She screamed to get their attention. "Don't give in…keep fighting!" She yelled. Argon turned his Element-gun up and began to fillet through them like a sushi chef while trying to keep his composure as he watched them fall from the sky. Condac's watchers jumped from one steed of the air to another slashing their way through the ranks of captains and creatures as ash spilled in heavy breathing from running on backs of dragon-like-steeds misaligned. The fight became definitive of purpose. Amen yelled for Danica to turn them back to better conditions as the enemy swarmed like hornets in a maddening world. She turned suddenly and saw Amen fell from his Condorsorous of dragon-like-fashion and felt Danica's heart drop right out from under her. Danica's eyes filled with terror as she dropped off the same way into the blackness of the night to find the youngest of members…

When Danica woke, her whole body ached from top to bottom. She hung somewhere in a darker place of putrid smells. She felt like death hung in the air as vomit rose up in her throat. Her hands were tied to something above cutting through wrists, leaving her numb and disillusioned of where she was. When her eyes focused, she realized she was blindfolded to keep her from seeing these creatures that had bound her and tied her to poles hanging over a pit of some sort. She could only see a small cut of a corner facing her right eye. Her body was extended over the top ready for supper was her thinking, her last dying words held tightly on her tongue. On closer revelation she could see the hole was filled with sharpened stakes in the ground while dangling ten feet above them. She saw nothing of Amen anywhere. She thought, He must be somewhere else I haven't had a chance to see. Her heart sank knowing he might be dead or dismembered or crying in a place he didn't know where, just like her. She'd made a mistake by bringing Amen along for the ride. She should have left him in the star ship, was her thinking, but now it was too late, he was here for the duration of the fight. He would be vulnerable just the like the rest of them. Yet that fact didn't seem quite important at the moment. She was facing her own demise at the present time, and then she'd worry about him. She tried to communicate the best that she could but Renee and Torack felt so distant and who would even be listening. At the moment, her very life past by in memory, thinking of her family, of her world left behind in all this mess. Everything that seemed important at the time was fading. She suddenly heard someone coming. Even with the blindfold she could slightly see through the lower corner of her right eye. She was spinning above this mystery grade below. And the smell that rose above made her taste the vomit rising in her throat. She was tied to a four-inch-thick pole laterally with two other poles on the side holding her vertically. If she were to fall the stakes below would run, her through. Danica felt a warm swish of air flow across her body which caused her to tense. Someone was looking down at her. The pull of her own weight on her hands started to cut into flesh. She cringed from the pain but remained focused on the body that had just entered the room. At each turn of her hands, she felt a sting of blood dripping down her wrists and off her arms. She thought to feel dizzy but shook her head to stay awake. Each moment that went by felt like a lifetime when suffering, but she couldn't think of that, she had to think of the others to keep her going steady, keep her motivated, to stay alert, ready for anything that came back her way. Yet at the moment she could only think of this creature that stood over her. Hearing it's heavy breath in ragged grunts of frustration. Suddenly feeling dirt kicked toward her face. The smell of death came from the wisp of air that hit her nostrils. Danica looked from the corner of her right eye. She noticed the stakes below had blood stains from another victim, assuming someone died before her wasn't good news when thinking she might be next. They were jutting into the air as a reminder of where she was headed—this thought caused her to cringe and pull up on the ropes. She wanted to cry but for some reason she knew it wouldn't help her get free, if anything it would only finish her off quicker of a beating heart. So instead, she got mad, mad as a hornet disturbed from her nest. Suddenly, a sparkle of light came from the stone held gently around her neck. The reminding courage-stone that had saved her before. She'd given notice of still breathing, still pushing air in and out of her lungs. It was an insignificant prompting she wasn't out of the game yet. Swiftly, it felt like a chain of hope hanging about her neck. Once realizing she was still one of the gifted, a tear leaked out of her right eye, but not because she was scared, it was because it gave her hope that she needed to get back on track. Only thinking of Amen who had clung to her side, she was his only connection to a world gone mad, along with dead and detached from showing any signs of life—feeling she had failed him when he'd fallen to earth on the darkest of hours. Looking at the stone around her neck gave a quick flash of memory, as Amen's face came to mind…

Amen had fallen a few thousand feet yet somehow; he was still alive. His arm hurt a little and his knee felt a twinge of pain, but for now he was still in one piece. From what he could gather he had slipped through the roof of something soft that had covered some type of well. How he was able to hit this mark so perfectly without hitting his head was all a mystery when wondering where his mind had been. Lucky he could swim underwater and had the use of gills in his neck. The well was part of an underground reservoir system that pulled him toward a lower end of some type of tunnel. He swam in a downward direction as it caused him to feel alive like others of his kind, moved by his emotions through water gave him a sense of hope, a sense of power under control, through this course of action of forward progress. Noticing right away that it was fresh water and not salt water when first entering. He was well hidden in the dim lighting of the tunnels wall, pointing the way to something at the lower end of some type of water storage. The water was cool and clean and gave him a fresh sense of being alive. He didn't mine helping himself to a few swallows of coolness. Being Aquerae had its pluses too. From time-to-time he held a heightened sense of awareness giving him strength. Amen realized the fear of before had left him when entering a world of water. He felt a connection with water swirling around him when before it had gone unnoticed. Understanding it was far from a world he had ever known, yet familiar. The awkwardness was gone, the heavy breathing had left him, when thinking of his present situation. He felt safe for the first time since starting this trip.

He kept swimming his way to another place held at a lower end of a sudden welcoming. Amen saw a sharp glow of light up ahead, and slowed down as he came between a crossroad leading in two different directions…

Coming to a world of their parents, the Circle of membership brought along added strength from a place of healing elements. Stronger than a normal human would feel from experiences of healing elements, stronger than ever thought possible from the handful of gifted that had come along on this trip. They were Gambits of a different kind, shedding light toward a darker world turned inside out. Skyward—each member, along with the watchers, fought fervently through acetic smoke and the burning of air. These winged beasts screamed a cry of vengeance toward these foreigners of a red-dwarf-star. Named as the gifted by those called the ancient ones, somewhere else, uncounted for while watching and waiting for the chosen few to find the answers they seek.

Argon's face was covered in black soot. His shirt had been torn from his back, but he kept on fighting with no will of giving into these decrepit beasts of the air. Argon became a fierce competitor. Ismael wasn't far behind as the watchers were a force to be reckoned with as seen from both sides of this fight. The others stayed close together pressed soon to leave the scene. Ismael used his telekinesis to keep the Dark-Angels from getting too close. Tory had used explosive tipped arrows that caused her enemy to depart on contact. Condac, with his watchers, fought with a strength and agility not understood by these blackened creatures of the world now overspent. Jacob sat with sword swinging to and frow across the tide of this enemy. Renee used her mind of manipulation to confuse them. Even with a thousand sets of eyes connected to a thousand sets of hands jointed to a thousand-winged steeds of the air, they were over come from the many who were slowly taking control. But the eyes of the enemy could not see what would follow...

Suddenly, a reign of terror moved toward them from the heavens, an immortal host came to greet them on this dismal day of the dying. The sky parted right and left of billowing clouds gave notice of something magnificent and beautiful and powerful beyond any natural power of light. Argon's face lit up from surprise—a boy of his youth staring toward an inexpiable conundrum. Ismael's color was not recognizable as it paled in the brightness coming from above. Jacob almost totally exhausted looked up. Tory's face had beaded sweat mixed with blackened smoke and soot, as did the rest, the effects of war left its mark on the few. An elite class of angels, not seen of previous by this

Circle dropped from the sky. Their eyes were blinded from the greatest of light. The elements of weather had stopped, and the brightness of heaven's soldiers pushed the darkness aside like it held no meaning. The Fallen scattered to the four corners of the earth seeking shelter away from light. The Circle, and its legion of watchers, and dragon-like-steeds, left the area towards ground to rest and regroup. An angel like no other stood standing tall, a blazoning light of an unnatural sight. They were overwhelmed and under prepared from such a greeting. Torack stood with young and old as a representation of his kind. That's when he understood the light, it was the key. For darkness could not dwell where light remained. This angel stood twelve feet tall, and wings that stretched twelve feet abreast. Talons like curved hooks graced each corner of dangled bone of jointing appendages. His body was as golden color of light shining from the brightest corner of the heavens. His eyes were the deepest of blue and shined in brilliant radiance never before imagined. His form was one of a majestic making with heavenly cogent. His presence established dominance and control with light over this darker world. His movements were of grace and agility, to serve a kings purpose in a form representing the many. He was not afraid; he wouldn't be denied. He walked with authority and held his head high. He had plans of a greater purpose held to a greater esteem. He looked about this once beautiful place and knew of a conclusive end. Torack understood his message. He looked down at the Aquerae leader with a touch of consideration and asked who was in charge. Tory took a step forward and answered.

"I'm in charge until our leader can be found. We don't know of her direction."

"And you are one of authority?"

"I am the gatekeeper of this Circle—one who guards those from entering the world of the dammed—and you might be?" She asked.

Michael raised his right eyebrow showing an ounce of contemplation of her words. "I am who I am, shown by the markings in my neck and back, as you can see, these are markings of a King's servant and captain of warriors." He bent down and turned to show her. "I'm a leader of the first an oldest that dwell in a place not of this world. I was the first and will be the last. I am one who gives direction and wisdom."

Argon thought it would be okay to enter into the conversation. "Cool dude...then you're the man...awesome...hey is there a way out of here? Because we kind of got lost...and then these big guys from out of nowhere started a fight, and we don't know which way to go at the present." Tory reached over and covered Argon's mouth. Ismael spoke in Argon's defense.

"Don't mind him Michael of...of the first, he's just nervous." Tory showed a nervous twitch while Ismael improvised with mixed up words. "By the way, who were those guys anyhow?" Michael seemed a bit annoyed yet seeing he was surrounded by young adults lacking experience. He held them in high regards even though they were just children to him. It took considerable courage to face those devils of the air was his thinking. He knew that without asking the first question.

"And where were you headed?" Michael asked.

Tory looked up with a bit of hesitation glittering in her eyes. "I was trying to talk to our leader...but then she and one of our own dropped from the sky...and we were so surprised when turning back and finding them missing. I think that would be better answered by our leader, if we could just find her again." Tory informed the first with a host of confusion trailing behind. Michael raised his hand for he had heard enough. He knew why he was here in the first place, but he didn't know where to start with all the confusion and misguided talk.

"Those of the air took her." Michael said. Tory shook her head like she didn't understand. Michael already had heard the story of the gifted by the Indian princess. He knew who they were. "Your leader was taken to an underground tunnel system used by these creatures for years. They at one time were as my brothers. But they have broken rules and regulations of the highest order." Michael stopped because he wasn't sure if this group of young people would even care to know about a history not of their planet. He looked at Tory with eyes of serious intent.

"Does your kind wish to hear this account or were you more pressed for other things more important?"

Tory looked at Michael a bit confused about the question but tried to give an appropriate answer. "Yes, if it would help us to see the whole of this experience, please continue."

Michael showed a settling flutter of the eyes as he sat on the nearest rock with a flat surface. Each member gathered around and listened in on the bizarre account of the elite of heaven.

"These beasts of the air you were fighting were of heaven at one time. They have reverted to evil ways and have taken a path of least resistance. They turned to devious ways not of a king which held their best interest at heart, deciding their own pathway was of greater importance, started by the jealousy of a brother's evil heart." Michael looked around into each set of eyes as he spoke. He saw what a king might have seen, in the eyes of youth through purity and trust—his aura was filled with their character. Their eyes gave them away as being teachable, and goodhearted, and full of energy and promise. This made him remember his days of his youth expelled from a king, a father of love and commitment. As seen in front, young minds following the path of leadership. He remembered playing as a child with others like him. His old heart fluttered from the memory. This aged leader of the first began to feel these same gifts that he once expounded from a king had touched his own heart. He knew his purpose of being here, right at that very moment, it was a reminder of love and commitment that stood out to him, all through eternity. The gifts were passed on to their children and to their children's children and furthermore. The memory's caused his old heart to perk.

"I too was once young as you." A friendly chuckle came from the warrior with a love-filled- heart. Argon got closer like his was impressed with the biggest and brightest. He reached over and touched Michael's sword—a wave of power flowed in his direction. It felt like a bolt of electricity as he jumped back.

Michael looked to his left and touched Argon on the top of his head, comparing him to such lads in heaven. "Be careful." He said then looked at the others.

"Our brother, Cornelius, brother of another leader has taken his own path leading away from light." He then looked back at each member, not sure what to tell them next.

Tory turned a curious eye toward Michael. "If you have such wisdom, where should we look?" Michael wasn't sure if he could tell them, considering she wasn't the only one missing. Ismael realized just then his brother was missing too.

"Hey…where's Skippy?" Everyone turned toward Ismael with a look of bewilderment.

Amen kept swimming toward a dim glow of light drawing him like an allusive presence taunting him to come near. Noticing the water was almost transparent, clean for a reason he hadn't figured out just yet. The oxygen in the water was of a higher content than what he was used too. He took slow flumes of air through his gills trying not to get lightheaded. A few hundred feet behind, he saw something swimming towards him, but it didn't look like anything he had ever seen before…

Danica tied to the ropes noticed a force quite large was hovering over her. A shadow below took up space all around. In her mind, she tried to reach for the others the best that she could. But then the stone around her neck began to glow. Quickly, she turned her focus back on Amen. He was the one she was after. She didn't want to become a casualty of war. Never thinking she would ever end up at the bad end of a stick, tied to a post of all things ready to meet her maker. This had to be the last straw, then suddenly, someone slapped her across the face. It stung at first, but more or less elevated her heartbeat, causing anger to rise up in her throat as her heart pounded and her mind raced. This of course, jolted Danica out of the stupor she'd been in. And presently, this young leader, wasn't really trapped by poles above a hole with tightly fitted ropes for an unheard-of amount of time—remembered she had the ability to slip between doors without a moment's notice. She stayed still, because she had learned from a father's best friend that sometimes putting yourself out there, looking all vulnerable gave you the upper hand, especially if they weren't prepared that she could use her gift at any moment. Well, the slap came back her way, but this time she heard it coming. With only having her hands tied, Danica did a quick swing of her legs to the top of the pit and grabbed this not so smart creature by the head with her feet and swung him toward the stakes below her. Yes, he was surprised and quickly dead, was her surmise as she'd quickly said, when noticing the blood. "Wow…he went for it." Danica went back to looking all helpless as if she had no way out, a damsel in distress, waiting to be rescued by someone coming along to make things better, when unexpectedly hearing more footsteps. She closed her eyes and held her breath. Then she heard the shouting from a tunnel further away.

The confused beast of wings looked her way, once entering the room. "What did you do?"

Danica took the role of a dumbfounded damsel. "I didn't do anything...I think he tripped?"

The second in response. "Look miss...I know you did something to cause him to fall...he couldn't be that clumsy."

"What could I do...I'm the one tied up and blind folded, or did you miss that part?" The second of lesser intelligence considered her statement by the obvious and reached to scratch the back of his head. By then, Danica reached for him with her legs and repeated what she had done to the first. He followed suit of the other before him as shadows of a brother turned to ash. Then more footsteps came down the same tunnel. The sound of feet running to meet her current position. A third shadow unknowingly bolts into this room. Danica couldn't explain the warriors missing so she stayed quiet, knowing, someone tied up couldn't accomplish such a feat. And being blind folded on top of that, who was to know for her to do any harm? The third looked back and forth before commenting.

"Hey what happened to my friends?"

Danica considered the dumb question and answered with sarcasm. "I didn't know you had any friends, and what friends would that be, if you had any friends at all?" She paused to give him a minute for it to sink in. She then finished her thought. "I think they were dying to get out of here and took the wrong door." The third winged beast seemed to be stifled by her tactful words and didn't know how to respond. She waited for him to say something, but he'd only turned and walked back where he came from. She let out a slow breathe of air before saying.

"It's tough to fine good help these days..."

Amen appeared to be trapped. He looked behind him, then front, contemplating if there was any way he could elude this shadowy figure coming towards him. Furthermore, the water continued to pull him to a lower place unknowingly of where he'd end up. He was being siphoned to a greater pool. Not sure he wanted to continue this downward path leading to a darker place than where he had come from. Where would he go from there if caught between this thing coming toward him and this place he'd never been? Swimming backward wasn't the way to go either. The current was moving faster than he could swim backwards. Amen noticed the tunnel was rounded like a giant tube ten feet high with handles above in the ceiling that led to another place through what appeared to be a hatch, a door of some type, comparable to a ship or submarine. They were spaced at least one hundred feet apart, and otherwise there was no other way to get out of this place once at the end of it. He was stuck here until finding an alternate route, now knowing where it would lead him. Then quickly seeing the top, Amen swam upward. He tried to reach while passing each hatch. Yet timing had to be just right. Missing the first, then the second, he was running out of time. Amen looked behind and saw the shadowy figure getting closer, understanding if missing the next one, this thing would be right on top of him. He focused and looked at the next. A steel hand railing was coming his way. Then he reached far enough above to grab a hold of it, just ever so slightly swinging his legs toward the top. He could imagine a curmudgeon beast coming closer, moving faster than first noticed when looking behind. Then quickly trying to reach for Amen and then missed. Amen's heart was about to exploded. A steel circular trap door with handrails at the north and south position of the hatch. Knowing, if getting the hatch open, he would be free of the tunnels water and the thing behind coming closer was now gone. He put both hands and turned with all his might, yet the hatch wouldn't budge. Amen thought of Danica, thought of the training with the boys when some days were harder than others. He wondered if Danica was even alive when he looked and saw her falling just as he did. Trying to wipe that from his memory he started to get mad. Then he opened his eyes and tried again. The hatch started to give way. Amen finally got the hatch to open. He poked his head up out of the water and looked going left and right while holding tight to the top. The force of the water was strong, but not strong enough to keep him from getting free. He had no idea where he would end up. He cleared the hatch and closed it behind. His heart was beating out of his chest…air came in heedless gulps while blood pounded in his ears. His hands were shaking, and his shoes were wet. With his head pounding, and his confidence almost gone, he was still alive, still breathing in air, even though it burned in his lungs. He felt confidence building from knowing he was free. Dragging himself passed the entrance and dropped the hatch lid closed. It crashed with a ringing clang. Then noticing the lighting was dim, and his breathing sporadic, but he wasn't out of the game by any means. The Aquerae were meant to spend much of their time in underwater cities of hidden catacombs, of other worlds that none of the humans had ever experienced. Amen felt a strong emotion of getting free from the burden behind, he had lost his way on a perfect day, headed in the wrong direction, without showing any sign of leaving the scene behind, yet he knew of his mission. Amen sat for a minute to catch his breath. Looked north, looked south, and not knowing what would come next. He was soaked through as a chill in the air hit his skin. That's when he felt water building on the back of his eyes, to no surprise he had felt like shedding tears—quickly swallowing the emotions rising in his throat, thinking of Danica, how tough she was. Would she give up as easily as he felt like giving up? He stood and shook his hands and cracked his neck, took a deep breath and started walking in a direction of an uphill climb, away from the sound of water from below. Now in another tunnel, out of the water, another maze had picked him to be the smartest rat to overcome the dilemma of being trapped. It caused him to smile for a minute when compared to a rat. Remembering they were the hardest to kill back home felt like some type of test fronting him. A rat, just a rodent, but hard to get rid of, just like him. Amen's confidence started to build even more. Another walkway going both directions. Motion sensor lights overhead popped on when he started to move towards a southern slant. The tunnel was in tomb like form with moisture and mud and roots climbing up through concrete of another world, and broken tiles of another form. Garbage strung out across the floor, giving clue that chaos walked this path at one time. Then he saw the bones of a carcass with a broken form, a lost life missing an arm, a skull caved in. It was a vivid picture of a life now gone. Amen's heart was beating in a steady rhythm, thump, thump, thump, as it rose in his throat. He walked around the bones carefully not to step on them. The more he moved forward the further he got along. He was on a mission to finding their leader. A hushed-out whimper came from him, but when hearing it he thought it had come from somewhere else.

Yet it was him making the noise in the back of his throat. He was making the noise to ward off any fear that might keep him from focusing. Amen started humming a familiar song when thinking of brother, and Jacob, and that big idiot Argon. Then he started to miss them. Argon was a pain in the butt, and annoying, yet somehow in a deeper part of his soul he knew there was enough love to go around for all of them. Then Amen's thoughts went back to where he was. The tunnel was damp leaving heavy moisture in the air. It felt better in the water, was his thinking—at least he'd been used to that type of world. These tunnels didn't make any sense. Counting at least six when walking for a good while. The tunnels went forever. Amen sat for a minute and put his head in his hands and tried to think. Something he usually left for the others to do. He left responsibility and planning for the adults. Then it hit him, like a shovel-nose-shark from darker waters. The courage-stone was still in his pocket. No other ideas had come to him, causing his heart to hurt and his mind to wonder. But then he remembered the stone had given him courage back home, when being tested. What was so different now, than a few months back? Then he remembered. He was in the company of five other members who'd helped him along the way. Now he was really being tested, being alone. Amen pulled the stone from his pocket and held it up like a token of good will, a smart little light that could shine like no other on the worst of days. And today was no different. He needed saving. When knowing in the past it had helped him find his way on the road to their leader. So, he started calling her with the light held high. It worked before, why wouldn't it work again? Amen decided to stand and face each entrance of each tunnel when passing them by. From what he could tell, it looked like he was inside some type of hub as each tunnel spewed from one to the next. He remembered Danica reviewing a map to such tunnels when traveling toward earth. But he hadn't thought about paying attention. The adults had tried to prepare for such things as this, and he hadn't. It was the thirteenth tunnel that Amen counted. There showed a little sparkle of light from the stone suddenly. Then he perked when pointing the way. Amen walked a good hundred feet into the thirteenth tunnel to the right, with the stone held out in front of him. The stone flickered even more when going further, and then he knew. He should trust the stone…

Michael sat for a few more minutes surveying each member while his warriors above waited in patients—the brightness of light put off parted a trail through a darker world all around them. For a moment, the Circle of members felt safe in the company of heaven's elite. The storm seemed to have recognize their angelic form by giving them passage without standing against them—respect, was Tory's thinking. She felt it in her bones when the storm parted, and the Dark-Angels fled. Michael looked curious of these smaller humans, and the few aliens that had come along for the ride, causing him to raise an eyebrow of suspicion. Torack looked over and saw his expression. That's when he knew they were here for a reason that lay beyond the gathering of clouds in the sky. Michael turned and raised his eyes, trying to get Tory's attention. "Where are your parents?" He asked. Then he stopped her short by asking another question before she could answer the first. "And why have you been given passage to this world and not your parents?"

Tory looked around before returning an answer. She couldn't speak for their parents, but then she'd remembered what had been said.

"Well, we've been told, a long time ago that this was our destiny... to come here and make things right, was all that was said."

Michael looked over, not surprised that they were on some type of quest, and sent by their parents, still not knowing why? They'd looked determined to do something, or anything of something important he wasn't quite sure. He heard the stories told by the guardian, Thaliana, and James and a few of the others had talked about what the other humans had done of earth, but then heard them fleeing that place where the valleys sank low, and the mountains rose high.

"The ancient ones," Tory said, "they're not here now, and I'm not quite sure where they'd come from. Who would care once coming back to earth?"

Michael measured her statement showing a bit confusion in his eyes. Since he'd lived his many years, from a place so far away, would she even understand his point of view, when his point of view was never imagined by children of their youth. They were the gifted on their way to a destiny imagined only by those of the realms. Maybe they would find resolution by the end of the day...

Michael wondered about using children to face those creatures of the dark. What was his king thinking? He was usually only involved in spiritual warfare matters of the realms. But now he'd noticed their interest was perked. They were leaning in to listen to his every word. Then Michael noticed the Aquerian leader standing by their side. He knew there was wisdom in the guidance of such a fellowship, connected to a leader that had lived many centuries traveling the stars, to find peace and hope and love in some inept part of the universe. With guiding hands stretched out to lead them, in finding a better way of living, from a place so far out in space, next to a Red-Dwarf-Star shining only for the few. Michael measured a world set a part of his own world was given a future of the gifted on another planet set for greatness, as he could feel it in his heart, and acknowledged in his head he looked down at Tory. Knowing of their account, mistakes as children were unaccounted for of the past, because they were given a future not yet recorded in any books of history. They were the gifted as foretold so long ago, to shed a little light on the few, was Michael's thinking. Tory looked over at this warrior of heaven's elite. He was positioned to lead an elite set of angels, commissioned of a king to do a king's bidding. He was the one standing tall to represent. He would lead by virtue of position given to him.

"And you're the next in line?" He asked.

A flutter of eyes with hands on hips she looked up at him. "Yes, I would be the next." Tory said. Not wanting to disappoint, standing on the side, trying to think of what to say next. She was nervous, showed by her lack of experience.

Michael looked at her, thinking she was the oldest, maybe she would know what to do. In the universe they had their part played out in each planned sequence, stretched out beyond the thinking of a handful of youthful children. They were the gifted bound for leadership. A piece of each member was theirs to teach of a king's purpose. Embedded into each young heart standing tall at a dreadful hour, holding on to the last bit of knowledge they had, but staying close to the inside of old leadership. Torack gazed toward the gifted and youthful followers he'd taught well, knowing they held a special place in his heart. He was attached in a way they'd never know. Nothing written about the beginning of time was revealed of a better way of living, than by these young people of wisdom acquired through an Aquerian teacher. It was defining of heart to listen and learn from such leadership. But who would know of a king's will and testament than one so old and wise of heaven's leadership, than the one standing in front of them?

Torack looked at Michael as if queued with like thinking. Michael understood the part he was to play would keep them going in the right direction. "And what one of history could be so vibrant of knowing a king's heart, than of his servants? Who would be your master at this appointed day and hour?"

Tory careful to answer, remained somewhat hesitant, especially when feeling uncertainty.

"She is the door to those other worlds like her father. She's well trained to fight. Trained by the best. Yet we don't know where she could have fallen. She dropped from the sky to go after the youngest of our members."

"Yes, they are quite the duo. Do you know of my king's purpose without her assistance?" Michael asked.

"Yes, we serve a king pointing toward light for darkness scatters in the light has no place in our world. We know such light will show us the way. It's written in our destiny to follow such as you portray." Light is the answer.

Michael smiled at the sparkle of her words. "Rightly so, you've spoken well of direction, young leader. But every pathway can be altered by the conditions of the road. So, which road will you be taking?" Tory felt the leader of realms was right on top of his game when it came to wisdom and leadership. That was the impression of his words.

"We will be taking the higher road for a better view."

"What about those who have eluded you?"

"We will face them again, if we have too. But we prefer to find a better pathway than the one leading away from light."

10

The Way of the World

"They'll come again…mark my words…they won't stop until the world changes to suit their evil hearts." Michael turned with a loud voice signaled his soldiers to set down and pay attention to what followed. They spread themselves thick throughout the lines of defense. Miles of light lit up this place that used to be a coastal city by the sea, at another time called Long Beach, sending out a dazzling glow toward the heavens. If anyone was watching, afar or near, was certain to marvel at the brightness of light out beyond the borders of misconception. A model of the gifted was standing away to the side of heaven's elite out on the edge of this once beautiful place, now lost to oblivion. Tory thought the lights paralleled to a stadium filled with thousands of people during an NFL football game. She could hear the thunder of voices all around, reminded by the lights and these creatures of heaven by her side. Uncle Drew had reminded her of such stories. About warriors in a field of battle making history, on fields of grass, with lights and noise beyond comprehension. The darkness of the night was blotted out by light, and the light took over the stadium as if deemed necessary. The night all around watched in anticipation of what was to come. Tory imagining, their hearts rising up to the occasion, sitting on the edge of their seats, taking in what was before them. Each watching their favorite team, fitting of a king to entertain them, in the light of challenging foe—none threatening of a rival from either side with swords and weapons, but only the challenge of each physical man taking them to soar above the clouds on feet with grass, inspired by the limits of physical aggression. He shared about a leather ball floating on the wings of the air, who'd be the warrior to catch it and run toward victory? Then the vision left her. She felt the fading importance in its meaning, not aware why such a meeting would ever take place. This world was different now. A Circle of light surrounded them all, as darkness edged away from their existence. Light—an impetuous way of causing pain to a darker world, without words, causing self-inflected depravity in misery, without pointing a finger, but felt in the air, as seen from the movement of the wind. Showing them a direction, they did not want to go. As light sometimes brings about hope to the heart, brings emotion to the surface, leaving no doubt of purpose, a settling comprehension.

"So—we're here to help those left behind of the gifted." Tory said.

Michael looked over and nodded. His officers stood at attention out of respect for their leader. Argon acted like a gimpy child that got neglected.

"What's the plan, Stan...I mean who's the boss, apple...?" Argon's mouth was quickly covered by Tory. He pulled back while crossing his arms. An impression he'd seen some rockers do from studies he'd seen on Dr. Zimmerman's computer back home.

Michael raised both eyebrows wondering the boy's frame of mind. "You—young fellow. Are needed to stay in the rear and let the experienced be the guide." Argon, losing a curious stare of misunderstanding, melted between thin lines of confusion, like he'd been dropped from the roaster of a famous football team.

"I thought we were doing okay—they're too many of them—that's all." He said standing tall as he could stand, with soot in his hair and ash all over him.

"Exactly young warrior. Those that have left this place were only toying with you. They have the nasty habit of sneaking up on you in the dark—without much warning. It's best you heed my words young warrior. This fight wasn't meant for one such a young warrior."

Argon lifted his head in disbelief. "But I killed a bunch of them—did you not see?"

Michael leaned in toward the youthful boy full of inconsistencies. "Yes, you did, and I saw, and we're all proud of you. But there's more to fighting than just pulling a trigger and blasting away." Michael paused and looked down at the boy. "War is fought by those with experience.

Not by children with a mission on their mind and two member's missing. Besides, you've got to find those that weigh heavy on the heart as part of this Circle that completes you."

Tory reached and put her hands around the disappointed fifth. "Argon—we don't have time to disgust this with one so wise. He's, their leader. We're on a mission of finding Danica and Amen. We have to find them, before it's too late."

Argon looked up like he'd been scolded. "I'm not a little kid—you know. I can make intelligent decisions just like you."

Tory looked over with a raised eyebrow of concern. Whispering so Michael couldn't here. "Be quiet before you upset him and he leaves this place, making us vulnerable to those creatures of the night."

Argon wasn't having any of it, the scolding, the brush off from Michael, and the creatures coming back. "I didn't start this. They did. But I'm not going to sit around and wait for things to happen. I brought my weapon of choice. Just wait till I see them again." He lined up his sights going north-west and closed his right eye. "I'm going to break some bones and leave them moaning and groaning." Acknowledging it, like it was soon to happen.

Tory couldn't believe her ears. "We've got to find Amen and Danica." Tory said, "Argon, stay focused and do what Michael says."

Argon wondered what he had done wrong. He was standing a few feet away trying to find out what the old leader would say next. Jacob had a worried look in his eyes, and Ismael was viewing a handheld computer screen with Renee of underground tunnels. Michael stood suddenly because the sky was changing, and something was headed their way…

Amen kept walking through tunnel thirteen. Wanting to feel like he would be rescued at any minute. Yet somehow, in the back of his mind he knew he was on his own for now. Amen relied on internal instincts.

When thinking of it, it left an empty hollowness in the pit of his stomach. Keeping up a pace set to a rhythm, making up ground without looking behind feeling something not recognizable might be following along. When nervous he would hum to get his mind on other positive memories of lessor importance, usually not involving sore feet or a mind racing a mile a minute—so he started humming, a song quite familiar among family and friends, yet today was different from any other day experienced of a past shortly lived. Amen was in trouble, from the word get-go when taking the tunnels to find his way back to those that loved him. If taking the wrong path in front or headed in the wrong direction couldn't be an option. Sensing danger, sensing being at his wits end, thinking, Danica could be hurt or stuck in some dark hole needing his assistance, wishing she had never fallen to go after him. Lonely and afraid, small in stature of playing the right roll in the right manner, tired and deluded of finding answers, full of incomprehension of where this tunnel would lead to next. He had to find her because she was important to all of them. With a heavy heart, and his mind racing while wondering about her condition, about how she could survive the drama of being on her own. Within minutes, his feet started to give out, and the water in his water-skin was almost gone. He'd forgotten to refill it when leaving the water world behind. The tunnels were a bit confusing when dehydration started to set in. It was too late to change the direction he was headed. That's when he decided to sit down and take off his right shoe. Then he took off his right sock. Right away he saw the raw toe that turned a dingy purple color, which wasn't his normal healthy color of blue. He'd forgotten to take his shoes off once on dry land, to let his socks dry out. Amen looked down the next tunnel that held a dim glow of light and saw a sizable rat walking toward him. He never even noticed them before until today when being alone. The rat was like him, stuck in this maze looking for a way out. He got up to avoid the rat and walked around him with a disguised look from a glance, but then for some reason he turned back around and looked at the rat as it scurried away. The rat was a survivor. He'd survived bombs and chemicals, and unbearable winds, and those things of the sky, and now he was running through mazes, just like Amen. Amen wondered if the rat might have a better plan than he. All he knew was his feet were on fire. Every time he put his foot down, he came up limping, like a wounded dog pulling up lame. He contemplated if going back in the water might be a better way to go. At least it was cool, and he wouldn't dehydrate. From sitting on the ground, he felt vibration coming from the floor. That's when Amen's thoughts went back to the courage-stone. Quickly, looking down he noticed holding it tight as a faint flicker of light started to glow. With everything happening on the strangest of days, he'd forgotten how important it was to even have it. Understanding the flicker of light was a reminder of past memories. Suddenly, the vibration below began to turn into a rumble. Hastily standing to his feet, with one shoe in hand and a sock hanging out of his front left pocket of faded jeans that were still not quite dry. Amen noticed the shadows growing, getting closer, making him nervous, as the shadows quickly climbed the tunnel walls. He didn't know what to do. He couldn't go back where he had come from that wasn't an option and running straight ahead was out of the question. He was stuck in the middle. Looking front, looking behind, with his right foot aflame and blisters forming on the bottom of his feet he couldn't just let this thing run over him. Looking down at his big toe, made it hurt worse than it really was. Amen thought of war-week with the others, he thought how tough the others had been on him, to finish each part of the obstacle course, to not be lax when it became difficult, or give up trying when feeling pain past what a normal boy of his age would go through. Condac was always close by watching all of them, to make sure they were all doing their best. He was an elite type of leader that didn't stand for insubordinate actions, even by children such as them. He was tough on them, not excepting tears or excuses when fatigue set in, or when their muscles refused to move any further. Amen shook his head from the memory, stood solemnly and huffed out a steady stream of over-heated air. The floor was cold on his bare foot, his head was throbbing, and his heart hurt without really knowing why. Then Amen looked down and held the stone in his hand loosely. Without warning it began to heat up in his hand. He tossed it in the air a couple of times thinking maybe he misread what was really happening to the stone, after wanting to cry and then wanting to die when being lead down the wrong pathway away from friends, away from family, where others of his kind dared not go. It was just some crazy rock when first thinking about it, but it continued to glow, burning his hand when first feeling it. He almost wanted to put it back into the pocket of his jacket and forget he had brought it along.

Then the weirdest feeling had come over him. Swiftly, feeling Danica calling to him. Her audible voice distinctly in the back of his mind. Definitely redeeming him from earlier, now readable through a telepathic connection he'd known to have with her all along. She inherently telling him to hold up the stone and point it toward the direction he had been moving. Amen turned his head to the front of the sounds and noticed the shadows were getting closer. Whatever it was started making these high pitch screams as if they were not human bearing in mind what they had already been through. Nothing at the moment would surprise him. Amen stood there trying to make sense of Danica's thoughts that kept pushing him to be brave. He wasn't sure if he had the strength to listen. He could barely contain this hot little rock in his hand, blinking back the thoughts of being close to their leader, and yet sensing somehow Danica was screaming in his head not to turn around on her, but keep moving forward, keep pressing toward the prize that waited around the next corner, getting ready to lead him towards his destiny.

The stone was hot, but he held on tight. The shadows were getting bigger, moving quickly with greater purpose toward a boy lost out on his own too far away from his usual friends. The rumble of feet was more definitive of purpose as he stood facing something that was moving at high speed…

Danica sensed Amen to be in trouble without knowing which way to turn. She needed to get to him at any cost, even if it meant to give up her life for his if that was even possible. She knew he needed to have courage at this very moment. She knew if he took a minute, to find hidden strength, he'd find his way no matter what. Danica screamed inside her head for Amen to pay attention. She could imagine him sitting there watching something overtake him. Picturing him hiding his head in his hands, sitting the hours away without finding a solution to his problem. She could hardly contain herself. Learned memories of Orbitus began to flash before her eyes. Danica sensed the end was eminent, but she couldn't do what she needed to do because she felt so far away from the boy of his own elements. How could she help him? How could she reach him before an ill-timed fate came and took him away? Then suddenly realizing, he was one of them. Amen had inherited the same imbued gifts passed on to the other generations of their kind. She knew this couldn't be happening to such a delicate boy on his own, too far away from those who cared for him, too far away from anything recognizable of being home. They had spent so many days together as a unit, and all of them were beginning to feel complete as they grew to love and share an altered life. She loved Amen like a little brother, if ever having one she'd never treat him any different than she treated Amen. He was a special type of boy who was led by his words and acted out their conditions. Yet her thinking was not on personal issues of losing focus from her pain or leaning toward the fact that she might die at any minute. She was still their leader, even at the distance that separated them.

In the past, Amen had been quite the troublemaker getting under her skin. But she never imagined losing him. A lingering tear leaked out of Danica's right eye. She signaled mentally for him to hold up the stone to light a pathway ahead. To let the courage-stone be a guide back to those who loved him.

She sensed all along that that was the right thing to do. When thinking him trapped, she had to do something. Danica moved all her inner strength toward one place. She swung her legs toward the top of this abated hole like she was on parallel bars at her local gymnasium. At the same time three of the fallen burst into the room—to her it was all bad timing. Amen needed her right now in the worst of ways, but she didn't even know how to get to him. He wasn't very big and didn't really know how to protect himself. Danica screamed when they overtook her. She fought and kicked and screamed some more before slipping through a door evading her captors…

Torack signaled for the Circle to head for the hovercraft. Michael blew a klaxon bade signaling his warriors to head for the clouds. The sky quickly filled in with those of the fallen, a darker place a part of a world that had faced sacrosanct order. They'd come back better prepared, leaning into an imperious side of life, purgatorial in remittance, not seen or experienced by these warriors of light. Light of heaven perfunctory of existence as the dark inanities were set to confuse. Michael's legends had no time to regroup. They were like the no-huddle offense of Payton Manning debut of the Denver Bronco's smothering opponents with no time to set their defense. A warrior like no other standing strong convivial showmanship of an opposing foe. They were gambling their hand to meet them midair. Though Michael was not counting on the watchers doing their part, he knew their presence would be preempted to what followed. This alien race was skilled in the art of dismemberment. He welcomed their assistance like having a big brother backing his front. He spread his wings and led his soldier's into obscurity. He fanned out his massive form, catapulting straight up into the air, like a rocket headed for the moon. It caused a sweep of air to zip by like an eighteen-wheeler flying down a country road. Michael pulled a weapon out beneath his belt that caused Argon to turn his head with widened eyes.

Argon quickly climbed into the hovercraft as the others of his team followed behind. Torack was yelling for the others to leave the scene in a direction the enemy could not follow, opposite of the direction fronting them. But it was too late for the others, they were surrounded on all sides. Numbered like the sands of the sea couldn't begin to explain what was seen with the natural eye. The sky turned black, darker than the night. Each leader, standing tall, viewed the caricatures of movement, steadfast, floating on air, with a vicious stare all around. Panic developed when looking back at their leader. Cornelius of the darker world had prepared wisely and efficiently. Michael was caught unguarded with less words used and more gesturing of hands. His legions spread out as the watchers and Condorsorouses fronted the enemy, who were duped by their size as they moved in a desultory way. The dragon-like-steeds took them to higher elevation as the watchers set the bait, with bone-knives and swords, and a rote chant building of attitudes in confidence, a rhythm in the making, setting the pocket of leadership, honed to the inside of a better attitude, pumped with adrenaline, they moved in as a team...

* * *

Amen stood with one shoe off with the imperiled blister burning on his right big toe. The shoes he wore weren't for the foot-soldier that he had become. He felt tears pushing on the back of his eyes, but he found them not to flow at the moment on this day of all days as he was quickly followed by the dead. All he could think of was Danica, was she okay? Would she be there at his final moment when he needed her? They were attached by mind and heart that interlopers of this world would never understand, being those of a healing planet. The emotional memories of the Aquerae way to fight were two-fold in meaning. Set the bait and start the rhythm of the dying. The vision of Amen's showed a different side of life to the extreme. The Conquerites revealed scorching and dying of an enemy not ready to give up at a moment's notice. Amen understood they would work in the pocket, set in a rhythm of swaying an enemy past confusion. They were set apart from any natural way of fighting.

Amen felt a scorching heat in the back of his throat. He felt dizzy and shaky when pushing past fatigue on fragile limbs. His bottom lip moved with emotion, as his heart flooded with devotion with getting past the fear. The Conquerite sealed his fate, of a true member, of all members, included in a fight walking toward freedom. He'd envision those memories of heaven's warriors. Hanging onto the loose end of denial of not making the cut of bigger boys. He was leaning towards courage and commitment. Amen used such memories to help him see past the barriers in his way. He limped toward the end of the next tunnel. His was being pulled in a direction he did not want to go. Smoke and blood and mud from rain had scattered his thinking in moments of dehydration, moments of shakiness and dizzy spells. He had to get a grip on his reality. His heart was heavy, and his strength almost gone on this road leading away from a previous life. Death held a unique smell left in memory, filling Amen's nostrils of crossing the line. He raised his eyes, along with the stone. He moved toward what might be freedom, freedom of life, freedom from pain. The stone was set aglow when burning in his hand. His ears were throbbing, his heart was hurting, his foot was burning, in a mixed-up maze of marching with courage. The fear of being alone left him, and the tears he shed before had stopped. And dying was an agenda left on a road now behind him. Memories of the ones before kept him company, not thinking he'd been forgotten by family and friends, he had a mission on his mind but never missed a beat of opportunity. The courage-stone stood out like a smart little light that it was, lighting the way, giving him a nudge of courage to keep moving. The eternity of making the wrong choice overwhelmed him once causing him to stumble on shaky feet. There was strength now when first there was none. He stood stationary for a minute to catch his breath; he could feel his heart beating in his ears. He was getting madder by the minute when thinking of being tricked. When looking forward he saw shadows getting closer, closer than he wanted as he still faced them. Amen felt the rumble of trouble headed his way. The light of the courage-stone took over obscurities. Memories of blood and rage ran rapid of mind. An evil opposing of wills was centered now coming his way. Amen put his head down and closed his eyes and raised the stone as high as he could. Courage was something he needed. Believing in his members of friends was his starting point.

Abruptly, a beam of light shot out in raining brilliance. Amen opened his eyes and almost couldn't believe what he was seeing. He saw the light move like a cloud bursting with energy. He could envision Danica not so far away past the light, past this enemy that stood in the way. Light of the stone was dominant over the dark heading his way. His courage caused him to stand taller, caused him to feel something stronger run through his veins, giving him a moment of confidence, showing him an easier pathway up ahead. The fallen moving towards him was destroyed by the light of the stone. Amen dropped to his knees and let out a slow breath of air. He was finished. The enemy blocking the way was gone...

When Danica opened her eyes, she was surprisingly in another tunnel. Yet this tunnel was one of a cemented kind that would carry water. She felt the sting of blood oozing from her face and wrists. Drained, dragged, and beaten. She was a sight for sore eyes. She had water on the back of her eyes when seeing she was free, yet her hands were still tied together. She looked for anything sharp on the ground. A few feet ahead, among debris, she noticed a broken piece of glass from a time of another past. Yet she couldn't hold up the glass without being cut. She could feel her life flickering on the balance of that other room she'd just left. Leaning forward quickly to throw up, an emotional appeal of trouble now gone. Her head was spinning, her heart uncertain of living past another day. She had fallen from a few thousand feet to an assured death, yet she hadn't died, still breathing in air. Where to go from here she didn't know. Tired past weary, broken and alone, she had her memories that filled her soul like quenching water. They kept her company as she moved along the pathway of an underwater passageway. The tunnel was like how Amen had seen it of a similar place. Danica traveled without knowing where she'd find a place to rest her head. A place of vines and moisture surrounded by overgrowth, with loamy conditions as water from before ruining a good man's day showed evidence of being here for no particular reason. A toilet-seat with dingy brown stains, absent from apartment 3A, a broken doll with one eye missing, a cracked face, a shoe of a passer-bier, sunglasses bent beyond recognition. And then she noticed rats and bugs bigger than any normal size she had ever seen. It was a world underground turned upside down. She was caught in a world of bugs and trash and vines all around, sewer lids closed tightly to drain off water from another rainstorm of a missing day. She felt the mood of the tunnel as she took part of the reality as if a dream. Danica felt to be a lifeless form plotting along in this pathway given to her. Her mind went past worry. Covered by some miraculous miracle that saved her from those devils of the sky, left dirty and disheveled, left alone and lonely, too far away from those she loved. Her soul felt purged and turned inside out. Walking steadily on the tunnel below. Through corridors and memories, keepsakes too lost to keep her company, from some other souls left behind without memory. Left only footprints of another life that was now gone. She was pleased when thinking of her disgruntled members of membership. They would never stop to listen to her. They seemed to have a better plan than the one next to them. She imagined looking behind and saw her Circle in her imagined rear-view mirror. They smiled back when walking toward the light…then something slapped her awake.

Danica was staring in the face of an elongated foot soldier with a funny looking baseball cap twisted to the side, with one shoe on and the other shoe missing. Then noticing one draped around his neck by shoestring ties. A face of faded dirt and tear-stained eyes, with clothes messed up from her angle of perception. Something green staining Amen's mouth, with hair stuck out in all directions without knowing why, but he was still genuine, still hanging on to the last bit of effort of trying to get along. Amen clicked his fingers to get Danica's attention. Staring down at her in his usual informal way. Wanting to snap her to a standing position.

Wanting her to recognize the current fact that she was still alive, still kicking, still listening to the small voice in the back her head. She slowly moved her eyes toward this strange boy who offered her drink from what he had left. Danica took the gift without saying a word, then she choked and coughed before sitting back up. Then realizing Amen had found her. He freed her hands from the ropes that bound her to blood-stained wrists. Helped her gently to her feet. Then she began to focus where they were at.

"Hey…you look tired." Amen said.

"Yeah…more than tired…I'm drained."

"Do you know which direction we need to go?"

"No, but I've been following the courage-stone."

"Me too." Amen smiled. He felt the connection to their leader.

She looked down and noticed Amen's missing shoe and sock and looked at him. "What's up with the foot?"

"I forgot to let my socks dry out after being in water, before walking. I've got some blisters and a raw toe. It hurts pretty bad." Amen pointed his toe toward up to show her.

She looked down and wrinkled her nose. "Well, we can't have that."

"I knew you were down here somewhere." Amen said. "I heard you calling to me, but I wasn't sure which direction."

Danica put her arms around him with an endearing hug. Amen sat down and Danica applied the blue healing-stone…"So, what happened to you?" Amen asked.

Danica looked over and saw the worried look. "I got captured but it didn't turn out to well for my captors." She said. "They left in a hurry. Of course, they skipped introductions."

"Don't figure." Amen said while brushing off the rudeness of such unlikely gentlemen.

"All the gentlemen of this place aren't any gentlemen I've ever seen."

Danica raised an eyebrow to show her approval. "Yeah, their quite the dogs they insist on being. And I don't particularly like dealing with them. They're a waste of my precious time."

"Yeah, a waste of time." Amen mimicked. He reached over and took her hand. Shaky fingers and a heart full of love had gotten to her and the tears started to flow. Amen put his head on her shoulder in the joining of comfort. He learned of love that day was something more precious than anything else ever felt…

The battle above continued for what seemed like forever. Michael pulled his wings in and dropped from the sky. He had to make room for the Morning-Star needing to pick up speed in thirty feet of space. A weapon different from any other ever used by the elites. Each Circle member stayed inside the hovercraft under a cloaking device that, the Aquerian leader had devised. Michael held the Morning-Star similar of that in Greek mythology, used by warriors of a time period long gone by those of a past far hence removed. He held it above his head and started swinging it in a circular motion. As it picked up speed it put out a high-pitched whistle. It was the simplest tools of a rod, ball, and chain in simplicity. Yet it was a weapon of the worst of its form. The blackness of the night was pulled toward the ball of steel and spikes tore through flesh and bone of their enemy. Like hurricane Katrina ripped through New Orleans on that dreadful night. The Morning-Star stood out as a symbol of power and quaint resolution. Heaven's elite stood staring down at this weapon of change. The Morning-Star took no prisoners and told no lies. It was the coming together of current retribution. The blackened winged beasts were pulled toward pandemonium, greeting them quite efficiently as brothers culled from their duties away from home. A demystify storm began to light up the sky above the warriors. The fallen were seared by strikes of lightning. Flashes of light brightened the sky turning night into day. Michael twirled his weapon of choice above his head. He was the master of disaster, pulling them in. Appendages and bones brought up the dead as they were dying by the thousands, dropping from the sky. Michael became an exterminator of infectious limbs torn from bodies in the embodiment of the dead, giving away their lives as payment of a day of reckoning. The Morning-Star tore through their defenses, like a siphon draining the runoff from a dams overflow. More Morning-Stars were raised to the heavens, creating a wind tunnel while waking the dead of their recent departure…

Danica looked north and south of the tunnel. Two rats walked across her foot as she jumped to her left, almost toppling over Amen and knocking him down. "Sorry squirt…I'm a bit jumpy after facing those creatures."

Amen looked up and gave her a smile. "Don't worry...I've got your back. I know you wouldn't intentionally step on me. Besides, I've learned quite a bit from our Circle of friends to avoid such occasions of error."

She looked down and nodded. "Thanks Amen. I know your motives are divine."

Amen reached to help her step around him and looked back at the rats scurrying away.

"Don't mind them, they're looking for a way out, just like us." Danica looked back at the rats before facing forward again.

"Well, I guess you have point. Maybe we should follow them."

"I don't know if that's a good idea." Amen said.

"Why do you say that?"

"They don't look like they want to face what's out there, you know, out on the barren land above us, besides there's no water up there." Danica brushed off the rats like they were on a different journey than the one they were on.

"Maybe so...let's keep going like we are."

Up ahead, Danica saw something above them. "Look, there's a hatch coming our way."

Amen looked up in surprise while blurting out the words. "I see it!" He said while raising his right hand to high-five their leader. Danica accommodated by a slap of her hand.

From behind a glowing sapphire color of water shot down the tunnel, catching the rats and trash and debris while rushing toward them. Someone had opened a valve somewhere without letting them know. Danica screamed when turning around. The glow only lasted about ten seconds before catching them. Amen reached for her hand as the water took them off their feet.

"Hold your breath!" Amen yelled.

"I know..." She returned while going under.

She reached up and grabbed Amen's hand and held on. Amen let the water take them without a struggle knowing Danica would struggle enough in the moments to come. He breathed in the water naturally before realizing Danica was in a panic when the tunnel filled to the top. Amen took over, knowing this was a natural way of existence to him. From at her side, he'd seen her sword swishing back and forth from the force of the water passing by. The water picked up speed on a downward push as debris and rats with floating pieces of wood moved at a speed not recognizable. Danica, an hour earlier, was being tortured by an enemy, now forced to go in a direction she did not want to go, in the worst of conditions, an altered day of recognizing anything being of a normal everyday occurrence. She was being challenged in an unfamiliar world, with Amen at her side—attached more like it, like a leech holding on. Still weak, still struggling to get her strength back, hanging on the loose end of leaving this old world behind. Yet she held on to the boy misconstrued on most days that held any meaning to this disillusioned girl at his side. Face it, she'd been saved. Amen saw her face turning colors. He grabbed her head while they both turned in circles to keep attached. Amen moved in and covered her mouth. At first, Danica didn't know what Amen was about to do. Then seeing his gills move on the side of his neck, she understood. He cupped his arms around her head and his legs around her mid-section. Danica could feel air being forced into her lungs. Relieved to be saved again by the smallest of members. She focused through rushing water to notice him looking back and blinked understanding. Amen didn't want to close his eyes because of floating objects, each item of driftwood and trash moved in discordant order all around them. He took advantage of this moment to save her life, she was the key to everything they'd fought for. There wasn't a greater mission than saving their leader. Knowing she would be dead within minutes; he didn't hesitate to do his job as appointed by the Conquerite. Amen was meant to go through what he experienced. But in Danica's frame of mind Amen had showed up at the perfect time. Then she opened her eyes and noticed him staring. But her view was not one of a curious little boy having his way, it was eyes of concern from a certain young man of membership, doing his part, even if being the youngest of seven. He showed courage. And noticing Danica's skin was a bit pale. The pressure of the water was building as it moved to the lower end of a pool. They were victims of someone else's circumstances. And nothing ahead made any sense because of the constant churning of water caused chaos to take them toward an end of a darker place. Amen held a worried expression when turning his head. Danica's hair was covering her face as she pushed it back and tied it behind her. Her arms and legs where tiring from splashing about as she relaxed and moved them in close to her body. Amen used his webbed feet to keep them from hitting the sides of the tunnel as the water picked up speed, it developed unusual currents not expected. Danica's clothes clung to her body, causing her to shiver from its onerous chill. She would have dressed more proper for the occasion, but her plans had been altered by those creatures of the air. A recalled memory brought a bleak remembrance to her character when remembering her swimming back home. Nothing from home could compare to it. Amen wondered when making the connection of danger and held on tighter than usual. A raised suspicion in the back of his mind caused him to think things would get worse as they moved toward the lower end of an underwater aqueduct. Suddenly, a sizable piece of wood shot past them just missing Danica's head. She looked back and noticed Amen staring in bewilderment. From the corner of Amen's eye showed a hesitant doubt of which way to go. Danica could feel Amen pushing at her to keep her moving, keep her focused of finding a way out of here. He paused to blow more air into her lungs as she gulped it in, feeling like her lungs were about to burst. Danica twisted her lips to one side to blow out used air. Amen, immersed up to his neck with trouble this day as it caused him to wonder, caused him to think of his training with the unique members of membership. He was not his usual color of blue as when first starting through this maze of liquidated reunions. The tunnel seemed alive, giving way of the dark held a deeper meaning, held to the circular bonds of being caught in a trap not seen with the eye or understood with the heart. Surrounded by circular walls as they passed along on the darkest of days draining them of energy, draining confidence and courage. Holding no bonds of likelihood that held any thinkable meaning. Yet Amen's thoughts came in at an angled consistency of making any sense as the hours and minutes went by. Depleted of energy while lost in direction not feeling up to par. He wrapped his hands and feet around Danica as she clung to him like a leach on the surface of skin. Held on tighter, to last a bit longer, on this dismal day of finding a moment of hope. Thinking for a few seconds he suddenly knew what to do. They had to find a way to the top…

Ismael leaned against the glass bubble of the hovercraft and mashed his lips against the glass. It fogged up as he looked on. He was worried about his brother. Argon reached over and put his arm around his shoulder knowing a worried member was at his side. He might have said something sarcastic, but would it ruin a good friend's day if pushed any harder than losing a brother? The fighting above just under the clouds was starting to get to him. With ash and blood raining down from the sky the view was almost impregnable. Torack's cloaking device of invisibility left them unseen, as they sat at a lower indentation of land, out of the directed fight from above. Tory looked over at Ismael and new he held a worried expression for his brother.

"Argon was the one that saw him fall off the Condorsorous." Tory said. Then Renee reached up and put her hand on his shoulder. "He's with Danica now."

Ismael turned to look at her. A bleak guise showing on his face, "I wonder where they are?" He said, as Renee returned with a worried stare toward darkness.

"They're alive. I can feel them but look at the sky." The fallen kept pouring in all around them from above, and hundreds of hellhounds have followed after taking up the slack where their leader's had missed. Ismael was so frustrated from what he saw started moving things just outside the window. He saw a sword lying on the ground about thirty feet from the hovercraft. He didn't see anyone attached to it, so he picked it up with his telekinesis and sliced the face off a Hellhound. The creature dropped in remission and turned into ash. Tory saw what he had done just looked at him in bewilderment.

"Did you do that?" The Aquerian heart of emotions was quite different. He showed a smile and thought to stay awhile before answering.

"Yeah…it was me!" Pondering being stuck in an elevator with no easy way to breathe.

"Why'd you do that?" Tory asked.

Ismael looked in her general direction of sword, and knew it was timing. Then Tory noticed the gleaming sword with blood stains. "I used my gift." Ismael said. "That's all." Argon looked back at the weapon sitting next to him. Taken by surprise, a bolt of lightning came from the sky hitting the top of the hovercraft. Glass exploded in all directions. Members moved left and right to duck and cover. Michael fought his way toward the explosion of glass, while faintly hearing screams, he saw movement a hundred feet away. No one was permanently injured, but Renee had been cut by some of the flying glass to her cheek, and Argon had a slight cut on his arm. He picked up his Element-gun and turned it on. Torack looked over and raised an eyebrow. "We're in this fight now..." Argon said with a grin plastered to one side of his face. He was suddenly focused with a mission on his mind from one previously missing. He looked over at Jacob. "Let's go find our leader." He said.

The Circle of members got out into open air and walked into darkness...

Amen and Danica kept moving to the top of the tunnel reaching for a hatch coming up. They were trying to get on solid ground before dropping to the lower end of this assured water basin.

She didn't see anything, was her thinking. Danica focused to get a better view, but then she realized her view wasn't on something behind them, but above. Whatever they did they had to do quickly before running out of time. They could see the shadows of darker water coming from the lower end ahead, mounting and building of the currents force, with debris all around pushing at them forcing them away from the walls. Amen, worried about dropping below before reaching the top. Yet knowing, thinking that way was not a good way to be thinking in their present situation. They had to be moving toward the same goal. Leaving this place is what he needed to be thinking about. But how? What can we do before it's too late? Amen thought.

Suddenly, Amen saw another hatch coming up ahead.

Danica had a troubled expression cross her face as the water continued to whirl around them, pushing her left, pushing her right. She couldn't understand how weak it made her feel. Then she understood why the courage-stone wasn't working at the moment, it only worked when they were apart. She had an idea and would pass it along, with a certain stare of movements of her eyes, to get Amen's attention, then movement with her hands she pushed him in the direction of the top of the tunnel. Amen looked above with a curious stare and knew they were thinking of the same thing. Danica closed her eyes and thought of taking them through a door, if it was even possible, but where would they end up? She tried to make connection with Renee or even Torack, but she had trouble focusing because the force of shadows coming shortly ahead of them, not knowing what it was she didn't know how to respond.

We have to go, was her signal, as she pointed Amen near another hatch about twenty-five feet away. The ceiling was hard to judge running at a decline by three percent, give or take a few inches from looking either way. An eerie feeling crept into Amen's mind when seeing the dark water coming closer, closer than ever. They had to time it just right. Seeing the handles leading up to some type of roof-hatch, twenty feet, ten feet, and then five. They reached for it together. Amen moved his webbed feet and hands in a circular direction, once procuring the handles. He pushed off debris and anything else floating their way and tried to grab for Danica's waist as she suddenly caught the last handle before sinking towards the bottom. The water moved as if alive, set to change the stage of their future, set to give away life at a moment's notice. The darker water was only ten feet ahead, and the water behind picked up speed while pushing toward them with a purpose, forcing all who took part in this journey, not giving them a choice of which direction to go.

Thinking this was a way out of all this mess, getting in over their heads. They were way past the two-minute warning of making it, ten feet past seeing another way out. Danica looked up and noticed the round cylinder shadowing in a distance of just a few feet. She made the ladder first and started pulling past debris. Amen at her shoulder, grabbed Danica's waist and pulled her in. He turned to look back at where they'd come from. He stopped to give her more air. Then quickly seeing her gulp it in. He watched dim shadows moving behind eluding them of purpose. He signaled with his eyes toward the top. They were tired, overspent, wanting to get past this challenge. Without further hesitation, Danica opened the hatch, thinking they might be headed for more trouble once freed from the water. The hatch fell open. Danica reached for dryer ground. The pressure almost knocked her off the ladder. Amen grabbed her arm to keep her from slipping further. Danica pulled through and reached for the top of the hole. She reached behind and pulled him up. Then once getting on solid ground she closed the hatch leaving the noise of rushing water under their feet. They sat a few feet away to catch their breath. Danica's heart, felt to beat past recovery. Amen looked over wondering her frame of mind. "You, okay?"

Considering his own self-preservation was intact. The pressure of the water was gone now, rushing by in that other world. Yet the vibration was still felt beneath their feet.

"I'm okay," she said, "kind of light-headed from the lack of air," holding back a sparing goodhearted laugh. Amen heard it in her line of breath.

"Where should we go now?"

"That way." She said as light from ahead would take them south…

Argon cut a trail in the obscurity of the storm. The lightning helped spread ash and a tinted smell of the dead. They trudged away from violence of that fight left behind. Their time to act was now. The watchers and their steeds-of-the-air stayed with a mental connection with Torack. He was left with the Circle of membership, to keep them motivated, to keep them moving toward finding their way of the present mission. It wouldn't be accomplished without his input, his leadership, giving pointers when needed, staying towards the back of the line, as they walked on dirt roads of this world left behind. They were set in the sight of their commitments of servitude. Not giving in to the misalignment fading of purpose. This world of bleak arrangements was covered with war and famine, covered with unrealized finalization seen from the stare of eyes all around them. The setting of emotions was to meet an end. They were better suited up of not giving in to the chase, not giving up by what was seen with the natural eye, nonconforming, not committed to their lack of sensibility, sensing misery could be around the next corner of leadership. They had to stay focused. The sky was scarred with an onerous feeling of being close to an end. Yet the world yielded only moments to breathe in the dust and take seriously the form of those creatures left behind on roads not too far away in greeting them. Ismael pushed against the wind with his telekinesis as they stayed close together, not giving in to the pressing of the wind, as it pressed on all sides of this journey's beginning. Torack had caught up to them with an Element-gun attached over his left shoulder, and a hand-held-computer screen lit in a color of green. Argon turned around and pictured him like a Commando out of a soldier-of-fortune magazine, then smiled when picturing him on the cover of the latest issue with his bluish sharp teeth glowing in unison of a mouth full of teeth, and then the thought left him...

The Circle stayed closely knitted together, no more than a few feet between them. The windstorm made it almost impossible to see or hear or find their way without the guidance of their electronic device of the world they had come from.

Tory held her hand up. "We need to find shelter!" She said. They'd been walking for about three hours before acknowledging the wind wasn't letting up anytime soon. They were drenched of sweat, tired from walking, and all hope was almost completely gone. A flicker of light was seen up ahead. A touch of rolling hills from what Tory could tell on a computer screen. She turned to tell the others one by one. They stood in a valley, with wind and dirt filling the air and ash was covering every inch of clothing making them invisible from the blacked-out sky. The smell of burnt cinders remained in the air as Tory tapped Jacob on the shoulder to get his attention. Torack touched base of where to go, by pointing south, just above the first hill. Within minutes they'd found a place of rest burrowed in cave like form just two hundred feet to the south. Tory took the lead as Jacob, Ismael, Renee, and Argon and Torack followed after. Once past the opening Torack blocked the wind with a force-field. The howl of the wind receded, and Argon turned on a flash-light to get direction without tripping. Tory clicked on a LED light on just above a baseball cap that she was wearing. She stood at Argon's left shoulder. Argon waited for their second in command to turn and look at him. Tory saw him standing next to a puddle of water and gave a courageous smile of recognition. The air was clear as far as they could tell, and the temperature was cave like, not hot or cold but somewhere in between, causing all of them to relax a bit. The ceiling rose a good thirty feet in the air, and rocks of stalagmites and stalactites whirled above in Gothic like form. Argon broke out his canteen as others followed suit. He was first to take off his backpack and find a place to sit as he brushed off ash and dirt that had covered him. Jacob came over to sit next to him. Renee was next, along with Ismael. Ismael was breathing somewhat heavy, not used to the surface air of what was left of earth. None of them were doing very well breathing what was out there. Nothing had happened the way they had planned, it was a world of reform, nothing like expected. Jacob was pulled to the entrance suddenly, something seen of the sky. He could see what was left of a red-blood-moon reflected off ocean waves of another time. He could hear the surf, of memories past, hidden in the rhythms of gentle waves spanking the shore. The top of the water gave him a sense of peace. But now it was gone. What had gone wrong? A sparkle of hesitation was seen in Jacob's eyes when seeing the moon give off a touch of reflected light. Renee grabbed Tory by the hand in a sudden jolt of realization. She turned to meet her glance with the LED light shining on her face.

"They're gone" Renee said. "The Dark-Angels are gone. For the time being." Tory looked over and understood Renee was seeing them leave the fight left behind three hours back. They were now in a resting place to gather their thoughts and strength, and to give in to the comforts of friendliness and casual memories of the day almost gone. Needing the strength of each other to make sense of this disconnected way of life. Argon's face was sealed in the experiences of the night. He felt no hope to guide him further. What was left inside of him was fragile in the wake of what had already happened. Argon felt the chill of the air, not knowing if it was day or night, as it burned its sting across his face from the outside elements of weather.

They rested up for a few hours before getting back on the road...

Tory stopped to look over where they'd come from. "Where do you think Danica ended up?" Argon asked when turning back to look at her.

"This is where she would have headed." Tory mentioned.

"How do you know which direction Danica would go?"

"I don't know, but her family is from San Diego. We're about fifty miles from there!" Argon pulled out a compass he had in his coat pocket. He watched the needle move south, and then it moved north.

"If we keep heading south, we might run into her." Tory turned to look at Renee for some type of reassurance.

Renee glanced to their second in command. "He's right...this seems to be the only logical place she'd go." For some reason Renee felt going south was their only option. Torack sat back of this small group of members making sure everyone was together and no one left behind.

Suddenly, Jacob grabbed Argon by the arm to hold him back as he was first in the group. Argon turned around and gave him a bewildered stare.

"What's going on?" Argon asked.

Jacob pointed at what was below them. A deep ravine wasn't felt or seen to look any different than solid ground. They almost walked into it as a group. Jacob, paying attention, recognized the ground appeared to move like liquid smoke. Heat rose off the top of something seen below. Argon, only inches away from death, pulled away from the edge. Pulling him back to solid ground, he wiped a bead of sweat from his brow. A befuddled look glazed the boy's face, tired and testy over the long haul. A rift lay only a few feet away. He turned with an unsettling hesitation. "Hey…thanks…that would've hurt." Jacob didn't understand his humor.

Argon nodded in retreat of Jacob's response. "A thank you would be good. I think you would have been more than just hurt." Argon had considered as much and let out a chuckle of acceptance—by then Torack had caught up to the group of members and stared in the darkness of the rift. Something was brewing that caught his attention. Argon looked down after and wondered what Torack was looking at.

"Which way do we go now?" Argon asked.

Tory pulled out her handy green computer screen and looked on the map of direction they were headed. She explained their situation within minutes to get their attention.

"Well, if we go east for about half a mile, we can make it around this ravine, then we can head south again." Tory turned the handheld to show the group as the wind whipped at their faces. "Below the area here is some type of underwater tunnels." Tory pointed with her finger at the map. "According to the schematics there's something under there we haven't seen yet."

Everyone circled in to get a better look. Torack, from behind, leaned forward and turned on a really bright light that shot down into the rift. The rest could hear the movement of earth and a thin line of lava viewed hundreds of feet below. Torack measured the hole and knew it was a path leading to a certain death. Then he turned the light out so not to attract those of their enemy, leaving them in a dimmer light would be a better choice. The group turned east and kept silent to save time and energy that was soon to quickly fade from the pressures of walking for hours.

Argon kept looking back time-to-time in the direction of the ocean as it started looking smaller as they moved on. Quickly fading behind from the last of flickering light covered by the raging sandstorm…

The water was gone for now. No more pockets of hidden air to contend with. Amen and Danica were both drenched from the tunnel below. He reached to take Danica's hand. She turned and looked at him. Amen saw her paling face, once tense shoulders began to relax. Shedding tears crossed her mind, yet instead a fluttering heartfelt relief of a small boy of alien decent overwhelmed her thinking. He put her life above his own to save her. Now knitted to her side was showing the same proclivities of life, so love appears to have no limits. Danica thought about how they'd been carried away in the night by water and war and certain death from the fall, with no knowledge of where they were going to end up. And somehow, they were still alive with a mission on their mind. A sensing peace floated around them taking up space. She felt blessed. Some cosmic force had intervened, taking over the difficult turns of each situation. They fit like one in a pocket of courage, as it coursed through their veins and burned like adrenaline. The concept of love was learned of that day. It was of self-sacrifice to gain freedom; it was staying in the fight no matter the circumstances. It affected each individual personally on a physical level of acceptability, like it did Amen and Danica. Without hesitation, without recollection that they might not live past the next five minutes, capitulating them beyond the notion that they were facing an end, seeing now this was just their beginning. Around the next corner another wave of water took them off their feet…

The wind continued its onslaught, its combative sting, one dreadful foothold at a time. The Circle finished traveling east before Tory signaled everyone to start going south again. Torack, not being of his youth, began to lag behind like before. Renee turned and saw the aged Aquerae leader being held back by the wind, and-wear-and-tear of age had slowly crept up on him. Within a few minutes, the wind began to taper. Up ahead, Tory could see a long narrow shape of hills strung across desert land and what used to be the California Aqueduct just up ahead. Carrying water underneath where they were soon to stand. Water that flowed from the Colorado River once traveled here, but where was it coming from now, they didn't know. Looking below, the water was clear and clean unaffected by war. The natural color of water submitted standards of the highest form, from a purified filtering system not seen at their position. Tory looked both ways where the water had flowed and saw nothing in the dark that was misleading of what she'd seen. But there was a presence she couldn't describe with words or signs by movement of her mouth or the use of her hands. Ismael turned back around to get Torack's attention, slowly catching up. Suddenly, Ismael saw darker shadows swooshing overhead, causing all to duck and cover before knowing what it was.

Somehow, with all that was going on in the confusion, Condac had made communication with Torack on a mental level. The Condorsorous, the dragon-like-steed of the air sat down to the right of this rushing aqueduct. Condac looked at his endeared friend of many years. Torack glanced up with a returning smile on a bleak day of war behind them. The watcher looked worried. A second before realizing they'd finally caught up together at an appointed place and time. Torack looked spent, and the watcher looked on with concern. Argon understood the quick arrival of the watcher and wondered where the rest of them were headed. He looked around and only saw the one.

"So—what do we do now?" Argon asked, still a bit confused. No one answered him but—Renee looked in the water below, after hearing the rush of pressure building from an open tunnel ten feet below. She sensed something of fragile existence coming their way but wasn't sure if it was of a good nature. The watcher suddenly reached into the water and snatched forms from its fast-moving flow.

Each member turned to see what was pulled from the water. Ismael noticed the familiar blue frame of a younger brother right away; the other physical form was Danica. Everyone's hopes had perked that the watcher had solved this mystery, by listening to Torack's summons. Right away everyone knew Amen was alright, because he started in with his usual way of bringing on attention.

"Put me down you overgrown jolly green giant!" The watcher's face turned to a grimace while he thought of throwing the scoundrel back in the brink of rushing water. Condac was shocked that this smaller than normal rodent was talking to him. He stood there confused for a moment. Amen repeats himself.

"I said put me down you one-eyed-want-a-be. I'm not a doormat!" Condac made a deep grumbling sound and dropped Amen on his head two feet off the ground. Amen feeds the crowd with a bit of attitude. "Careful with the merchandise you psyche-clops I'm breakable!"

The watcher turned Danica right side up and sat her on the edge of rushing water. Danica was shivering from the cold of water and the cool air wasn't helping. Amen was unaffected by the cold. Torack reached in his pouch and pulled out his blue healing-stone and placed it on her forehead, without saying a word. The healing-stone began to work its magic to a soft glow, in an early morning light coming up over the horizon. The group of members gave hugs where appropriate, laughed about having members back, and gave relaxing sighs for finding their leader. Then Amen looked up at the watcher and gave his two cents worth of thankfulness.

"Sorry for being hard on you Condac…I mean you're big…what I mean to say…those big green hands of yours…well, you came at just the right time." Amen turned to look in Danica's direction, a confused expression flickered in his eyes. "Is Igor even listening to me?" Amen scratched the top of his lip. "I mean…he never says anything…and he's always looking like he has extreme constipation by the look of it." Condac shook his head in frustration, mimicking a bag of hot wind. Danica reached to cover his mouth. Anything to shut him up. Amen pulled away and looked up. "I saved you from drowning and this is how you repay me…trying to smother me in front of the one eye watcher who can't even talk, talk about bad calls. What's goin on around here?" Ismael reached over and put his arms around little brother.

"Cool it Skippy…Condac just saved your life." Amen turned towards his brother, in the early morning light. He held a hesitating acknowledgment of thankfulness, for maybe a minute, before going south. A lump was felt in the back of his throat while hugging bigger brother.

"Yes, I know he did," Amen said, "but I don't think he likes me." Amen dipped his nose below his underarm. "It must have been the sardines I ate yesterday, because I haven't had anything since. I couldn't help it…I was hungry… Lost my backpack when the water took us." Everyone laughed and circled around the two that had gone missing. Even Condac dipped his head back and made a gurgling sound in the back of his throat. They had survived another day. Jacob took off his coat and wrapped it around Danica's shoulders. This was a night they would never forget…

The sun forged its way above the horizon, showing a field of shadowed ash, left behind as burnt memories in a life now gone was lost through the Winds of Time just behind them. Then fronting them, lay wasted mile-after-mile of dry windy plains, cracked and submitted to a new way of life. Amen reached over and grabbed Danica's hand like that was where it should be. He was close to their leader, where he felt conformed to a better way of thinking, after all they had been through, after all gathered around. They were soon to walk in the distant land, all but sand and dirt and memories. They had no clues if there even anyone was left behind to greet them once arrived. They would find out soon enough.

Amen turned to look at Tory, "Hey…you think there's a popular eatery close by, because I'm getting really hungry." Amen dragged his feet through the sand, as the giant Condorsorous slowly overshadowed them…

Michael stood in the early morning sun with a blazoning look of concern from what was left. His heart went out to those who had lost their right to exist. Thousands of winged creatures both of heaven, and the Fallen, lay in fields heaped of bodies and bones disheveled, detached, flowing of blood was the natural cause of war when dying by the sword. Michael put the Morning-Star back into a slinking sack he had draped under his belt. His second in command stood by his side waiting for orders. Then he looked up at his leader.

"They'll be back…after they regroup." Michael's second in command said while looking on. Michael, lost in thought about his youth. When a boy, he used to play with the others like him from where he first lived in a kingdom thought only of legend yet growing up in such fields left memories of love and commitment of brother's in a king's court of safety. No safety was left to view of the moment. Death never made sense to him after becoming an adult male of his kind. A churning sickness welled up inside causing him to heave what he ate earlier that day. The larger-than-life leader of realms lost his composure. His second in command looked bewildered that their leader had taken war as a personal gesture against his army of soldiers. Michael lifted his eyes toward the heavens as his heart sank to its slowest point. Regiments of flight-ridden-troops turned to stare, trying to comprehend the scene. Astonished by their leader's emotional appeal of personal gut retching flexion. A silent understanding was felt in their ranks. His emotions were understood by such soldiers committed to a king's army. Even the strong have their vulnerabilities was his second in commands thought.

Michael reached down and touched the hands of dead brothers, with tear-stained eyes compromising in least resistance, brothers of both sides had fallen that day. The air was full of a stench that burned his eyes and raised emotions hard in his throat. Michael stared into the eyes of the dead and knew that war and death was a formality of the living, giving insight only where needed, mixing misery with pain, taking life for restitution against their enemies. It caused him to feel vulnerable. He couldn't remember why he used to want to stand before the many and show his talents given of youth. Waging war didn't make any sense to him at the moment, and the wisdom he had gained from the many years of service left his heart feeling heavy. An emptiness was felt when looking into eyes of the dead without emotion. He would carefully measure a better way to live, to remove the bad, the indifferent, and the ugly memories of the not so lucky of such visuals laying at his feet. To be guarded by each influence all around him. He remembered his brother Lucian who had always devised the best ways of bringing honor to a father that loved him unconditionally. A father that looked to his sons to find meaning in life, without saying words to confuse, a father with a heart full of wisdom. He was the one that showed promise in his youth—yet now his brother was gone. Emotion spilled from his heart for brothers lost. Some days he would stand waiting at the gate wondering if he would ever see that young boy of his youth, just one more time. Hoping he could hear him laughing or touching his shoulder once again—to feel the love of a brother. The gate never returned the smiles and camaraderie once held of a brother's love. Michael wiped back a tear while standing before his army. A shudder of emotion went through the crowd of warriors. They were standing on the shore next to the sea. Many of their numbers were replaced when death rolled through the clouds of war, as they dropped from the sky by the thousands.

Suddenly realizing, those of a Circle of members were here on a mission appointed by a king of realms. Michael stood and looked toward his army, seeing a quick glaze of eyes all around. He bent and whispered words of leadership to his second in command. After a brief moment, his second in command signaled several warriors to take flight. They were on a mission of finding the lost Circle of members. Three took flight heading south. Ash continued to fall from the sky as blood flowed from bodies like a river.

There was a price to pay in taking one's life—a picture execrable of meaning. The dead had been cast through the winds of time, carried away like clouds lifted of dreams. No elegy was said or a proper burial to take place, no friends or family standing by to pay their respects. As soldiers waged war it was just the beginning. Michael finished with his point of the day; he signaled the rest to move skyward. The winds of war carried them to another place at another time...

11

What lies beneath

The sky moved with signs of clearing. Even though there seemed to be a pinkish glow that hung about in the firmament, it revealed a peaceful settling of an early morning start. The wind calmed to a gentle breeze keeping the temperature at an even keel. Torack had gotten on the back of the Condorsorous, he was worn out from the fifty miles they had already walked.

Ahead, Danica could see an oasis several miles ahead blurred in visions of rising heat. The desert sun floated with shimmering waves of warmer conditions in the middle of another day. It was hard to tell if what she was seeing was actually there. Before leaving the area of the California Aqueduct, the Circle had filled all their water skins and the Condorsorous had gotten his fill of water too. The air and sand was heated to a mid-day warming, without anyone noticing right away the change was unusual for a normal type of day. The effects took its toll on each individual when walking for hours. Amen was the first to start slowing down. The extreme heat was getting to him.

Ismael turned to see his brother drop twenty feet behind. Condac's steed-of-the-air circled round as he reached and scooped Amen up, sitting him atop his trusty ride of the sky. Not noticing any added burden to the bird of the air. Danica looked up after feeling the lift of wings. A place of palm-trees and water moved her with emotion just beyond a natural way of thinking. She perked from the chance of changes up ahead.

"Look over there! There's a place to rest under the trees!" An oasis, a place to find a bit of comfort in their time of need, held under a shady clump of trees at the base of rolling terrain backed up by craggy boulders all around. Joshua trees lined of indentured shadows throughout the land, with mountains behind of dried out conditions. Condac smiled and dropped Amen directly above a pool of a cool plunge.

Amen, not expecting a sudden awakening, settled to the bottom, breathing in air through gills of cooling comfort. Others gathered around to get their fill of cool relief.

Tory acknowledged the time of the Twelve O'clock hour viewed on her computer screen. They were seeing earth for the first time without stormy conditions, a subtle reminder of fading beauty. Danica looked up, shielding her eyes. Looking for anything of a resembled enemy, fluttering in unannounced, making a run for the hills above them. She turned back and looked at Tory. She was busy looking through several screens viewed on a map showing a lay of the land, but something looked a bit strange from her angle of perception. It didn't quite match up with the land below their feet. She had guessed, through the storms violent reform, changes of the land had shifted, twisting and pocketing a world below in hive like form. The map had an infrared camera showing an area not quite readable, just past a mountain range fronting them. Something around two-hundred meters away, of layered earth was drawing her. The rocks with dirt above this sheltered place wasn't small by any means, something gigantic lay just beyond beneath their feet. To Tory, it looked like an underground dwelling place showing movement of life beneath them. Danica caught her staring for more than a few seconds, not knowing she'd come across some type of lead, maybe leading to what they were looking for.

Amen popped his head up out of the lagoon. Shooting water out of his mouth like a dolphin coming up for air. He flipped over and did the backstroke across the strip of water. Looking up at Tory from over his left shoulder, he was the first to ask. "So—where are we going now?"

Ismael reached down and pulled his little brother out of the water toward dryer ground.

Tory not paying attention, didn't answer him because she was still flipping through screens on the handheld. Then she enlarged one screen to the next to get a clearer picture. She wasn't sure what she was seeing.

Amen looked at her while drying himself off. "Are you okay?"

Danica stood and looked a bit annoyed from a further angle. "Skippy—let Tory figure out what she's looking at—she'll tell us when she's good and ready."

Amen glanced back with a puzzling devotion. "It was just a question." He said.

Danica gave an impatient glare back. Wondering of little boys with annoying words.

"Be quiet Skippy—and let her finish." Argon piped in.

Amen pulled back from saying what he was thinking next, noticing everyone staring caused him to raise an eyebrow.

The only thing Tory did say was, "let's go—I found it." She pointed southeast of where they were standing. Each member revived from hearing a determinate direction, noting each one was past fatigue on weary feet. A lack of sleep was beginning to set in, along with dehydration caused by the sun. They gathered their small amount of gear they had and headed southeast.

Argon looked up as the shadow of the Condorsorous swooshing by, with Torack and Condac hitching a ride. He'd draped his right hand over an eyebrow, to block out the sun—then Tory yelled for everyone to stop. Noticing a blimp on her map started blinking...

Before she could share of her discovery, half a dozen hellhounds and a dozen Dark-Angels came moving in at a fast speed, causing each member to duck and cover, without given notice. Without thinking, Condac jumped off the back of his trusty steed and skewered two Dark-Angels with a spear. A hellhound flanked him to take advantage of a tail holding a stinger. Ismael used his gift to pull this particular hellhound directly in front of the draw of the Condorsorous mouth and crunch, a taste of blood ran red on stained teeth. It left an awful taste in the big bird's mouth. The steed-of-the-air better beware of nasty poisons, bit the hellhound in half. Spitting the beast out not wasting a moment. Tory put her hand-held computer away and pulled her trusty bow from behind her back and lined it up. Danica had already placed her sword in a fighting stance. Argon held up his Element gun in the direction of those creatures closest to the ridge.

With his telekinesis, Ismael forced the hellhounds close to the Condorsorouses mouth. An automatic reaction from the bigger bird of dragon-like-fashion to make use of well managed teeth. The Condorsorouses jaws flexed before the crunch. The taste was a reminder the enemy was bitter and black. Ismael smiled, enjoying the moment of breaking bones without missing a beat. A stream of steady air breathed in, suddenly spitting them out almost right away, by sending the remains to a darker place. Amen, hidden behind Danica's right shoulder, finding protection under a well-managed girl given of the gifted with usually long blonde curls, but since landing here combing such curls went out the door. Torack took out two devils of the sky coming in from the west, sensing more over the next ridge. Condac summoned more of his kind to come to their aid. The sky moved with movement, bringing further chaos to a group of members on this memorable day, as the dying were soon to give up their dead. A darkening hour passed the time by quickly, in the light of this dismal day, suddenly, turning dark from the swarming of an enemy. They were at a loss of what direction to go to find cover. They were pressed on all sides, no way out, nowhere to turn. Torack looked in Danica's parallel gaze thinking the same. Two hundred and fifty yards later passed the ridge, they saw an opening. Noticing a small area surrounded by fence and cemented slab, worthy of hiding them. A quaint covering surrounded by trees that read 'keep-out high voltage.' Danica seen a sealed covering, leading to another place, away from those winged creatures who'd come to greet them in the light of day showing no fear. Amen already knew of her thinking from the connection. Everyone drew close to Danica, and she took them through a door, to another place right outside fronting a small building. Noticing right away a covered hatch in a cement square lying beneath their feet. By the look of the hatch, it dropped into another world, where they'd elude this enemy nipping at their heels. Not to draw attention from the sky, two-hundred and fifty feet from behind them. It would be short of a miracle. And where would it take them? Tory looked back to notice the fallen quickly to follow after. They hadn't noticed their departure. Where did they go? Confused of direction, no sense of where they had gone or which way to turn. They'd become frustrated and heated, misplaced and defeated for the moment for retribution was fast on their heels.

Condac, the strongest of his kind, would help when assisting those of the Circle to a lower level of this hidden place. He would close the cover when signaled from behind. They would be sealed from within once past this line of safety—it would be locked, no turning back. Danica took over. Appearing on the other side of a pressurized door, she unlocked it, and opened it for others to pass through, letting her bewildered crew to regroup. But something else was seen slipping past her vision. Just in time to say good-bye, just in time to slip past their enemy. They were one chocked up for leaving the scene, one less meal to provide for, for the unfriendly foe fronting them, made other plans. Knowing their unwanted friends of the sky would be dying to get in. She looked over at her second in command. "Tory—can you find out where it goes on a map?" Looking in the dark beneath tunnels of a putrid smell rose in the air, certainly something to beware of. Tory looked over, still bewildered by the scene they were leaving.

"There's something else coming?" She said.

Everyone turned to look up. She pointed toward the Western sky. She could see three dark spots slowly moving right of the sun. Showing from a satellite position blinking on a computer screen. Each member looked to phosphorescent color of gold and black dots, remitted in planetary form. Each viewing three black marks moving toward an Eastern sky. Suddenly being aware of what it meant. Danica hesitated for a brief moment. She looked up toward the sun, with one eye closed and the other twitching. She made her best impression of what she saw on the screen, matching the same images as the ones in the sky. "Yes—I see them, why…what is it?" Tory glanced at the others. Torack, Ismael, and Renee caught her gesture too.

"Something is on its way—not too far—maybe three days from now."

Danica remembered stories told by Dr. Zimmerman from youth, and suddenly understood. "They're Asteroids," She said.

Tory showed a bleak expression in her eyes. "Yes, I know." She said. "It couldn't be anything else. Their moving too fast. Nothing ever seen like them before."

Danica looked over with a sense of hesitation in her eyes. "It's the Octum that the Aquerae were talking about." She said. Danica looked down in Torack's direction, who just dipped his head below the hatch moving fast. A nod was what she saw. No lingering disapproval.

Danica's face drained of color when reminded of a previous conversation. She knew they were running out of time. Amen wanted to see what was coming too and became so preoccupied by the blurred black glitches in the sky he couldn't see what was coming from behind. Two beasts of the air swooped down and grabbed Amen right out of his shoes. All Danica could see was one of Amen's shoes rocking back and forth from coming off his foot. Danica screamed while looking up. Torack grabbed her from behind when seeing the shadows overhead. He cleared the door just past the leader of watchers. Condac fought off a winged beast trying to get through, trying to reach any member of the gifted. The watchers at their backs as they tore them from a direct path leading to this place of safety. A spear, out of nowhere, flew toward Condac and skewered him through his left arm, a trickle of blood came oozing from the back of his arm. Condac took out the warrior that had speared him, then snapped the arrow and pulled it out without flinching.

From the other side of this abated hole to rescue, Argon sealed the pressure door leaving the Circle in the dark, and something of a drifting smell greeted them on their quick arrival of bringing up the dead. Sitting there, unaware of where they were headed, trying to regain their composure, breathing in fermented air, trying to figure out what had happened in all the confusion imposed of this other world below. Amen now gone was in their memories of only moments before. There was no changing that. Danica's face paled at the implications of losing the youngest of members for a second time. She played the scene back over and again. Nothing made sense.

This tunnel of another life was black like pitch. It gave them a sense of loss without direction, not knowing north from south. Ismael and

Torack heard trickles of water coming from another direction. Inside lay memories of the dead, pieces of another life, shattered, and scattered beneath desolate land. The temperature had dropped forty degrees. Tory turned on her headlamp flooding tunnels of moisture and over exposed debris, with twisting vines among bicycle parts, and old car tires blown out from better days gone by, a broken baby carriage twisted and bent. They were in another world of hidden secrets. The ceiling was twelve feet high, and just as wide, but where it would lead them, they didn't know? It was big enough for vehicles to make their way to lower levels. The air was richer at this level than the air above. They felt relief on their lungs. Danica was not herself for a few minutes. She'd seen Amen pulled out of his shoes, knowing he would be afraid around those beasts of the air. She kept replaying this scene in her mind trying to find some logic in it. Why was she not paying attention to the things around her? They were so overcome by the black dots in the sky they were frozen from surprise—that's when they took him. She leaned up against the wall with silent tears rolling down her face.

Tory looked over and seen her disconnected. "We need your leadership—without it this isn't going to work." Tory said. "You knew what was at stake. We're all vulnerable to this place. And the creatures that roam here."

Danica wiped at her eyes and stood to her feet. Ismael looked at her in a comforting way as she informed the rest about her personal feelings. "Amen's braver than you guys give him credit for—they need him alive, and they know there's no other way. A king has his way in everything of the air. 'The wind blows where it wishes, and you can hear the sound of it, but cannot tell where it comes from and where it goes…' Danica quoted from a biblical scripture she had read said by a master. She was thinking of heavenly circumstances, and not of earthly dimensions. "Amen's role in all this is not for us to know, but to move in the direction better suited for a purpose of a king will soon be exposed." Danica didn't waste any more time, she pulled out the blue healing-stone from her pouch. And applied it to several members who were lacking strength. Argon with several cuts and a slash across his chest from being attacked from the side. She placed the stone on Argon's forehead next. It lit up the corridor with a beam of hope while healing him. The stone gave strength to the body, drawing pain away from the mind, healing beyond any natural reasoning.

The Circle sat and waited patiently. The corridor was dark and cold and filled with a smell that didn't sit so well on those affected. Below them, they were hidden of a world held to secrets, as glittering lights exposed a different impression. It was a place of remembrance. The tunnel went two hundred feet at a lower incline, still moving them slowly on Tory's computer screen. It ended abruptly at an elevator shaft that lead nowhere else but down. Looking around, there was no indication of where it would take them. So, trusting their leader they all piled in. Danica helped Torack back on his feet while shouldering him towards the elevator. "How do you feel sir?" She asked.

Torack showed a slight sparkle of hesitation in his eyes, "I'm okay… just need a minute to get air back into my lungs." Yet he was reminded of leaving his friend behind, left in the hands of those creatures of the sky. To fend on his own, in the brightness of the sun, and the heat with no relief in sight. Condac would not fall easily, when fronted by these beasts, was Torack's thoughts. His legion of warriors would meet him in the air, as those attacking would be unaware.

The elevator moved with speed and purpose. Tory looked at the screen in front of them. A blinking light kept them mesmerized, once behind closed doors. She took over by bringing up schematics below their feet. The computer screen on the wall of the elevator was part of a panel in front, showing a layout of something of another world below.

Argon was the first to talk. "Where are we going?"

"Somewhere none of us have been—or did you miss our exit?" Ismael said.

Argon scowled an unblinking stare. "I'm just making conversation, we're in a dilemma not knowing of our direction, or had I missed something else?"

"I agree, you missed something since we're all at a loss." Ismael said.

No one else paid attention to the brief conversation between the two boys, because curiosity brought them all up to par with the screen in front of them. The elevator moved like it was on its own personal mission. The smell of an enter-city made Danica's nose sense change was coming, and her eyes widened when seeing a schematic of a vibrant structure. A metropolis not expected spread out more than six miles in hive like form, most likely they would find those they were looking for were somewhere near. Whoever was down here was preparing for some type of end. Hoping to survive those creatures of the air they'd better beware of needing someone's assistance. The ground below changed of color when moving to the next. The deeper they went, the more Danica worried of what would come next. It was evident, Amen was a part of her thinking, as one member missing, yet she'd never mention her troubled mind to show weakness. She'd find him. Whatever it took. Wherever she needed to go, she'd go there. The floors flew by like passing memories of another time. Danica remembered when she was a little girl at the age of ten. She used to play in the City of the Aqua Ring's jungle, without feeling danger being at her front door. Nothing like here, nothing like her world where she grew-up. Every corner of well-hidden trees of unique creatures never imagined before, trees filled with deadly bees, or foliage of poisoned plants never kept her concerned, but these creatures of that gulf that lies between the living and dead concerned her much more. Those with the blackened hearts, and wings that give off a fragrance of the living dead, left behind them was more of a concern. She touched the courage-stone hanging around her neck, knowing this was her way in to find where Amen had been taken. Within time she'd find him and pay a visit to those who'd visited him on this terrible day. The youngest of their group had to be somewhere. A glint of light flickered from the stone reminding her she didn't stand alone when thinking to find answers, even if it took a while to find the smallest of members. She remembered Amen always being the one that would make everyone laugh, telling his silly stories to pass the time away. Being bored at times he'd find moments of joy in sharing, doing what he thought was needed to cheer them up, with no hidden agenda marked by others of his kind. Only wanting to grow-up under better conditions than the average boy gone missing. They were unique. Amen wasn't big by any means, unable to fight back like those creatures did, but he had courage, and lots of it. At first, no one noticed the tears filling Danica's eyes, after spending several dreadful hours with the boy that clung to her only a day behind. He saved her life by sacrificing his own, filled her lungs with air, and hugged her close to keep her from drifting too far away from safety. Silent tears flowed from her. Knowing how cruel this world was of those circling the globe were wanting to cause pain, even to the smallest of members. She was worried about Amen. They were anticipating a place they had never been. The elevator suddenly stopped, jolting Danica back to reality. Trying to clear her eyes she wiped at them. Ismael standing close to her side noticed the tears and draped an arm around her shoulders. The elevator opened to an enormous, cemented sweeping warehouse. It gave the impression of being below the deck of a ship. There were workmen running around in military attire, and small electrical vehicles being used to take people from one place to another. Office buildings were seen off in the distance, and a row of lights had turned on just above their heads. They walked down long corridors filled with a smell of efficiently working machinery. Sounds of computers and fans blowing cool air, showing doors to different rooms that housed different offices. None of this made any sense to them. A world underground, not above in the chaos even though close at hand. It was comparable to waking up inside a world you've never been in. Where your surroundings had an altered purpose, one that didn't include your normal way of life. A world within a world, controlled by the government, but worked by the hands of laymen ready to do a service or die to protect the little bit of life that they had left. Hidden from the turmoil from above, with no creatures fallen of heaven taking away their security.

Tory stopped to view the up-and-coming map on her computer screen. Trying to figure out where they were going. All she could tell were squiggly lines made up a world of pockets procured of small living spaces by desperate people. Water and power were slim resources used sparingly. Then around the last corner, before entering the biggest of rooms—along corridors leading to open spaces of standing thirty feet high, fourteen city blocks long, and the same in the other direction.

Quickly, Danica is greeted by a well-mannered young man with suit and tie, and a smile that could light up the sky, if there was such a sky of giving notice. The Circle of members turned to look at each other. They felt like children needing attention, left behind for someone else to deal with, then this well-dressed young man came fronting them. They shuffled to a stop and looked at him. The young man blocking their way, looked straight at Danica, knowing somehow, she was in charge of this sad looking bunch. They looked tired and depleted and somewhat beat up, compared to other members left behind in better conditions. He knew what he'd been looking for all along, being assisted by someone of the realms.

"Hello, my name is David." He said, as the others looked on, feeling somewhat left out of what to say in return. "I've been waiting for your members of membership, for quite some time." He looked down at his wrist like he was on some type of eternal clock ticking the time away, needing to be quick and precise about what was on someone else's agenda. Within moments, to express his point of view was the expression seen on his face. The Circle of member's weren't quite sure what they were in for.

"I was hoping your Circle could get passed the enemy above, and find those of the gifted, and take them to safety. I was hoping far away from here, towards a red-dwarf-star, twenty-one point three light years away. This as I say...is my wish." David said, without saying the most important part of the conversation. "Those creatures above are the worst." David began to explain when Danica, all of a sudden waved a hand into the air. David blinked inappropriately, then looked at her, cut off midpoint through his words, losing his train of thought, being somewhat new at this new job of leading simple humans of earth to a better way of living. Then she insisted to be told where they were, before busting at the seams, at what seemed senseless. Being of another world underground past good reasoning. She nodded toward her crew to reply and give answers to the many questions that graced her lips, on the way to the tunnel of safety. Once being left behind, when members of membership became stranded on dirt roads, and leaving places behind of no comfort, now leading away from those creatures of the sky. A bit confusing was her thinking before mentioning they were tired, overheated, thirsty, and depleted of a good pair of shoes, and a comfortable chair to sit on. And maybe a good massage could ease the pain she was feeling between her shoulders, and a good room to rest in, to clear her troubled mind, when suddenly stopping on a dime, to make a call to no one there, to write down all of her complaints, and jot them in a book for someone to read on a lazy day. That's all that she had said in her head before David realized she had anxiety. He looked at her all bug-eyed, and no sustaining like she was speaking out of line, after not saying a word. Only body language said what she was thinking. She hesitated, raised an eyebrow, thought of a better way to word her thoughts, but never said anything, lost from losing a member just recently. She was ready to give an account. Then the young man took the floor, minus confidence, to give his point of view, before running out of time, he insisted. Their group of members, flown across time and space, just in time to meet a deadline.

"And what is your title—if I may ask such a question of good reasoning, before we move on to more important issues concerning us all?" Danica asked.

He avoided the question in question to set the record straight that he was in charge when facing the end, as it appeared to be. David dressed in a uniform of blues with stripes and bars on shoulder pads. A nice clean haircut for a man of his stature, short wavy brown locks, trimmed close to his head, and a bit of attitude seen in his walk, and the words from his mouth, backed up that. Bigger brown eyes of an abnormal size of a person of his rank and title. He looked around at all of them fervently, taking in personal appearances, being graded by their looks and bad haircuts. But who was likely to see them, on a day below ground, in darker corners hardly ever viewed? It was to make a personal statement. Danica had never pictured any young-men, close to his resemblance that ever mattered. Not considering him, being in charge, of a hand full of the gifted being shifted to take orders of the likely form in front of her. She showed a mounting quiver of a smile while looking back at his apparel. He stood about six feet in height, and narrow at the shoulders, and his suit arms didn't quite fit right on a warm afternoon of no sun, feeling they were on the run with no answers answered of questions still pending. They were in the dark literally, about everything so far, on this trip across the universe without knowing really why. His face paled, but darker highlights in his eyebrows and hairy knuckles on fingers, and nails longer than needed. She glimpsed him looking back. The light of this busy room ran with shadows cast against the wall to their left. Danica considered not only him lacking confidence yet good-looking to balance the scale, even though a bit odd on introductions "I'm David," he repeated, like it needed to be repeated because no one was talking, of course accept him. "This is Ark City—not to confuse you about any Biblical Ark mentioned of ancient history." David said, "Ark City—is a safe haven for the blind and weary, for the old and the young, and the not so lucky of the gifted that have been left behind. And others acquired by skills of their trade, to do a good man's work by the end of a day." He looked over at Torack and gave a nod, and wink, like Torack couldn't think he was a part of some list. On a wall or slate of another date and time. There were no dates or times on any wall they could see of pending weather. It was the first level of Ark City, according to David. He was their host, pointing the way when needed, addressing certain elements of surprise past any normal way of getting his point across. Danica, and each of her members, looked bewildered by what was seen and was shortly to say, with no demise or surprise when thinking. Their stares gave away any secrets not revealed by words, only body language.

There were trucks and airplanes and motor cars never imagined by those of youth and membership. There was sky walks on second levels just above their heads. There were dump truck, SUV's, and POD's of a different kind. Argon never imagined seeing so many people at one time, working together for a better world left on their minds.

Danica pushed out her hand in a gentle way of greeting, then smiled and shook his hand. "I'm Danica, their leader." She said, when looking back at her mesmerized crew. "We are the second-generation Circle of members of the gifted, as told so long ago by those called the Ancient Ones. Where they are now, I do not know." She emphatically said. "A few friends of ours came along for the ride." Torack stepped forward with a wave of a webbed hand. This startled David to blink without saying a word, then pulling back his hand. The look of the alien said it all. David grasped that several animals of the alien type would soon be exposed, later on, coming from above without notice of direction. Torack was standing behind the youngest of leaders. Danica put an arm on his shoulder and smiled. Torack approved of her introduction and left it as being members of a greater calling not recollected. Obviously, their blue color through David off a bit. He, by no means would be rude and stare back, not without Danica's approval. He smiled efficiently with an approving nod. Careful not to step on any toes fronting him.

Ark City lay below desert crust from above, five hundred and fifty feet beneath the surface, functioned without lights from above. It was totally dark from that perspective. Yet light was solidified from an underground power plant provided by the California Aqueduct. The water had been circumvented to run Ark City underground lighting and commercial use for business efforts to keep the city running efficiently. A perfect plan keeping the enemy from starving the last remaining few from coming to the surface.

Danica, puzzled by David's stare, looked back and wondered why he was dressed like a professional guru scoring points for the main man upstairs. David stood at the front of the largest room without going inside past doors. He was to give directions of the up-and-coming tour of the city. Each member felt the rushing of air like recent memories. A trolley was their welcome wagon of recent history. To take them further into the central part of Ark City. Compared to a tour, one of the local variety, like the San Diego Zoo had run of years earlier. They climbed aboard and got comfortable, while David gave a brief overview of the scene coming up. There was a purpose for them being there. There was a plan in the works. David held to the front of a driver side pole, as the driver drove through the tunnels circling below. Lights left and right, in the distance, thirty feet apart lighting the way. The air felt filtered on each ones lungs, nothing like home, nothing close to being normal. It was processed air from a world in total despair.

David's eyes moved back and forth, thinking of what to say next, noticing they were tired, thinking of other things, wanting to pull to the side of the road and start all over again. A glazed look was seen in Danica's eyes, missing the smallest of members.

After carefully memorizing his speech, David lost his train of thought. He saw the blank stare in several sets of eyes. Torack looked directly at him.

"Anybody have any questions?" David quickly said wondering if anyone would answer him.

Torack raised his hand and took the floor. "Who runs this unit below?" It seemed like a reasonable question when first asked, but David hesitated to answer, because so much had happened to them. He felt they had too many distractions to think clear and knowing who was running

Ark City didn't matter. So, David avoided the question with another question.

"Who should run such a city with knowing the end is near?"

"Someone with a sense for the people and having a purpose of saving as many as they can!" Strung along in a surge of emotion, Torack answered back. David realized their frame of minds would be set in a fighting motion, like warriors on alert. Thinking, they'd been chased, chastised, shot at, burned by the heat, frozen by the cold and now taking a ride on the inside of a Trolley, no less, like they were headed to a local baseball game, and were running late, for a date marked on someone's calendar of recent history. But this was no ordinary time slated on a calendar you'd buy at the local liquor store. It was a time of facing the end of the world. Being patient, looking into each set of eyes, feeling quite different for seven members hiding from the chaos above. They were slated for extermination by those creatures of the sky, without trying to give back anything in return. "I'm sure that all of this will soon make some perfect sense, and maybe then I can answer all of your questions." Danica stayed neutral by the words said, and David inadvertently went around answering their questions when asked. Yet truth to be revealed wouldn't put them in a better position than they were already in, lending a hand wouldn't change the end, and caring and sharing would only prolong the agony of breathing in filtered air. And at the present moment David felt lacking any better way of communicating with the lot of them. Once back on solid ground, he continued the tour of Ark City, pointing at certain highlights of the best places to eat, or corners of the city to avoid. He looked bright and cheerful from Danica's perspective, even though he said very few words.

"Now, up ahead," he said, "is the downtown district of Ark city. Shops and open markets of canned goods and marketable foods are where most people go to get what's needed. Actually, it's quite the experience." David said, without really going into details. None of it really mattered to any of them. Their minds were still floating up where there was war and chaos and the worst of conditions. Yet something was left out of the conversation that David wasn't saying, and Danica, along with Torack didn't miss a beat. Danica looked back with a blank stare and Torack moved into place putting a hand on her shoulder. He was done hearing about a place that would soon be erased from memory. Danica and Torack wanted to hear about the problems before them, not about the comforts of this place. By now, Danica had had enough of the tour guide too, and projected a scowl of indifference, wanting to prime the air with proper words for a world gone mad, wanting her and her crew to get back in the fight, soon to face those demons up ahead. No borders were safe for any of them, to find hope or comfort in this cave like city. She stood as if to confront David in his comfortable looking suit and tie, seeing their host leaning in toward a hidden world, where anything could and did go wrong. Polite at first, Danica raised her hand in order to show she still had a bit of patients yet hanging by a thread of confusion.

"So, David—I'm wondering, when all is said and done of this tour, and we become well informed of the ins and outs of this place. When do we take up arms against this enemy and crush them? How do we get out of the mess were in and onto a clearer pathway of seeing our true purpose here? One of our own was left behind up in that chaos above." She said. "We're not up to hiding from our enemy without numbering those missing or wondering when they'll come and tear this place apart." Danica said, as her eyes lit up with fire and adrenaline. "Not knowing how to tell you, we're not here for the comforts of this fading city. We need to save those on someone else's eternal clock, before the three days expire. What I've seen of the sky, there's not much time left." David eyes widened so vividly by Danica's words. She was on to something, not of the same reasoning of a young man hosting an event beyond anyone's wildest dreams. He knew she was right.

"Where are those we came for?" Danica said without wanting any further rebuttal from this man in the well-managed suit. "Why are we being detained by you?" She said further.

Suddenly, being caught off guard from Danica's harsh words. He appeared to lose his words to be said in certain order of concern. He knew the girl of leadership was trained by others far superior in the training of warriors of a different kind. Standing up to par, leaning towards shedding blood and breaking bones, was David's thought. Danica was right for confronting David. She reached out and grabbed a pole that was mounted in front of her from ceiling to floor and pulled it loose from the wall it was attached too. Taking it like a weapon in her hands and flipping it into the air. A building of wind and attitude caused the pole to look like a blade from a helicopter chopping at the air, biting and bidding to take charge of this day gone missing. Danica held an entrusting look in her eyes. She stood there glaring at David, wanting for helpful information, to get past the confusion set to motion. David looked at each of them, trying not to lose their attention from not speaking clearly. Appearing overwhelmed at the moment, not wanting to exchange blows with this girl held to her internal prodding, realizing true leadership was within her grasp. Her eyes gave away her true intentions of the day. Knowing her crew would stand and fight by her side, without hesitation, without considering they could be killed in the numbers that once had fallen from the sky.

"If you would be patient—I'll tell you about the most important subjects of this meeting, and those of the realms have their place in this." David said. "Your true purpose of being here will shortly be exposed. Here the words said. Draw your conclusions, only after I've said what I've come here to say. And then you can judge me accordingly."

Danica raised an eyebrow at these words, so she asked. "Those of the realms are drawn to this place?"

David looked over suspiciously. "I thought this would be information you'd already have known?" His eyes narrowed at the thought. Each member would have their part done by the end of three days. "Yes, heavens elite will have their say in all this, but they will not interfere."

Danica comprehended stories shared by their parents, of past judgments and endings that involved winged beasts moving about in the heavens, involving angels and demons.

Then David responds, after once holding back to saying what was needed. "They are the means to this end that you talk about in three days. The wheels that turn involving us all is but at our very door. We are the very parts of what's written —in all certainty your questions will be answered within time."

Each Circle member looked at each other in confusion. They thought most stories told by their parents were of legend, more than that of fact. Argon stood and grabbed the pole attached to Danica's hands, with a scowl and a bit of attitude. David acknowledging, he couldn't stale anymore. Knowing this Circle of members would not go down a road leading to misleading statements. They were headed for victory in their frame of mind. Destined for a different journey than the one seen by this procurer of common reasoning. It was time for David to put all the cards on the table of what was to come.

"That's enough!" He barked out, surprising the rest. "I'm not here to mislead you in any way, past these borders that contain temporary comforts of a time held on shaky feet." He said. "We're ready to do whatever it takes!" He implored, "A clearer picture waits for you beyond these walls of rock and hidden stair wells. Lying in wait are secrets soon to be revealed of an enemy unprepared. None of you have the heart to listen to my words, for the hours hence facing us are not illusions but real as the heart that beats in each ones chest. The miseries of this fading world effects all who walk the streets and breathe in air. Nothing left of mortar or stone will be left of this place. It will all fall in the darkest of hours. Don't be fooled thinking there is no way out of our dilemma, because there is always a way out that is not without cause or solution. Your experience is placed by a King, worked and molded to fit a certain plan that's not written in any book of history, but only placed in the heart of a supreme being calling the shots of these few days left, for our world is more than ready to feel relief from the coming retribution."

David walked back and forth while trying to hold their attention, for an immediate show of emotions past confusion, past not knowing what to do when getting their attention, on a cloudy day of misconceptions. "I expect each of you to understand your mission into leading you against those demons of the air. They are sure to take this world in hand and crush the very life from it, with slaked disregard of the innocent dying in the streets by the thousands. No breath held back will save them, except the breath in you that has been saved by a King so cunning in forming an army never seen of numbers filling the sky. He's not held back by the conditions of those of earth have been through, yet if you were a part of families and friends left behind, you wouldn't be so quick to facing what's headed your way, at the darkest hour—when the Winds of Time will take the very life from this place. Those left of this world, still have hearts that beat with confidence, even though their world collapses all around their feet. Each fleeting moment of time leaves them wanting a better way out. Yet what's facing them, draws character and courage from a place not seen with any natural eye. But seen with the heart of a man or woman with courage lining the roads hence forth they walk, without anyone leaving their destiny to be worked by an enemy of the air. Show yourselves to be the people you were meant to be and stand together!"

A wave of emotion had its effect on each member bonded by their training and upbringing.

By now, each member was getting the point of David's words. He was somewhat angered that the Circle was not open minded on the road to his unmatched words. Danica saw the rage of passion lit in his eyes, pointing to further commitment of arms. Then she speaks.

"Look, I'm sorry. At first, your words were too nonchalant in commitment of facing this enemy. Your words were not getting to mean what now you proclaim. We are geared for a life not having the comforts you use as illustrations to pass your time away. It doesn't come without a cost. We're here to stay until our mission is complete."

David expressed a moment of hesitation before putting a hand on Danica's shoulder, which held a meaning of trust, expelled by those said in high regard.

"Young warrior, your concerns are by far considered before any decisions take to roads hurried with life. The Indian princess will clear a path for you to take that leaves no guesswork of who waits to find favor in this Circle of members. Trust is the ingredient we hope for to get us through, and that of courage and commitment." David said. "Your parents are set on a path to a world far away, in darker places held of secrets soon to be revealed. It will test the very life that flows through their veins. It is not my purpose to become misleading in any way, but only to encourage you to believe there is a way, even if none is seen. For a way starts with courage, moved with motivation through thoughts of never giving in to the restlessness of this place."

With that said, Danica felt the soft glow of the courage-stone held around her neck. David with a parallel gaze saw the sparkle of light too. From looking further, to remind them of who they are to apprehend of a certain mission.

"Are you not the children of those who fought with Gabriel in the fields of blood and water? Your own parents bore witness of those of the realms fighting for the right to lead by spilling the blood of brothers, were they not? The leader of the second, and his brother fallen from a kingdom far from earth. In this same field as your parents, witnessed of another time, but remembered?" Danica's face showed a bit of hesitation from a man in a suit and tie standing for truth and justice for all of mankind...he lacked stamina more than confusing.

Amen felt as if dreaming was slapped awake, bringing him back to reality. Noticing right away his hands were tied to two poles above, left and right of him. And his feet dangled below as a drifting stagnate odor, overwhelmingly pungent, brought him to a place held to the dark of a deeper meaning brought on by something missing from memory. This place felt to creep under his skin. The pit reminded him of one that Danica had experienced just one day hence. Amen felt an immediate pain run down his arms, throbbing and repeated a constant pain throughout his body. A feeling of stinging blood at his wrists was a constant reminder that everything hurt. His arms stretched beyond their natural length to meet an end of each pole, causing his heart to feel weak and his body to shudder.

The thought of slowly dying crossed his mind. The pain was great, his words were lacking, as he tried to figure out where they had taken him. He was lifeless, hopeless to a cause not understood from a boy of innocence. A lump was felt on the back of his head now throbbing. He had never felt this much pain all at once. It caused his eyes to leak with tears without wanting them to fall, but the tears that fell from his cheeks were not of a natural kind. They were tears of blood. His emotions drawn from him like dripping blood from his arms, and falling from his eyes to no surprise, with the feeling of dying without really knowing why. Trouble had taken him to this point of drawing the very breath of life from him, without reason, without notice, without telling those of importance he had a purpose of being here, out in the middle of nowhere buried under dirt, and rocks, and mud, on a dying day of this planet left for the dead. His weight was unnoticed in his small frame. His heart started beating with a slower rhythm of now fading beyond recovery of a boy so mislead down the wrong path leading away to death. He coughed blood from somewhere coming up from inside his tiny frame. He shook, not understanding the pain to be so great. He was going into shock, taking him to a slower level of feeling his end. His face was bruised and beaten beyond recognition, not looking like a boy anymore, not recognized as the cheerful child of his past he had been. He was too weak to call out to anyone that would come to his aid, leaving him stranded, leaving him alone. Whoever slapped him was standing over him trying to get him to focus on words said, that felt misleading of any truth of being here. But Amen was past the point of being able to respond. His senses of reality had left him because his pain was beyond what a boy could endure, as if to feel the weight of a man on his back, nothing lacking what he was feeling, worth a thousand words of discomfort, but nothing said could be expressed of him at the moment.

It was cold where he hung sapped of energy left limp. Not understanding why, he was even here. This beast standing over him pulled a blade from behind his back. Ready to carve on the small frame that remained quiet. Just before pulling a sack like cover off his head tied around his neck. He blinked from lights blinding him. He was so afraid he let his urine go and anything left in his stomach turned to water, leaving an awful smell behind him. He felt humiliated, and defeated, and naked in the brightest of lights. He was on display for everyone to see, hearing voices all around, hearing murmuring of mocking him, and spitting his way. His tears so far gone, blood dotted his eyes and ran red on his cheeks. Yet in the back of Amen's eyes, he felt something else there, giving him a nudge of don't let go. Excrement running down the back of his legs along with stains of dried out urine, blood-stained tears burning on his cheeks, reminded him the cost of life was more than he'd comprehended from mere words. It was a total sacrifice of giving every pore, every ounce of energy and blood for a cause beyond words that couldn't be said by a boy overwhelmed. But somehow something else was holding everything together for a reason. His strength was gone, he was cold and naked, away from friends, away from family. He looked up and smiled. Suddenly, the noise in the crowd grew silent. No more jeers or snickering of watching this boy die. Just silence…before something crashed through this room of confinement and took them. The chains fell from his hands causing him to fall forward. Amen felt gentle arms reach down and scoop him up into the comfort of warmth. His heart started to beat a steady rhythm. He looked up and saw what looked like an Indian girl, all dressed in white, except she had Indian cloths and jewelry of another time, with wings, and a robe of an angelic form so clean so bright. His strength slowly returned, and bruises and pain left him. Amen raised his eyes and noticed his captors were gone. He had remembered seeing a beast in darker clothing with wings and teeth and attitude not far behind. A thing of the air took his breath away when moving towards the sky, now nothing, he was free. Amen wanted to speak, but something caused him to hold back, and rest from what he had been through. He closed his eyes and let this Indian girl take him to some other place of safety, a place he would feel warm and not ashamed of being bare and beaten and bleeding. The experience would always be remembered, too painful to fathom what he had been through. When waking again, he was in a room, a quiet place he could rest and put on a few pounds before leaving this place. A place he would find confidence, and strength, with nourishing food, and soft moccasins for his feet to keep his toes warm, and his heart glad, and his mind rejuvenated of a boy that was saved at the last moment from death. He dreamed about his brother laughing, about something said between them. And a circle of friends all around greeting him in a comforting way. The fear was gone, his strength returned, he was on a better path. In the back of his mind, he thought of calling his brother by name, the farther he walked in the dream the more he felt compelled to call louder and longer. He was pushed to get his brother to respond. It didn't make any sense to him why he kept calling, but he did, and his brother was soon to answer at any moment, if he could just understand where he was... then he knew...it was heaven.

12

Separation

Condac swung his club while leading by a mastery of strength. He smashed through the ranks of Dark-Angels who had not experienced such a creature as this that stood before them. His Condorsorous lit their enemy to the flame as this beast from a world they were not familiar with ripped and tore through bodies of black. Condac soldiers brought war and havoc to each blackened beast of the fallen as they lay waste of blood and blundering, as wings of war fluttered past relief of a different world. His soldiers had come to his rescue. The Condorsorouses burned the enemy into cinders not to return. The smell of scorched flesh filled the air with a putrid reminder that death took no prisoners, it took the very life from them instead. Condac jumped on the back of his Condorsorous while his lines of defense cut a path of fire through skies soon to relinquish the dammed, pushing their filth from the corners of this world gone mad. The watchers lived of another time from centuries long ago, learned of wisdom, through strength and courage, were their greatest attributes of all to behold. They were saturated by the healing elements from their world left behind. They had super imposed strength in beast-like-form, along with not informing this enemy of their true intentions. Their dragon-like-steeds of the air left a lineage of fear set in the eyes on those inflicted.

Their leader, Cornelius, called his forces to draw back from this front line barrage by fire and brute strength. As the air thinned of the enemy, Condac sounded a horn in victory toward this enemy that was caught off guard, fleeting to recover from their latest barrage of these war-like creatures, forgotten of an enemy, from a greater world held to a greater esteem.

Their trolley had stopped in front of a building cut out of rock that showed a living quarters. A place that replicated the old capitol building was meant to give an appeal for some type of governmental structure—yet somehow it didn't. Even Danica recognized this place seen of youth, from studies given to her by Dr. Zimmerman. She had seen its form once or twice before when studying. This was in some type of miniature form, from what they could gather. It didn't have the same appeal of the USA capitol, but it did draw their attention, to stop and take a brief look in its general direction. Argon was the first to acknowledge they were at their first stop. "Where are we headed?" He said.

David quickly answered. "This is what we refer to as the Hall. A place we get together and solve any up-and-coming problems."

"Well, I guess you've got a few of those…don't you?" Argon said. David raised a hesitant eyebrow in the boy's direction without rebuttal. Danica stood and viewed this rather strange looking building as if it held the answers, she was seeking but didn't know how to put it in words. Her democratic way of politics was not known—just a look, just a stare, of comprehension that it was temporary. The trolley stayed behind on curbside, waiting to take them further into this abated world of new discoveries. If regarded to do so by David, they'd move further, but at the moment no one moved past the entrance because of what they saw. The building stood as a silent reminder of being on a mission, one with purpose when the opportunity presented itself around the next corner. It reminded them of a past not lived by those few seeking further education of why they were here. They had to be patient, waiting for something to prod them along, to move them in some type of direction making it clearer than when first seeing what the eyes could see. Danica turned to look back at David. Maybe something was missed by a certain suggestion of the hands, or the movement of eyes strained of further negation of clarity, maybe something overlooked or left out of incremental details in importance gone missing, left out as the faintest of details, until now.

"So, what are we doing here?" Danica asked.

David's eyes were stuck viewing the Hall, stalling for time. She noticed the look but didn't say anything further to prod him along. David raised an eyebrow just before saying. "They should be here anytime soon—I mean we were expecting her, and those of her kind, maybe something else had gotten in the way—before getting here." He said it like a question or a misstatement of what he really meant. Then David looked at Danica like he was confused about something misread.

"What? Waiting for whom?" Danica asked. David wondered if she would even understand his frame of mind. He'd try to read the confused look in her eyes, before saying what needed to be said.

"Well, they were stopped from getting in here by something else… from a secret place of coming to Ark City. Those creatures could have detained their trip of reaching this place, but all considered, we should hear from them at any moment. Be patient and you will see."

Danica's eyes moved in his general direction, wondering of the misconstrued words.

"Who or what is on the way?" She said.

"We were expecting the Indian princess and her legion were supposed to arrive at any moment. But henceforth, since her second in command made a call about an hour ago…we were disconnected."

Danica's face drained of color. "Where are those of the gifted held of this place?" A bit of anger flashed before her eyes when thinking of them. Being eluded of where they'd been taken. David didn't know how to address Danica's flash of a heated stare. He tried to lead them toward a place of rest, next to the Hall. Where they could gain their strength back, get something cold to drink, take off their shoes from walking so far.

"Follow me please and rest assured of finding fresh supplies and something to eat." David said.

Argon's face lit up. "Way to go, David!" Argon raised a hand in high-five form to Jacob at his side. Jacob was still trying to figure out everything in this cave-like-world while missing his queue of slamming palms together. Argon swung at open air, to recover, he said, "Swerve… you missed me!" Jacob hadn't noticed the mistimed action of his latest travel companion. Argon, reacting so quickly almost fell, running his fingers through his hair completing the swerve. Danica looked over, wondering of boys missing parents, rolled her eyes before turning back around. Ismael, gone somewhere else, looking in a different direction altogether, possibly thinking about his little brother missing.

Each member, led to a room about two hundred and fifty yards from where they were first dropped off. The Hall was a reminder of the world above from years past. The air felt treated by some type of heavy processor filtering system, ridding the air of poisons from above. Ismael took a deep breath and moved his gills like he had trouble getting air into his lungs. They had all left their backpacks behind when the fighting began just before they entered the underground security door. Argon still had his finger on the trigger of the Element gun he had in his hands. As they walked toward the room, Jacob put his hand on Argon's shoulder, and looked up at the bigger boy to say, "You mine taking your finger off the trigger…I think we're okay down here at the moment." Argon glanced back at Jacob before taking his finger off the trigger and put on the safety, expelling air before relaxing. All members looked stressed from missing a small boy of membership. The Circle entered a room that gave the appearance of being a lounge with several couches and chairs with a large video screen showing about fifteen different camera angles of security, at all the exits of this place. Danica paused for a second, reaching for the healing-stones in her pocket. They were still there.

Amen had a dream: As memories led him down a path that caused him to feel left behind. He tried to decipher if what he was experiencing was real or not, yet after considering all angles of what he saw, he knew it as a dream. The size of any physical presence couldn't be right by what he was feeling. Definitely not seeing himself in a prominent way after being exposed to his fellow students, those considered pure of heart. Amen was caught inside a labyrinth, moving in all directions. When first entering feeling alone, secluded, partially confused, somewhat deluded in which way to go. He was facing some type of crossroad in his life, testing his intelligence, testing his ability to comprehend something unpredictable while under pressure. He was afraid, pushed to the side, standing alone on two weary feet, yet still game, not quite lamb. Now relaxed, he heard a familiar voice calling to him. A faint light shown through the other side of the passageway. Just a young boy, living his dreams, walking on a trail not quite what it seems. Learning from the giants of a world stood for courage, backed up by strength unrelenting. Coming from a deeper well of commitment as the light ahead would start to show. Making good choices, having a clear head held meaning. Amen looked toward the light and started walking in the direction of tall stone hallways, epic in size and dimensions, with vines of over-growth covering of green, moving halfway up the stone parapets, close to where the edge of the top could not be seen, left in mystery. Hydrographic charts were etched in stones along the pathway as if each corridor or turn told another story or had hidden meaning underneath each passage leading toward mathematical directions. He remembered studying maritime navigation when being schooled, being of an Aquerian background he learned to adapt to the changing of currents and pressures beneath the sea. This part of his studies he paid attention. Once realizing the stones placed in the walls were like a map speaking a language that looked all too familiar as charts, he spent many hours surveying. The light above gave the impression to be unnatural, coming from a source that couldn't be identified from his position, but sure enough the light gave him the ability to see just enough to get to the next turn, to see the next choices ahead. He had the ability to trust in the small expenditures of faith, and hope, and love, without taking a prejudice opinion of sight. Amen learned early in life that size of character was worth much more than the size of a physical stature. He had been walking for some time now, and then that once familiar voice spoke again. It was Danica, in his thinking, conversant like previous when he had faced the Demons in the tunnel from before, yet more distant, still faintly hearing her prodding him along. Reaching for an inside pocket, feeling for the courage stone well-hidden undercover, but quickly to be rediscovered, to guide him once again. When touching the courage-stone those maritime charts on the walls stood out, every time he graced his fingers a crossed the courage-stone the walls lit up from a dim glow of golden light. Pointing the way down one corridor at a time. Then the colors would change to a brilliant blue for another corridor, then green for another, but still drawing, still leading toward a brighter light. The stone in his pocket made a connection to the stones in the walls, like a ship being pulled by the currents of the oceans. Amen's dream continued as he made the connection of this enlightenment. The charts setting aglow, and the corridors guiding toward a goal he had no known knowledge of—yet it gave him reason to continue pressing forward. Amen could see numbered charts of the oceans flash statistics and formula's before his mind as he pressed onward toward a prize that was incomprehensible at the moment, but the onward push kept him motivated to keep turning new corners, kept setting new goals to find more success just up ahead. He sensed it to be effortless after a time, like waves crashing on distant shores set to rhythm—it was automatic. The charts lit up showing him the correct turn to take when reaching each corner. He was getting only bits and pieces at a time, but Amen let this draw pull him through what he thought to be an endless journey… connected somehow through the Winds of Time. Analgesic light flowed at the end of this current corridor he was facing as if light from heaven would pull those chosen into the light beyond the clouds of distant stars, marking a path for the journey to come wasn't anything ever considered by such a boy on his own.

Suddenly, the bluish boy having painful reminders came back his way, boldly his body slapped awake by the coolness of water being splashed on his face, he had returned to his body. Heaven would have to wait for another day. Amen pulled air into his lungs and realized he had been drawn out of this dream of corridors and hidden passageways stripping him of this world of the dream, a feeling of being slowly led back. Pain had grabbed him again, a reminder how comprehensive he was of being back in his body, which led him to belief he was still alive. Forgetting about pain in his back and fronting his ribs with blood porous of face while running in his eyes, yet nothing mattered at the moment but feeling alive. An ominous figure quite large standing over him, couldn't quite make out who it was—only knowing whoever it was to be was here to help. Amen blinked to get his sight back. Eyes glazed over by blotches of blood and darkness now gone. After blinking of moment's hence, he understood the massive form of muscles and mayhem fighting off those demons of the night. Amen hanging about from this hole in the ground, began to see the room torn apart and bits of light had started leaking in from somewhere above him. The depth from the sky was full of sounds of waged war and retribution, screeching of cries in mid-day light resounding off walls of air with swinging swords caused clanging above him, floating in the air of dragon-like-fashion, from Condorsorouses breath of burnt reminders that the living were here to collect the dead. Feeling change coming from movement of shadows flooding in space all around. He could see ash had covered this room, left in rubble, from those of that darker world were now missing, paying a price not comprehended with their lives. Amen drew focus, and realized Condac had broken through the top of the roof above him from this hidden place trying to free him from this place he was in. He was making an impression, making a stand against this enemy. Suddenly, Amen felt something hot light-up the inside of his pants pocket while burning his leg. Barely able to lift his head toward his savior pushed out the words.

"Hey, you big lug-nut get me down off of here!" Condac surprised by the sudden eruption from the smallest of members seen him as an inconvenience looked down at Amen. He could consider the boy already dead or close to walking towards some bright light—not taking in consideration his irritating little friend was not unconscious anymore, but wide awake.

Amen frustrated from hanging so long continued his abraded attitude. "What are you waiting for? Get me off this pole!" Condac reached down before anymore sarcasms flew his way—snapped the pole in half and gently slid him to the ground. Amen, quickly stood up, started dancing around like he had to use the bathroom on short notice, but not to say that he didn't, he reached for his right-side front pocket, bringing the stone toward light, burning in his hand now, holding it up high, repeating something he'd done in the tunnel before being rescued by their leader. The courage-stone shot light in the direction of the sky, guided by a different purpose. The light was perfect in form, guided by something not seen by the eye, yet understood as something of power beyond the thinking of a boy so young, so unprepared when facing his destiny. The stone tore holes in the sky like an atomic explosion, pushing air to all corners of this world, going off and rolling like thunder across the mid-day sky in all directions. The image seemed slow in the beginning yet building up speed and momentum kept it spreading in every direction, eating up distance without much effort. Seeing the light circumventing all around, in a protective type of form, moving past watchers and their dragons of the air—pulling them closer together as a unit, but pushing this decrepit enemy to the corners of losing bones and muscle, taking them out of the picture like a ghost pulled of weary souls go unwittingly, bodies held in a fragile state of existence, measured between thin lines of comprehension, removing bones and spreading of blood all-around of the dying. They were finished, of this day gone weary. When the light was complete —the demons of the air were gone. Condac looked at Amen, holding a worried expression. Covering his face with a raised hand of indifference and grumbled while shaking his head. Amen fanned at the air from the smell of the dead and dying. Condac found in the backdrop from quickly changing circumstances, put a hand on the shoulder of the abraded boy with weighing circumstances. Condac grumbled unwittingly when blinking his eye, he was almost happy the little pain the neck was now conscious not shooting insults his way. Condac handing Amen a healing-stone barely understood the watchers frame of mind took the healing-stone without hesitation and placed it on his forehead...

Danica reached for the cup of water she had been given by their hostess. She seemed a bit worried by the expression she seen written in his eyes. David tried to make conversation as everyone sat to get their strength back. The long walk from the night before in wind and sand left them more than dreary. Jacob was sitting across from their leader staring at her. Ismael slumped over in a chair in the corner was staring at the ground, thinking of his missing brother most likely while Renee had fallen asleep on one of two couches. Tory was still trying to decipher half a dozen maps showing the layout of the city. Ark City was the last stand of a people almost extinct. Their place of refuge seemed peaceful of the moment. They needed this rest.

David was the first to speak when looking at the Circle of members not quite complete.

"This place that you're from...is it beautiful?"

Not answering his question, Danica raised her eyes amidst the night's confusion. Wasn't sure if David's pleasant conversation would be in good timing of a people he never knew. The Indian princess was bound on assisting them, yet where was she? She rolled her eyes in his direction, thinking the question bad timing of this world almost spent.

Tory interrupts them when finding something coherently strange. "I found something beneath here in your city." She said.

Everyone that was still awake turned to view Tory's expression. "There's a tunnel system at a lower level...over here and here too. It leads out toward the ocean. What's it for David?" Turning to view his expression not quite readable Tory waited for his assistance. David's face seemed to flush a crimson color not usually seen by certain guesses. He wasn't quite sure what she was even talking about, after viewing his physical stance. Turning back around after doubting her question. "What tunnel are you referring too, young lady?"

Tory pointed to a bright spot on her computer screen. "The tunnel is here." She said. "It goes to the lowest point of the city then heads this way. See—Southwest?" Tory looked up to acknowledge an approving nod from what she could tell. "Maybe it's an exit." She said. "Does anyone else know about this place beneath us?"

David looked more than confused. "Well, tell you the truth...I didn't even know the tunnel was there. I thought all the lower tunnels were destroyed and covered up, until your recent discovery."

Tory couldn't believe what she was hearing. "The tunnel I see isn't on any schematics or maps that you have registered on anything I've seen just recently. What I found was by accident. See, look here." She said. "When I change the color on the GPS, I have on the computer screen, look what shows up on the bottom of the screen."

Torack stepped to her left to get a better view of the handheld computer screen. The mystery tunnel was a good five hundred feet below them. Then Torack looked up at the rest. "I can feel Amen's somewhere near. Condac is looking for him."

Ismael perked when hearing the news. Danica looked up from where she was seated, wanting to hear about a possible quick return of the boy she'd missed from a few hours back.

"So, my brother's where?" Ismael barked out. A bit of emotion was heard in his voice and a slight sparkle of hope seen in his eyes.

Danica got up off the couch to confront the Aquerian leader. "Where is he?"

Torack was still listening to the voice in his head. An all too familiar ringing was a reminder of such things of friendship from the watcher no less. Torack was slowly visualizing a mental picture.

A quick flash of Tory's eyes interrupted the conversation. "We could meet them on the outside of this opening. It is up over this crest, fronting the ocean."

David suddenly came back into the picture. "That's funny that you would mention this area because the gifted are not where you would think they would be…there somewhere else."

Everyone perked from the admission of where to look. Argon, asking the right question.

"You mean they're in the ocean?" David turned his head noting the boy was on the right track.

"Well, yes and no…to answer your question." David blinked before drawing his own conclusion.

"Under water?" Torack said.

Argon turned to view Ismael and Torack, noting both could breathe underwater having gills in their neck. Danica had reached back and bundled her blonde hair into a ponytail. She leaned in with her athletic frame against the back of the couch fronting her. There was a worried look in her eyes, wondering of their smallest member missing. Jacob reached to a table to pour more water into several glasses sitting atop the table from a jug he found in the kitchen behind the room they were currently in. David looked at them and suggested.

"I think it would be wise if your Circle of members could rest for a while before moving on to why you are here. And those that were trying to reach you will soon be here to greet you. Just relaxing a bit, take off your shoes, get something cool to drink."

"That sounds like a good plan." Danica said with still the worried look.

"They're in seven hundred feet of water?" David blurted out.

Danica looked over in a nodding approval. "How do we get to them?"

David shrugged his shoulders. "I'll give you the answer you seek when the time comes, before saying words to walls that have ears not worthy of hearing such secrets. Even a child would understand its meaning." He said. "Your mind becomes cluttered with those things of duty, instead of waiting for the answers to come back your way, at an appropriate time."

"Is this an answer or a parable to a riddle you seek?" Danica asked.

Answering a question with a question caused David to falter from lacking a good sense of thought. Torack saw the same expression in David's character, reached with an Aquerian hand and placed it upon Danica's shoulder to calm her. She turned to view his moment of surprising reprisal. She knew he was listening, and here to give advice when needed.

"Danica," Torack advised, "listen to what David is saying in his meaning of the question he asks for good reasons of facts we can't change but only react too. All creatures, great or small, in this world and the next tend to wander off course from time-to-time. Given the comforts one is soon to miss, straying too far from home is not everyone's calling, when it comes to what they will do. They become confused and overwhelmed, causing stresses of life we sometimes put on ourselves. The best way in finding answers in life is to sit still, gather your thoughts, and find the peace that had lead you before where you started in the first place. And animal from instinct goes naturally with the herd or flows through life with the seasons. We need to find that same place of fellowship from where we feel a part of those who are left of your species…as you know would be this place of refuge." He could tell he was making headway with the girl more than trained for such a mission—so Torack continued his thought. "We're all meant to find that one place we all consider to be home, not being led to wander this world so unwillingly. Let those you seek find us in a place of rest and relaxation, besides we have no other place to go. Being still, we will all find truth of a peaceful pathway in life is all that anyone seeks, as our timing is but in the hands of a King who sits and watches each moment."

David smiled at Torack's wise response…yet Torack knew there was something David wasn't telling of words. Torack's eyes met with the assistants eyes and knew. "If I may," Torack continued. "Those you seek are not who you think they are…" By then Torack had every set of eyes looking his direction, even Renee popped up her head to listen. He turned to view Danica now staring. "The gifted you seek are but only two members of membership thought to be missing—but not the members you think."

A confusing rebuttal seen in her eyes. "You mean there not the gifted who are missing?"

Torack smiled while nodding an approval. "I believe so…my dear girl—they're your parents coming from another place not known to this Circle."

Danica's eyes widened. "Why are my parents here?"

"Well young lady…I think that would be best explained when we find them, but first I believe our young assistant would best explain the how to on that subject."

Everyone then turned and looked at David. A glinting quiver of acknowledgment was all he insisted, before leading him back into the conversation again. "Well-spoken." David said. "But when the time is near, we will find those of the gifted, for certain, a special type of ship needs to be found that hasn't been mentioned, well, until now. You're to seek this ship hidden beneath water." David turned his view toward Torack and Ismael to say, "And that's where you and your kind come in?"

Ismael raised his head suddenly in curiosity, "Who…me?"

David smiled before responding, "Yes, you and your little brother, if you could ever find him again." David paused before finishing his thought. "But, to get there, you'll have to take a helicopter ride above water before getting where you need to be. On the next level below, we've stored in a hanger for such vehicles are made available. They will get you where you're going a little faster. On board, attached to the inside cockpit are a few special treats given for those who would try and take you from the sky. Those devils that seek your members of membership, along with coordinates of a hidden place. A certain ship will be waiting to take you places beyond the stars you seek in the heavens, a place where those devils that seek you will not go, for light follows you on a journey they dare not follow after, a journey that will take them to their doom. Head southwest on a baring 262 degrees from the heading indicator. The helicopter is loaded with machine guns and a few rockets we've been saving. Of course, only to be used if you are confronted by those seeking revenge. If they follow along after, and any of their friends, might want to greet you with open arms, without saying a simple introduction, before saying goodbye and leaving the scene, from recent departure of their members."

Argon perks from hearing of weapons, "Rockets! You have rockets?"

"Yes, we have rockets, but your focus is to find a certain ship that will reach past the stars that blink with life, soon to find a world of the future. Memories will take you there, so beware of any hidden pockets not procured by light and put away any thoughts not attached to your mission, while gathering those of your kind. Once finding them, seek only the guidance and approval of those who have come to help you in your hour of need. And do not engage the enemy unless provoked."

"And you think we'll have to provoke them to get them to turn on us?" Argon mentioned.

A raised eyebrow of suspicion was adhered on David's face. "I understand your point young man, but instead of using the tunnel system, it would be much wiser using Danica's gift to get you where you need to be." Then looking around the room he said, "Can anyone fly a helicopter?"

"I'm a pilot and so is Torack." Danica said. "So, what kind of helicopter do you have?"

David turned in question to answer with a clear conscious. "Well, it's not a new helicopter, it's from the 1960's, but we've modified the engine to suit our needs from a more aggressive perspective than one of any day previous. An old fire helicopter used by the forestry department when the world had seen better days. It flies nearly 265 knots and will go up to 10,000 feet. A lot faster than walking through the tunnels."

Danica held to her suspicions, "and who would be flying this aged piece of art ready for the museum?"

"Well, I was hoping you wouldn't mind going out on a limb and flying it yourself." He said.

David stared unrelenting. "Besides the crazies or whatever they called them, will be in the tunnels waiting to greet you..." David wondered why they hadn't had such luck in seeing them yet. "Back in the day, they called them CHUDS, but now it doesn't seem appropriate anymore."

Argon went ahead and asked the obvious question. "So, what's a CHUD?"

David decided to try and humor the young man with the loaded Element-gun attached to his hip. "Cannibalistic, Humanoid, Underground, Dwellers…I know that sounds kind of science-fiction but under the circumstances it fits their calling."

Everyone looked at David trying to make up their minds if taking the tunnels was such a good idea after all, and then Danica spoke for everyone. "I think we'll take you up on the helicopter ride David, your right—we need to rest before we head out, or none of us will have the strength to finish this mission." Each member took a deep breath and decided six hours of rest before daylight was a smarter idea. Danica looked over and noticed Renee was already asleep, and she knew the others would soon be too, if allowed to do so. "Okay…we'll rest here and leave before the sun comes up." No one answered. They all took to the floor or couches that they were to rest on. David left them while taking off on other errands of that evening. Danica closed her eyes and soon fell asleep. It was almost completely dark in the lounge. Even Argon had taken to the floor to catch a few hours of quietness. Torack and the two Aquerian soldiers that were with them laid on a rug fronting the couches with a slow burn of a fireplace next to them, to rest from their weary day of travels.

Then Danica began to dream.

She saw this maze ahead of her. This place reminded her of the castle from the great gulf left of earth, but not of a deathly origin. Looking down on a pathway before her she saw small prints of an alien-boy she was familiar with. Danica knew something was leading her thoughts this way, because it appeared to be too much out of the norm for her own imagination to take her on such a journey, without the elicitation of information from her subconscious mind. Knowing Amen had come this way on his own, vaguely he had been here before her, but not in a physical way. This was possibly his only way of communicating to their leader. The most important issues at hand had been overlooked somehow, leaving out all the important information that could become clues to finding answers they seek, and the rest left to the wind. Her face and hands and body felt warmth, as if she was walking in the wake of someone else's shadow, yet not of a small alien-boy, it was something else. Someone of significant position was watching her from behind or tracing her steps as she moved forward to be the second one inside this maze of conjecture. Whoever he or she might be was of a nonphysical presence slowly moving in behind her. Not taking too much to hiding or concealing their existence, lurking in dark shadows as they moved with a continued journey with each step. This mystical figure stayed closely knitted to her shoulder, without being found out, yet even then, Danica knew such a presence was there to keep an eye on her, like a protector. Even though she couldn't make out the face or be it a figure of a man or one of great knowledge was still all just a mystery. Danica decided to relinquish this image for but a moment of time that stood on her shoulder and take several turns on her own using her gift, as it was, to gain a little speed on the shadow taking up space, standing by her side. After passing through several doors, she had found herself alone once again, staring at the interior of Gothic walls that lay to her left and right, seeing the courage-stone delicately glowing around her neck, a reminder of where it had taken her over the course of the last two years. Something in the walls had attracted her to a gentle sparkle of light, revealing the stone of its purpose. The courage stone glowed while revealing hydrographical charts answered in return by lighting up within the walls of this place of secrets. Danica knew right away they were a clue to somehow in finding her way toward those of the gifted. They would lead her Circle of membership to a place involving the ocean. Charts set aglow leading to secrets not yet known. Then realizing the stone hanging about her neck was the key in extracting information off the charts on the walls, while still trying to not notice this shadow of a quick return. She waits to see what the shadow would do, yet somehow, she knew it wasn't here to cause trouble in this mixed-up dream she was in, it was here to help her. Once passing her by, Danica was jolted awake, closing the door to this dream behind her, without knowing of the information hidden in the walls…

Everyone in the lounge sat up quickly when hearing a siren. Danica looked up at the clock and noticed they'd been sleeping for almost six hours. She stood abruptly and started rubbing her eyes. A flamboyant bleeping came across a loudspeaker, some type of warning to alert whoever was listening. Men and women, soldier and civilian, came rushing by at all angles, all over the hanger when viewed from the inside doorway of the room. The underground streets of Ark City were in turmoil. Argon got up groggy-eyed reaching for his gun. "What's goin on out there?"

Danica's face became panicky. "We need to get on that helicopter and leave while we still can!" Everyone grabbed their gear, food, and water, medical supplies, then bolted out the door of the lounge, moving down a road they were unfamiliar with in the hangar. A good half a mile jaunt where Danica and her crew could see a group of military vehicles organized together, and then viewing this strange looking helicopter sitting on its own. They were ready for a ride on the wind to find their next destination. Then Danica smiled...

13

The Helicopter Ride

The helicopter barely got off the ground before the hangar became over-whelmed by the remaining forces of ground troops. After everyone was aboard, Danica warmed up the helicopter, and then told her crew to hold on while taking them through a door, a place reaching where the oceans of a particular plateau lay. Within seconds, they'd pulled through a door that came to greet them. The helicopter broke through hovering over the oceans coastline of San Diego bay. David came along for the ride knowing something wasn't quite right when seeing them as children needing assistance. Included were NOAA Raster Navigational Charts and those of a different planet were not familiar with the oceans in front of them, even though they knew how to read the charts. These few members of membership would be lost without David's assistance. A computer screen attached to the dash of the helicopter. Viewing charts and screens of a different making, while information blinked of lights and warning sounds going off, they needed heeding. The Navigational Charts were downloaded into the hard drive. David explained how the different colored pixels were like connecting dots moving in a direction they needed to be in—when placed in the right area. The pixels showing amber or green, red, or blue, that's probably what Danica was seeing when the stones in the walls lit up in her dream, something of memory was noted from what she was seeing on the screen. Each color measuring a different depth of ocean water or something laying close to the bottom. David was busy looking past rolling clouds building in front and behind, wondering if they might have to fly this particular helicopter IFR. The computer was equipped with a digital GPS receiver that was an added feature. Torack noticed the screen changing and wondered what he was looking at. Then the view below the waterline wasn't quite understood. And finding such a ship mentioned wouldn't take too long once the screen filled in with green. Gentle swells of the ocean became mesmerizing—something big was not moving but sitting on the oceans floor just up ahead. Ismael looked over at the younger of two captains and called out suddenly.

"Wow! What was that?" He yelled.

Torack looked over his shoulder to see the boy focused on what he was seeing. Ismael leaned in closer to get a better view. He stared at the screen in question.

"Did you see that?"

Torack turned to the boy in question. "No…what did I miss?"

"Something moved across the screen before hearing that bleep."

"What did you see?" Ismael turned to look at the others, but no one responded or seen what he had seen. "Nobody saw the shadow move across the screen?"

Everyone looked at each other and noticed Ismael still staring at a ghost he thought to have seen. "I'm not going down there until I know what I saw on the screen is nothing to worry about." Ismael stated. Danica was wondering what he saw too, but someone had to take the dive, even being a little apprehensive at first she would even try. Then she looked at Torack wondering if he might be up for the challenge.

"So, my favorite teacher… are you up for a plunge?"

Torack looked back when seeing Ismael's face drained of color. "Sure…but the boy is going with me. I'm not going it alone—just in case something happens."

"What could happen?" Ismael asked, "And besides," He said. "I need to use a bathroom."

"Bathroom? Do you see a bathroom out over the ocean?" Argon sarcastically said from the back of the helicopter.

Ismael turned to show his paling face. "It can't wait...I really have to go."

Argon looked up and smiled. "Well then, stick your fanny out the door and let it fly."

Even Torack smiled when hearing this. Danica had a smile crest from the corners of her mouth. "I guess there's no privacy among family and friends." She said.

"I'm not hanging my butt out a window." Ismael stated.

Everyone laughed at that bit of information. Even Ismael was smiling when trying to hold it back. "I got an idea." Argon said. "Save it for the enemy." Everyone laughed, including the victim of circumstances. "Wait till they get a load of how you smell...they'll run for cover."

Ismael held a blank stare when thinking of little brother. "Amen calls them butt darts."

Everyone present wondered where this had come from, but Ismael kept his poise...

Ismael turned suddenly when hearing the words, still half in and out of a daze-like-wonder, he raised a slanted eyebrow. "What?"

"I asked, if you're ready to do this." Danica said while noticing his hesitation.

"I think so...but we're still minus Amen. Am I doing this on my own or is the old guy going with me...and I still need to use the bathroom?"

"Well, yes, unless you think Torack sitting next to me can conquer the turns of the deep blue at his age, out on his own."

Ismael swallowed hard and look at her. "I'm doing this on my own...without my brother...without Torack?" He looked over at the aged and weary. "You can stay. I need to set an example." Then raising a slight eyebrow of hesitation. "But what am I actually doing?" He asked.

"You're swimming to deeper waters where the bleep ends...unless you have trouble going so deep." Danica said.

"The pressure affects us too, not just you humans. I'm not scared, just a little apprehensive in taking a cold plunge into an ocean I've never been in. You get me?" Ismael's eyes rolled towards her position. "By the way...what's down there?"

Danica saw the complete terror in his eyes, "I don't know, but I have a feeling you're going to find out as soon as you get there." Ismael didn't like hearing those simple words come from Danica's mouth. He could imagine, some strange looking creature, bigger than anything of a normal size sneaking up behind him and taking a bite of a perfectly manageable boy of delicious dimensions. Danica looked over and saw the worried look in his eyes.

"Don't worry...it'll be fun...besides your one of us." She said. But somehow, the words weren't much in meaning when it came to importance to a boy full of worry and doubt—then suddenly, thinking about having to use a bathroom. His stomach had turned to liquid. His current thought was realizing he needed to get into the water as fast as he could.

Danica saw the look in turn and knew something wasn't quite right in the way he looked.

Flying the helicopter, closer than intended to the waters swells than thought at a safe distance. She was trying to stay out of radar range. The water swished a trail leaving a stream of wake on the pathway behind them. The ones they were looking for were somewhere in the deep, somewhere in the silent darkness below them. What would actually be there when Ismael would sacrifice a fast-beating heart or maybe a perfectly delicious body part, to get to this so called star ship? The currents would test his strength, pull at his courage, lining him up to meet a deadline in finding others they were looking for. He would be safe from the outside world from down there. This was not a world he had ever been a part of before.

Amen got up off the floor and grabbed Condac's arm as he slung the boy with attitude over the back of the Condorsorous just behind him. The air was filled with acidic smoke burning of bodies and bones gone wrong on this dreadful day of the dead, this made Amen's stomach do somersaults when wanting to throw-up. He was able to communicate with the watcher telepathically. A one eye, one horn, Cyclops... breathed breathlessly in front of him. He pointed toward the ocean.

Amen was smiling just before saying, "Nothing like a good swim before supper." Condac wondered what Amen was up to. The Condorsorous caught air under wings as he headed in the direction of an open sea. From atop, the view took Amen's breath away. The mighty steed-of-the-air whispered his message of stealth wings swishing through the winds of time, in a close and coming sunset of a fading sky, leaving smoky ash behind them from waged war of a day gone missing. Amen's heart soared above clouds, when calamity left of memories, and tunnels torn apart by war and despair, ditches of dreary days lost of a darker world left a bad taste in his mouth. The sun was not far from rising in front of them. Death left a trail straight from hell behind—a place he didn't want to go back too. Amen reached to rub a few scales on the back of this creature from his home, a place to far at the moment to mention—he missed what was considered home, where the red-dwarf-star reflected peace of an enduring world, he missed his brother, and the friends of his Circle. Where could they be now?

He remembered those of his life that had become most important to him. Danica had been an inspiration and respected leader, a part of his life, branded in memory and close to his heart. He was thinking about his brother now, where was he? Though irritating at times, he still loved him. Making a connection with Condac telepathically he knew they were of the same. A young boy of an alien descent sucked in air and held on tight. The colors of the sky turned a light purple, and the black dots in the sky drew closer toward the horizon. Time was fleeting, time was almost gone. A legion of Condorsorouses and watchers of his world met them mid sky and followed along behind them. They were on a course of reckoning those left behind to find freedom…

After twenty minutes of swishing through the air with dragon-like-steed, Amen could see a helicopter flying in the same direction, lower at the water's edge, lower in the reflected shadows of swells set to a rhythm he couldn't quite follow. Then it came to him. Danica was flying the helicopter. Condorsorouses followed attune to a familiar rhythm and beat, with the same mission on their minds from those of youth were soon to explore. This was their third night on the blue-planet. They were not sure how many more nights left to wake up to greet the morning sun. The Condorsorouses turned slightly in the same direction as the helicopter was headed. The ocean swells here set to a certain rhythm, as a storm of a different kind was headed their way.

Specks in a trice form moved of light was seen through broken clouds west of a weary corner of the sky of a known retribution soon to pass their way. Amen thought it might be giving some type of warning. The Condorsorouses saturated the air like a flock of birds headed for a better place.

It was a race toward freedom. While floating above water, avoiding swells and birds of the air, avoiding pitfalls of another kind, avoiding some part of an unnatural deep, with valleys forged of building waves crest to the top of another beginning. Getting closer, Amen could see the silhouette of a boy standing on the edge of a helicopter foot hold and hanging on the side just outside its door, ready to take a dive beneath darker waters, knowing it was his brother, ready to fall into an open sea. His heart skipped a beat as he thought of a certain mission on his mind and knew he needed to be there next to him.

Amen patted Condac on the back and pointed toward the helicopter. "Take me over there!" He yelled. As Condac nodded an approval when guiding the Condorsorous to bank right and drop right at a parallel view of greeting his brother. Ismael, startled by the sudden swish of wings lost his balance and fell toward swells. Amen slid to the side and dove to meet his brother. They looked like small toys bobbing in a troubled sea. Danica looked up and saw they were not alone anymore. A fleet of watchers on dragon-like-steeds were here to greet them. The left side door pops open and Torack looks up to see his travel companion was there to assist, with peaking shadows overhead. The Condorsorous of dragon-like-fashion dove toward the oceans leading into a world of hidden secrets below swells misconstrued of a day hence here. Ismael and Amen met Condac midstream, slipping toward the crest of the deep that had kept them in mystery up to this point. Amen met his brother with an endearing hug at the top of a swell before diving under—Ismael clicked a light on he had taken from a side pocket of his jacket. Amen followed Condac as the Condorsorous cut a trail below between drifting currents. Each member looked on, from the tops of the rising swells as the helicopter hovered in readiness. Even though they could not see what was below, Torack remained in constant communication with his friend. They were on a mission to finding the others. Condac signaled the brother's to follow after. The dark of the deep conveyed a steady rhythm of currents pushed left and right as they moved with purpose towards the form of the deep. The wisdom and working of a watcher and his trusting dragon of the air, now dragon of the sea—they weren't unaware of any danger lurking of fathoms below. Fish and creatures lured past them of steady movement, moving with currents that swirled in S patterns from just 50 feet below. A worried look crossed the eyes of Amen's brother when seeing the product of the deep, and those of that other world above wasn't on his mind of the moment. They held respect for the creatures of the sea as they moved around them unrecognized of being any different than those that lived here. Amen's energy peeked when he saw whales and sharks of a different kind not of a world he had ever seen—a wave of emotion was seen in his eyes when considering life of a different kind lived in the deep. Both brother's knew what others had felt from finding a world construed of perfect form in the waters filled with life and movement. For the briefest of moments, brother's and companions side-by-side brought a bit of comfort to boy's aligned of purpose. Which held to a deeper meaning on this day given of their present mission. No one else could come to their rescue once dropping to the ocean's floor. Hearts of brother's focused on finding those humans, along with finding family members once again. Their emotions were high as they made their descent…

David's maritime charts view showed a rather large area below bleeping on his computer screen. The pixels were showing a darker color of red flashing to give some type of warning that something below was supposed to be there. Suddenly, two heat signatures of two boys came on the screen from a hundred feet from their target, and a watcher riding in style on one of those beast of dragon-like-fashion, moving with motion all around, like breathing in open air wasn't a common condition. The shape had them clueless. The darkness gave substantial cover to hide what was here, yet what was hidden wasn't dark by any means. David showed a loss of words, but then he looked in a parallel view to Danica and said the strangest thing. "It's the shape of a Pyramid?"

Danica looked at the screen and noticed the shape too. Yes, that's what it was…a Pyramid. Just sitting there like nobody's business, taking up space, causing everyone to stare and wonder. Danica glared at the computer screen not knowing what to say.

Amen was the first to see the star ship from an angle still thirty feet below them. He looked to his side when seeing Ismael and Condac stare at this strange looking form in front of them, lit up with a natural color, glowing. Condac reacted with a nod when staring at Amen toward this mystery ship, wondering why all of a sudden, giving him support in taking the lead. Amen understood the opportunity of knocking on the front door. But felt strange to see that he of all people was given this opportunity. Then thinking maybe, it wasn't an opportunity at all, he was just the youngest and dumbest of the group and picked by some strange reason. Then suddenly, a door below began to open. The star ship was enormous, to say the least, at least seven football fields long, and looked like it was more than seventy stories high. Ismael couldn't believe its size either.

The top of the plateau, which it sat on, was seven hundred feet below the surface in a perfect place for such a ship. It looked like it had just arrived for a late rehearsal soon to begin, yet not from earth, it was from another place and time when it came to fitting right in where it needed to be. Ismael's eyes seemed perplexed while Amen accepted it for what it was.

Both boy's wondered maybe it came from a darker red-dwarf star, from ten thousand years before settling on the bottom of this hidden place. Condac swam closer to its opening, following after a certain boy chosen to greet them. The doors entrance was twelve feet high and seven feet wide. They sensed a familiar presence on the other side.

David cut in to give an opinion of what was seen on the screen while they hovered over water. "This is no ordinary ship." He said. "Not made of any materials known of earth." He informed. "We've never fathomed such a star ship could ever exist. I'm sure from another time, suspended between our world and a world it came from."

Torack spoke next. "Our very own star ship has traveled to places we have never been, light is thought not to dwell where it has been. A place past the stars that we find to exist." Torack looked up to view David's response.

"Thaliana and Gabriel know of such a place." Danica said. Torack looked over to respond but said nothing in return. "And the Conquerites will go to settle differences brought on by the realms leading to such a place." Danica added.

"Whatever man…their creepy…I don't want to have anything to do with them, and I'm sure Amen would be of the same opinion." Argon said from the back of the helicopter.

Danica looked over her shoulder. "Don't worry about such creatures we don't understand. They're here for our protection."

"Yes, well, I'm sure your right and all, but—hey! Do you guys have anything to eat? I'm starving!"

Jacob, from behind, opened up a large cooler sitting in the back and throws Argon an apple, and a half sandwich of tuna and cheese. Argon looked down at what Jacob was handing him and took a wholeheartedly bite from the apple before Jacob had time to release it—almost biting Jacob's fingers.

"Hey! Watch the mittens moron, I'll need those for later!"

Argon smiled while juice from the apple squirted between his teeth spraying a little towards Jacobs face. Jacob waved a hand in front.

Then suddenly, everyone heard the bleeping on the computer screen get louder. "That contraption is talking to you!" Argon said.

David turned to view the screen. A smile was seen when viewing their numbers. The Condorsorouses filled the water all around them as they bobbed like ducks on a pond. David hit the print button and pages of information were being spit out from under the screen.

Torack, of an intelligent mind, wondered what was happening. David was the only one that could decipher their meaning, as the clouds rolled in around them and darkness proceeded to take away the remaining light of day—and those below would be left to the dark. By what he could tell, in an ancient language, prolific of form, a specific golden number stood out in the writing that drew his interest. Something used of a mathematical beginning made a connection with the star ship below, showing a perfect balance of symmetry, beyond the thinking of a few children of their youth. He was here to guide them. It was the key to everything. Torack looked over and wondered what David was looking at. Mysteries in petrography, pictographic charting of years ago held a clue to what followed. Recent discoveries of the last twenty-five years of study have pointed to some other race headed their way making connections. Torack looked up and wondered where they would go from here.

David tried to explain. "The ship was built somewhere else, by someone else, somewhere headed toward a Red-Dwarf-Star in the Barnard's Star system. Does that sound familiar?"

Torack looked over and gave a usual nod. "It's the second closes star to the blue-planets sun, the red-dwarf star being the closest." Torack reflected. "21.3 light years from here, a place we now call Orbitus—according to some of the charts they point a trajectory of lining up with the Ophiuchus Constellation. It's the largest of its kind, located around the celestial equator. Its name was derived from the Greeks meaning 'serpent-bearer.' It holds a profound connection to a race of people now gone. A fellowship called the Clodus had come from there. But why their star ship is here remains a mystery. Their language, repeated through these symbols shown on the charts here and here, according to what I can remember—this is not a consequential incident—it's written in stone back on our planet. Someone else, planned for a better future for those of tomorrow are running out of time." Everyone looked at Torack.

From the water below, Condac noticed a flicker of light coming from the open door. Amen and Ismael look past the opening and saw movement of the color of gold all around as if saturated with this feeling of safety was held by the entrance they were viewing. Condac, suddenly seemed lost in thought for a second as his mind drifted to a close friend at the top.

Amen got closer to the entrance and noticed no water went past the door, even though it was open to the sea below them all around, something of virtue was leading, drawing, and prodding these two boys to come near. Something from the depths felt like it was coming up from the bottom that caused both boys to hurry past the entrance, as the door quickly closed behind them. Condac looked to the side to find out what was causing such a vibration from lower waters and suddenly knew, it was an earthquake coming from deeper waters below. Condac considered the timing to be on someone's eternal clock that moved without giving notice of anyone nearby to greet them. They were rushed to move upward. Amen and Ismael, passed the door now, viewed Condac from the other side, couldn't go back once inside this ship of safety. They were led by a voice over a loudspeaker. The ocean floor continued to tremble. The light they viewed was unnatural bringing out a bit of curiosity of two boys of youthful beginnings, having questions on their minds of this mystery ship. Nothing assumed what the other was thinking, when seeing a light lead down several corridors, pulling them to a higher place. Something peaceful about the light gave way of a deeper meaning, making them relax, causing them to pull in fresh air. No one to greet them as of yet, on an ordinary day past recovery, certain to discover once finding their way. Feeling light all around brought warmth to their thinking. It gave off heat in a comforting form, bringing both boys to smile when viewing each other in the reflection of golden colors all around. It looked like a place they could rest a weary soul, giving them confidence, giving them courage to keep moving. Something cool brushed passed their faces. Something refreshing drove them to walk up several flights of stairs, without being concerned of the journey behind them. Amen felt almost tickled to be on such a path, to finding out the mysteries of this estranged ship. He pulled in a fresh breath while feeling a sense of satisfaction floating in the air.

Then suddenly, the star ship moved and broke loose from where it was resting, slowly rising from the oceans floor. Heat rumbled beneath their feet with a tumultuous beginning, waking those inside of hallways and compartments abroad. Amen tried to find something to hold onto.

A foaming of white froth covered the star ship from being discovered as it moved with purpose. Condac followed along attached to the Condorsorous, guided by an unnatural source. Amen and Ismael looked out to see what was happening. They could see right through this ship of corridors and hallways, like looking through walls of glass. The ship continued to move toward the top. Both boys scrambled to a higher floor...

Condac and his Condorsorous broke to the surface, shifting to the right, trying to stay out of the way of this risen alien craft. Though dark at the top, the sky was filled with stars all around, giving them vision of the surface, as the constant swells moved with rhythm. A welcoming sight for those of leadership. Condac pulled a fresh breath of air in, ready to take a break. In the backdrop of sight, they could see a nearby Island, only a few miles in reaching, only minutes for his legion of warriors to rest from the battles they endured. A telepathic connection was made with the rest as they took off for the Island straightway...

Ismael and Amen opened a door that appeared on the main deck of this magnificent ship. Bewildered to be greeted by someone they knew. Uncle Drew and Aunt Anna were the captains of this mystery ship. Both boys held in a suspended animation of awe. They looked at each other not knowing what to say. Then Uncle Drew smiled and walked over with open arms in greeting them with a fatherly hug.

Amen was the first to say what he was feeling. "Wow...nice entrance uncle, does Danica know of your arrival?"

Uncle Drew looked at both boys who showed a bit of confusion. "NO...and no one is to tell her because she has a mission to finish before knowing her father and mother are here, understand?"

"Oh...I see, and yes, I get it, no problem. We'll just stay out of the way, for now, I mean, if that's okay with you...uncle Drew?" Amen stuttered out.

Drew smiled and offered a high-five to the smallest of members, before Amen slapped palms. "Thanks, I knew you'd understand...we've a lot to tell you, but that will be when all your members are together at one time."

The watchers, on the backs of their mighty steeds of the air, took to the sky fronting the mammoth star ship rising up behind them. The Pyramid shaped star ship stood out drawing everyone's attention. Danica couldn't believe what she was seeing. Overwhelmed as the rest of her crew. Torack had his mouth hinged open. Condac and his legion followed along behind to the Island in bird formation. The helicopter got the jest and did the same, following along after to find a place to set down. Torack looked behind from the co-pilot seat and for a brief moment couldn't quite explain sensing Drew and Anna piloting the star ship.

"They're here...they've come to assist, but why, I'm not sure." Torack mentioned.

Danica sitting across from Torack in the pilot seat said, "Who's here?"

Torack held a slight hesitation in his demeanor. "Your parents... they've come back..."

She was trying to remember the last time she had seen them. It had been over three years. Without saying a word, she sat the helicopter down just in front, ready to greet her parents. With a doubtful expression she released herself from the seatbelt and opened the door after shutting down the helicopter. She was full of questions...

14

The Return

The Pyramid sat on a flat surface of the island that appeared out of nowhere. Danica, from a distance, could see that the island was the perfect place to accommodate all of them. When first seeing it, it felt overwhelming. What was this massive star ship doing here? And why, all of a sudden, was there an island unexpectedly moved up from the ocean floor, when before there was nothing here before? Danica was first to get out of the chopper as it landed safely at the edge of the shore. She blinked to draw focus and tried to comprehend what Torack had mentioned just moments before. Her parents, according to Torack were somewhere inside this Pyramid, but why they were here she didn't understand. David stood with his mouth hinged open completely surprised as everyone else that stood on the shoreline gazing up at its massive form. Condac got down off his Condorsorous and stood there waiting, as if a majestic sign would give him further insight of this grand illusion that stood before them all. The Pyramid appeared to be made of a golden medal, but it didn't appear to be as any material that Danica had ever seen in real life. The giant triangle reflected intelligence in the way it was made. She had seen this star ship before in dreams when traveling to come here. It was perfectly made from intelligent hands of a superior mind, not thought to be of human workmanship. The ship was very detailed, with annotated markings from numerical figures inscribed into every dimension. It told a story about each section with its hieroglyphics engraved into every perpendicular square, like a body of art filled with tattoos. The Pyramid took on the size of several massive sport stadiums. The base seemed to be 755.9 feet to each corner of existence, and 480.6 feet height. David looked at the Pyramid as if it would express some hidden secret between reality and a mysterious past.

"As quoted of others from Scientific and Mathematical history, studied and written long ago." David quotes. "The golden number is a conception thought to shape the entire Universe. The galaxies are shaped by the secrets of spiraling shapes of gaseous forms seen of space. The great masters, such as Leonardo Da Vinci, always used the Divine Proportion in their masterpieces. One can find the Golden Number in the face of the famed Mona Lisa's face if pressed to look." David had expressed his limited knowledge about the particulars of the Pyramid as they were getting out on dry land. Argon was the last to get out of the chopper, but then he noticed this monstrosity jetting in all directions…it made his mouth fly open.

"Wow…dudes…what in the heck is that?" Jacob put his hand on Argon's shoulder.

"It's a Pyramid dude, yet not originally from here—I think?" Argon turned to look at Jacob, a thoughtful friend was his thinking. Jacob seemed as awestruck as Argon was. David interrupts by giving of his knowledge from studies he'd been given, information he had read from uncovered secrets of past history.

"It's as your Aquerae leader has spoken, from the Barnard's star system…not too far from where you're from." Jacob cast a glance at this stranger who had become so formidable suddenly while shading his face with one hand draped over his eyes.

"What system?" David repeats himself for those not informed.

"The Barnard's star system…it's from the Ophiuchus constellation… the largest of its kind…around the Celestial Equator. The Greeks called the constellation of the "serpent-bearer." It's an ancient constellation, representing a man uncoiling a serpent." Jacob looked at David like he was speaking Greek.

"And where do you fit into all this?" David smiled and let out a laugh before continuing his little explosion of knowledge. "Well, I've read many books that focus on the studies of such stars, and I thought only to draw some interest toward them, maybe this thing that stands before us makes a connection somehow." Jacob's curiosity was perked and so were the rest of them, including Condac and the many watchers that sat around the shoreline. David continued to explain.

"I believe it was an American astronomer E. E. Barnard's who discovered some interesting facts about that star system posing some curious heads to turn. Barnard's star is of particular interest because it appears to show signs of planets encircling its rotation. Ophiuchus was the site of the last supernova seen to erupt in our Galaxy. I believe to have read that in a book called Collins Pocket Guide called Stars & Planets... 2nd edition by author's named Ian Ridpath and Wil Tyrion." Everyone stared at David as if he would continue making some type of point from his remedial knowledge he had attained from his studies. Jacob butts in.

"So, your point being..." David had to laugh again from this somewhat rude little alien-boy who never gave anyone the time of day.

"Well, its means that this ship before us is from that star system, to put it simply."

Everyone turned to look at this magnificent sight before their eyes. This was an alien ship beyond the imaginations of young minds and hearts, even Jacob's. Then Danica looked over at the oldest of leaders, Torack, with a bit of a wrinkle plastered in her eyes.

"So...how are my parents connected with the ship?"

Torack scratched the top of his head as he contemplated the unraveling mystery of missing parents.

"I believe...their inside?"

Danica raised her right eyebrow, "Inside what...inside the ship?"

Everyone turned to look back up at the Pyramid like this was some type of giant puzzle they were trying to solve.

"Yeah...inside the ship, they're not from our time."

Danica was now more confused than ever. Argon spoke like he had it all figured out.

"They're older…right…I mean they had to travel to that place… what did you called it, Barnard's star system…something they found back home led them to another constellation." Everyone turned to look at Jacob, and David laughed while placing a hand on Jacob's shoulder. "Well-spoken young man." Jacob gave David a dismal roll of his eyes.

"Jacob's right." Torack said. "They're not what you're expecting. They had to travel far, and many years. They couldn't see doing anything else except to save their homes and families. Traveling to find this star ship in the Barnard's star system before coming here, was there main concern." Torack acknowledged Drew wanted to see firsthand those called the Ancient ones and clear any questions they might have still had. Danica's bottom lip moved with emotion, dawning on her that her parents might be in a state that she wasn't ready to face. Suddenly, the ship showed signs of movement toward the center of a door opening. A center piece of this grand ship opened just beyond the golden medal doors, omitting light of a blue tint. It almost seemed to be blinding at first, but then it calmed to a dull color of light. Danica's father stepped from the door, and then Anna came from behind. They didn't look any older than assumed by Argon, in fact they looked quite normal. After stepping away from the doorway, a path began to develop below them as if a stairway was leading down to the end of the Pyramid giving them a clear path. Drew had a glow about him as if he had retained much knowledge from traveling across the universe. He held a different look in his eyes than when she had seen them last. Not a significant change to be considered old or worn by time as assumed. Danica didn't wait, she started running toward them as her eyes filled with tears. Argon followed along behind until Jacob almost yanked him out of his shoes by grabbing him.

Then Argon shouted. "Hey nimrod…let go of me!" Jacob reached down and covered Argon's mouth and shushed him. "Shhhh…give her a minute alone…you can see she wants to be with her parents." Argon quit struggling and got the jest of Jacob's message.

Danica met her parents at the bottom of the stairs and through her arms around her father first, and then absorbed Anna into the gap. Then Amen and Ismael came out in the background. The little family was all in tears. This made the big watcher turn his head so he wouldn't catch this emotion that seemed contagious. The big giant had a small wave of emotion run across his face. He considered being this close turned out to be a bad idea, so he backed up and took a long dreary look at his captain who seemed to develop a smile across his lips. Condac only gave him an indignant frown, and so his captain lost the smile quickly. Drew waved to the others as they slowly encircled their leader and his wife.

Drew spoke first. "We missed you all. It's been three years since…" Drew stopped for a second because he realized they had only been gone from the children a few weeks, even though their travels had taken Anna and him three years before returning to Orbitus. Then Drew started all over again explaining.

"I knew you all would be okay. We didn't want to miss the show." Drew turned and looked toward the sky, as everyone else did too, including the watchers. The three small specks in the sky seemed to be a bit closer. A blue blaze of light trailed behind them. It almost appeared to be beautiful in a way. Amen blinked twice, along with Condac who was curious about the asteroids that were headed their way. Anna stepped forward and put her hand on Amen's shoulder as if they had only been apart for a few days. She appeared to have a few more defining lines under her eyes. Amen grinned from the touch.

"So where have you guys been?" Anna looked down at Amen and thought to explain what had happened, she glanced over her shoulder at Drew for a brief moment—they all appeared to be curious. Amen asked another question before Anna could answer the first.

"Where are the others?" Anna answered the second question because it seemed much easier.

"There back at home. I mean those creatures came…so did the Indian princess and the Conquerites. It was awful at first, before she came to help." Amen looked confused and so did everyone else that had missed whatever had gone on at home. Drew looked at Anna and knew she still held a lot of the pain and anxiety inside. Drew took over for her about what happened.

"We found another ship beneath the dead-zone. It was different from the star ship first found. It had secrets that we only had a few days to react too. It had writings on it like the other, but we found something that showed us we made a mistake. We weren't supposed to find the ship that you had taken to earth. This star ship was supposed to be the ship you traveled in—not the other."

Everyone looked at the Pyramid as if it had revealed a hand full of secrets. Ismael stared at Drew and was the first to respond.

"Say what?"

"You have the wrong star ship. It was meant for another time, another place."

David stepped up and responded to what he knew. "Let me guess where you've been. You've been to the Barnard's star system."

Drew's eyes widened. "Who are you?"

David smiled and extended his hand. "I'm the guardian's assistant of the seventh realm. I handle all the messy stuff that's left on earth. My name is David. We have accommodations for you in Ark-City, if you and your spouse are weary from your travels." Drew looked somewhat puzzled, and then looked back up into the sky. Those three lighted specks were still there. David seemed unfazed by the three asteroids streaking toward earth set ablaze. Anna gave the impression of being apprehensive about responding to someone she had never met. The guardian's assistant had this big smile on his face like some cheesy car salesman from the early nineteen fifties. Anna looked into Drew's eyes to try and find some guidance from her husband, and then Danica vouched for David.

"He's okay—we should go back to Ark City and talk." Drew's eyes dilated some from his daughter's leading suggestion of rest. Condac and his crew would stay behind and find something to eat on the island, or from the sea at the water's edge, and of course, guard the Pyramid. Condac turned toward his friend Torack noticing that the giant watcher was fine with staying behind, and only gave a slight nod. Drew figured their communication more of telepathy than anything else. Danica walked her mom and dad toward the chopper, as they all piled back in and took to the sky.

Ark City was bigger than Drew or Anna had imagined. David set up Anna and Drew on the eighth floor in a suite while the four boy's had to share a room with two queen size beds. The rooms had the usual things like coffee maker, microwave, and small refrigerator fully stocked. The bathroom in Drew and Anna's room was made of a beautiful light tan marble, not that it really mattered much to have such comforts. It reminded Anna of the comforts of home, which she had missed the last three years of traveling through the galaxy. Ismael, Amen, and Argon all had to bunk up in the same room but being there together made them feel more as a unit than bunking separately. They had to share, but better than sleeping out in the cold desert by far. The three boys settled in without complaining, considering they had been through hell the last few days—in the literal since. Tory and Renee got to share a room, and Danica got her own.

Danica got undressed and took a hot shower first thing. She stood under the hot water for a long time letting this personal message of flowing water metaphorically wash all her anxiety away. Her hair was a bit longer than back home, still blonde curls of soft beauty. She was a bit leaner, muscular, modified like a fine-tuned engine. Danica was happy that her parents were here. Her mind began to relax from being on edge so long from the fighting, and the anxiety of knowing so many of the Fallen had flooded the earth. She stepped out of the shower. She saw the reflection of herself in the bathroom mirror. Her face showed a small amount of sadness. She had no idea about the coming event that was about to take place on earth. Her hands were shaking, and she became dizzy suddenly. She caught herself by bracing her body against the wall. Danica had turned eighteen two months earlier, but even being so young she had turned out to be quite the leader. She had become a very refined warrior through mental and physical training. She knew her limits and had this uncanny ability to flow through tough situations. Her eyes were a deep blue. Her skin glistened in the reflection of tanned muscle and beads of water dripping from her hair. It's the first time she had been able to lay on any bed for the last week since they had left Orbitus. She was hungry, but her weary body seemed to take over her ability to be able to move. Lying on the most comfortable bed she had ever experienced kept her stationary. The quietness in the room left a ringing in her ears, after hearing so much mayhem and the sounds of war forced upon her from the last three days. She had never seen so much blood and unforgiving terrain—all the things that her parents had warned her about had come true—yet she felt the worst was still to come. Danica fell asleep rolled in her towel. She had no clean clothes to dress in so she stayed as she was, and darkness and the pangs of exhaustion over took her in the silence of sleep. Danica began to dream.

She first dreamed of home. She used to enjoy spending time with her family and other members, memories that used to make her laugh or made her feel part of something grand, and then new memories would take place... Danica felt at first that everything was perfect for a while because she was home, in her own bed under the securities of her own familiar surroundings. The place where she laid her head started to change into something strange and elusive. Then noticing darker colors transformed into unbalanced shadows overtaking her room, then her surroundings out beyond the house, then overshadowing the city. It became a place where the dead became a part of every corner. A malignant festering disease laid in bodies lying in fields of dismemberment. A vision of something not meant for the younger minds of youthful beginnings. Orbitus had become a world turned upside down. Anything of a permanent normality had disappeared, and something more austere had reared its ugly head. Her heart began to pound as she jerked awake.

The darkness of the room made her feel alone. Cold chills of sharper pains of stiffness went running through her body. She was feeling the stress left over from fighting the day before. She got up and moved slowly toward the light of the bathroom of a small night-light plugged into a corner wall. Danica turned the main bathroom light on. Seen from the reflection in the mirror, she could see someone placed a stack of clothes on the other bed opposite hers, it caused her to turn quickly. Her hair seemed unorganized on first impression with meshed arrangements of tangled curls. A small stone from her necklace left a reminder from a sparkle of light dangled from the delicate lining of her neck. The courage-stone glinted from the reflection in the mirror. Gazing momentarily, she calmed her breathing to a silent pause—it reminded her of Amen when he found her in the giant tree across that great rift they had experienced back home. Her form was beautiful seen by her reflection, but vulnerable from being naked and the coldness of the room. She noticed someone had put a makeup kit, a hairbrush, toothpaste, toothbrush, and perfume in her bathroom, and a heavy leather black jacket placed over a chair at an open desk. She reached to turn a small lamp on over the desk, and slowly got dressed. The makeup was somewhat foreign to her, but with a few minutes studying the colors she had figured her perfect colors schemes. Danica even used a little bit of the perfume to splash on her body—it stung as it warmed her skin drying quickly. She heard a knock at the door, alarmed suddenly she stood from getting dressed. Danica tensed as she turned toward the door and waited. The knock came again, but she almost felt she wasn't ready to face a world like this. Noticing quickly the comforts of this place caused her to hesitate about ever leaving the room. She went to the door, and notice David was standing there, somewhat shy looking with a wrinkled grin plastered on his face. He looked at Danica's attire and then commented, "I wasn't sure of your size—your friend Tory told me." David seemed a bit embarrassed to say what was next. "I had to come into the room to drop off your clothes." He said, "But the room was dark, and I didn't want disturb you—did I?" Danica had then realized she had woke with only minimal covering on her lower end. She had rolled out of her towel and laid there naked. She looked at him piercingly but said nothing as David tried to change the conversation.

"Your members are to meet inside the lounge for dinner in about an hour." While trying to hold his eyes away from her. We have much to talk about." He said. There was a slight pause in his direction. He didn't know what to say as she stood there heedlessly, with her mind on other moments of memory. She wondered of his behavior while looking down, noticing her clothes were perfectly formed on her petite frame. She then realized he was staring.

"Well, you lead I'll follow," she said as he turned quickly from the loss of words. David turned to look at her now and then, realizing how beautiful she really was. Danica ignored the stares when walking at his side. Then suddenly she shot past him. David was young by the looks of him. He was drawn to her stunning features. He couldn't continue a decent conversation with her, when before he could never shut up. So, she just asked.

"Did you see me naked on the bed?" David turned a crimson red before answering, and his answer wasn't quite what she had expected.

"Well—I had to deliver you clothes…I didn't have any idea that you would be in such a state…my job is to make sure you're taken care of, and we're running out of time." Then David went blank about what to say next. Danica reached up and thumped him on the chest with the back of her hand…not to hard…just enough to startle him. David then apologized for his bad assumption that it would be okay to walk into her room without knocking. When they entered the doorway of the lounge David was still a bright crimson color. Danica only looked at him remotely as she shook her head. "So, you're the world's greatest hope to guide us to the end." Ignoring her comment, he then left her standing there as he was off to fetch the others.

Amen wanted to sleep right away, but his brother insisted he take a shower after riding on the back of the Condorsorous—he smelled dreadful according to Ismael, Argon through a pillow across the room, which hit the back of Amen's head and through him off balance. There was a knock at the door. Amen didn't hesitate he reached for the doorknob. Jacob was standing at the front with a sleepy disposition set in his eyes.

"Where you've been lug-nut…everyone's been looking for you?" Jacob passed Amen off like he was a fly buzzing over his head, after clearing the doorway he threw himself on the next bed without saying a word. The three other boys looked at each other, and knew Jacob was beyond spent and didn't say a word to him. Amen then suggested.

"Okay, I'll take a shower first, but I got the bed side closest to the door—so don't hog all the room." while looking at his brother. Ismael only smiled and passed off what the little turd was saying like he was a cockroach running from light.

Argon looked over with an expression of regret. He was considering this whole ordeal that they had gotten themselves into was more complicated than a few million creatures taking over the planet, but with the impending doom followed by three dark streaks crossing the sky—it didn't really matter much to him. Ismael then looked over at Argon, who was checking out his Element-Gun, making sure it was secure so it wouldn't hurt anyone, and laid it across the dresser. Ismael was the first to break the ice.

"So, what do you think of this Pyramid stuff and those asteroids headed our way." Argon looked at him with a bit of contempt. Since they landed on this mystery rock the last three days he was at a loss and sharing about it didn't appear to be the right thing to do either, since there was no control on their part as far as he could see.

"This whole place sucks—do you have an answer to make all this go away?" Ismael's face showed a bit of surprise. "No, I don't, but the more we know the better off we'll be—anything to get a jump on these creatures from taking control."

Argon's eyes were set in a state of confusion. "Why does it even matter—everybody in the next three days will be dead before we have a chance to save anyone." Ismael knew Argon had no mental connection to Torack or the watchers like he and his brother, leaving Argon in the dark about what's coming up in the next chapter of the blue planet.

"Well, you don't know about what's going to happen?" Argon tossed an unsettling stare back at Ismael. "No, tell me…what's going to happen besides the end of everything here on this planet, and besides all the death and confusion, we shouldn't be here in the first place. Our parents know more about this place than we ever did—so tell me what's so great about the end?" Ismael looked at Argon like he was facing some boy he had never met before.

"Dude…were not supposed to be fighting, we're here to help those from Ark City, or did you miss that part?" Ismael made his own calculations of what was to come. "Besides, having both star ships kind of worked out to our benefit."

"How so…?"

"Well, did you see how big Ark City was?"

"And what's your point?"

"We can take more people back with us…probably a few thousand more, according to Torack." Argon had this bewildered look on his face.

"So our mistake turned out to be a good thing?" Ismael smiled while shaking his head.

"Sometimes mistakes turn out to work in our favor—this is one of those times."

Amen popped his head around from the bathroom door. "Anyone miss me?" Argon threw another pillow his way, which caused Amen to flinch and bump his head on the side wall. Amen protested. The other boys heard the bump and laughed.

"Hey douphus...quit messin around." Amen had a towel around him that barely covered his mid-section. Argon reached over and pulled the towel off. The small alien-boy returned a stream of yellowish water from his mouth that smelled something awful. It hit Argon dead on from six feet away. Argon wiped some of the liquid off his face, and quickly knew that Amen had just inked on him. His brother turned his back quickly toward the awkwardness of the moment, with the nasty habit. "Euuhhh...Amen...that's nasty!" Argon glared at Amen as if this was the worst way he could insult him. Amen stood there naked with his little fin hanging out.

"You started it lug-nut!" Then someone came banging on their front door. Ismael's the one who answered. "Yeah...what is it?"

The voice seemed to be coming from their hostess. "You guys settled in?"

Ismael returned and answer. "Yeah, give us a few minutes to take our showers."

"No problem, dinner will be ready in about an hour." As the patter of feet left them.

Amen started looking for his dirty cloths and got dressed. He thought maybe they'd been heard, and he was about to get in trouble. Argon realized the stuff on his face had the same effect of what a skunk leaves behind. "How do I get this awful smell off of me?"

"Tomato juice and hot water!" Amen piped in. Then suddenly realizing about the forgotten stone in his pocket. He put his hand in his pocket of dirty jeans and felt the lump. He'd forgotten about it still being there, he double checked its authenticity of golden color by pulling it out of his jeans and then put it back. And Argon, across the room had to go to the sink and wash his face from being inked by his soon to be enemy.

Anna stood looking out the eight-story window. The troops from about eight hours ago were fighting somewhere away from this secure place. Light were flashing through the underground streets, and business as usual was going on like nothing had happened as the day wore on. She hadn't settled in about all the changes in her life, and it didn't seem like anything was going to stop this forward progress of the end. She turned to look at her husband with a bit of concern written in her eyes. She had enough unstable living to last a lifetime, and the next three days wouldn't give her much hope toward any of this turmoil all finishing anytime soon considering they had other planets that could be exploited with the drop of a hat. Anna was only about three years older from when Danica had last seen her. She still was beautiful and had been good to her body with all the vigorous training and constant changes, she stayed pretty thin. Drew didn't feel like talking anymore, even though they had spent their last couple of months in that Pyramid like a shooting star streaking across the galaxies. Anna had brought a duffle bag and had changed into some silky pajamas, and then lay strung out on the king-size bed. Drew did the same as the couple clung to each other while Anna fell asleep. Drew had his right arm snuggled around the front part of Anna as she pulled her legs in tight against his body. He began to think about that first time he had gotten close to this stunning lady, when they had first traveled back in time to Bristol, England. His heart began to beat like he was that teenager again; it made him feel somewhat out of body for a few seconds before he came back to reality. She still had that delicate fragrance he had remembered from before, and she was still the soft and delicate woman he had known back then, it made him smile within. Drew didn't know why they had two star ships here now, but he did consider a king of realms didn't make mistakes, like the Fallen had implied. There was a purpose for two-star ships, yet to figure out why.

15

The Meeting

David stood at the podium trying to get his thoughts rolling into the right direction. His face was shining from a thin layer of perspiration glowing about him. His eyes were big creamy cocoa colored, similar to Drew's, showing a pleasant or adequate amount of intelligence reflected in his frame of mind. His hair was a darker brown than Drew's, with that unusual curl that flipped slightly at the ends, with waves of curls throughout. Pale seemed to be his natural color, from what one could tell, probably from spending so many days below the surface without any natural sunlight, considering most available sunlight had perished by the wage of war and continued blackened skies. He, being a tall young man of about six two, and on the thinly side, most likely because of limited resources. He seemed nervous, a guardian hadn't made her position known of a visual presence yet, and he kept starring at this big sparkly watch that he had on his wrist, as if time itself was being blown aimlessly bye some unseen force carrying into another dimension. It was the last of the afternoon by now, around four precisely, and if she was to make an entrance, now would be the best time. David stalled for more time by asking questions instead of giving answers. Torack had enough of it and stood to silence David with a look of outrage.

"Okay, young man, I think we get that the Indian-Princess was supposed to be here, and she's not, so what's next on the agenda for today?"

David's bottom lip seemed too quiver as if being overrun by a higher power of knowledge. David then looked at each member and decided teaching would be the best that he could do to stale for more time, so he mentions the Pyramid.

"Well, I guess explaining how this other star ship has its role would be a good start." David got his hand-held computer out and began to flip through screens, as he came to an interesting spot exposing parts of this massive ship. He looked up with a raised eyebrow. Then it dawned on him that it would be of greater value to his audience if he could show the images projected on a much bigger screen. David stopped briefly to turn on a wireless remote connecting his hand-held computer to the big screen behind him. Amen caught the gesture of David trying to reflect a larger image got up and turned out the lights. As soon as the smaller computer made connection the whole back wall lit up, it showed this in-depth golden picture of hieroglyphics reflected back in vivid color and detail etched in every corner of this great ship imaged above the door. There seemed to be an obvious message to the masses or whoever was watching, yet somehow missed by these strange mystery masters of the past—whoever they might be. Then David proceeded with his thought.

"The star ship out at the island is yours to command, left in the watchful eye by your estranged accompaniment of alien friends. I believe a large number of the gifted will fit inside, thus hitching a ride across the galaxy—but those that are to make this trip back to Orbitus are not yet here. I'm sure being delayed by things not considered, assuming all war has its problems, and unforeseen details that change circumstances can become unending." Torack was assuming David was talking about the Indian princess, yet he appeared to be holding something back.

David paused for another moment because he had come to a screen that he didn't seem too recognize as familiar from before. Torack caught his gaze of bewilderment. David stared at the screen like he saw something for the first time. He didn't know why all of a sudden that this page had stood out to him, but nothing could keep him from seeing it now from a larger perspective. The visual was too plain to see. This hidden panel slipped up beneath the door frame, and a message brought out further meaning to what was already written in the Gallatin language, in this darkened corner that had gone unnoticed before, now stood out as a portion of light shown directly over this hidden panel—once so cleverly hidden. That mystery island left behind, being guarded by the watchers and their wickedly winged steeds of the air, and then suddenly the thought came to him.

"This ship was so well hidden into a perfectly natural formed Pyramid. It was by no ordinary thing to be viewed." He thought. It seems to be the beginning and ending of a gateway or means of travel, which appeared to be the obvious, and then David continued his message as if he were learning of the discovering for the very first time.

"According to the inscriptions located above the door frame, a secluded message left out or hidden above the door that is only visible by the passing of light over the top of its hieroglyphic indentations. It speaks of a race that showed no beginning of time, according to the words translated from a Gallatin language. It might be considered that these masters had no written beginning, thus being considered by the Clomends having no permanent record of their origin—to point that out seems to be a key issue—yet something is missing that's harder to translate, I can quite make out the words?"

Torack got up and walked toward David wanting to view what he was focused on that had become such a focal point of discussion.

Torack stood there for a few minutes examining the hieroglyphics on the smaller screen of the handheld. He reached over and touched the screen to enhance the picture to bring out indentations inscribed hidden in etched places above the entrance, and moved it back and forth, and brightened the pixels to bring out the engravings of this message written from another time.

"A gateway without light or one that bears no light." Torack looked up over the rim of his glasses to see if anyone was paying attention.

"They that had traveled from afar are of a different species, those who've come from this Barnard's Star system. They had settled there, and it being only six light-years from the blue-planet, yet they were not from that place. They are a type of life form that gives off an energy source, not human, not Aquerae, and not Clomends." Everyone gazed at Torack as if he would expound further on his findings.

"From there, I could only guess at what that translation inculcates." Amen raised his hand. Torack noticed the small hand from the side of the room, but only acknowledged by a sigh.

"What does inculcate mean sir? It's kind of a big word for me." Torack assumed his role of teacher was never done when Amen or one of the other boys were around.

"Well young man, it has a repetitive type of meaning for the persistence of teaching, to drive home a point so that little ones as yourself never forget or even those of a scholarly mind. My guess is that this message is said over and over again at the point of becoming obscure but hidden by the very ones who created its message." Amen scratched his head without trying to be any more irritating than usual, and then he asked another question.

"Tell me, what does that mean exactly?" Torack momentarily stared at the screen because he wasn't quite sure either. "I think it means whoever wrote the words did it out of fear or was driven to do so for personal reasons yet unknown, possibly so others wouldn't question its meaning or would accept it for just what it is." That statement got Anna and Danica to perk up. Danica, being young of heart and quick of mind, was first to expound upon the Aquerae leader's judgment. The young warrior girl said.

"Like the slaves that built the Pyramids back so many years ago. They were pushed to build such an archaic structure. It appeared almost impossible to build for those time periods, but here they are, and so intelligently built, obviously motivated by a more intellectual dominance." Torack looked up over his glasses again deeper in thought about what he had translated.

"Yes, but that's only part of the message." By then he had everyone's attention, even little Amen's.

"They're warning others through the message. If I understand the translation right, almost like they were over emphasizing the message, but hidden beneath the shadows of cover, so their masters would somehow miss it, but not hidden so well that others of a more intellectual time might find later of an educated mind." Danica implied, "yes, but your assuming this dominant race couldn't understand the slaves writings but have no proof of that." Danica explained herself.

"These hidden writings are similar to a lighthouse warning ships to port or like the flashing lights on a plane or sounding horn of a train warning of danger, only showing at the right time, and not giving any bearing of its message until faced with its impaling meaning, and to the right people." Anna stepped in and explained further.

"They were definitely slaves from this ancient time. Drew and I learned early that they were a species smart enough to leave some type of visual trail behind. This Clodus fellowship, who spoke the Gallatin language wrote the message repetitively hidden the hieroglyphics throughout this ship in different hidden panels. They had found enough character in their fellowship to reflect value in their species. They saw a purpose in the message hidden for others of the future—overlooking the motivation of fear. Probably their masters were very similar to the great kings of the ancient worlds that drove slaves to do their bidding, and that's how most of the great Pyramids were built—by shear forceful cruelty, pushing early man beyond human endurance. It seems to be the Clodus fellowship meant for others to avoid this type of following of entrapment."

Torack's eyes widened.

"That or a warning to future fellowships that this enemy would return and hoping this superior species wouldn't take their ship and make use of it." Amen jumped into the conversation.

"You mean like crusaders?" Everyone turned to look at Amen in bewilderment. Amen continued the spark of thought that had hit him. "I think maybe it means not to travel there because only darkness was there. No light was there, and no source of security—it's metaphorical in meaning, a place of darkness away from the light. Surprised that little Amen was paying attention, Torack whispered to himself, so much for big words. Anna agreed with Amen.

"I think Amen has a point. It was awful there."

Anna spoke about what they experienced in the Ophiuchus Constellation on a planet they called M, named by the slaves that had once lived there. Anna saw the name as fitting since the M4 Dwarf Star was named much later by scientist.

"This particular Barnard's Star has six planets that circle in its solar system. The star burns at 3170 kelvin was a precise measured power source, according to the ships computer. No significant planets had been recognized as orbiting this star from afar with the use of telescopes, and it didn't seem to have any planets of substantial size, until we got there. The pointed-out Barnard's Star has an infrared lighting with planets of substantial size weren't in view until within its solar-system. This place was hidden for a reason. It caused deception. I'm sure that's what their masters were hoping for."

Anna paused and looked at her husband. She had felt overwhelmed and under prepared pursuing the secrets behind this bizarre star system, and she was weary from the constant onslaught of danger. Anna continued.

"We were caught in some type of time-loop that we couldn't break free of, until just in the recent months. Drew and I, along with our other members were caught in this giant interstellar trap caused by a magnetic time warp, something pulled us off course. We got pulled into this dark-energy by something that these star-travelers set in our path. Bella saw their weakness. We broke free by finding its source of energy and worked around it. The gaps in time were exposed by what she saw. We couldn't do it individually. We had to work it out as a unit, that's the reason there are seven of us in our group. Our past dealings with the Great-Gulf reminded us of who we are. Our strength was our gifts as a unit. We didn't really understand how it worked until we found the secrets from within. Drew and I figured it out after a few months of observation and study, and then Bella gave us a little more insight through her dreams. We had to find the reason these ancient star travelers were here, in this Barnard's Star system, and why they had left. It was the key to keeping these star travelers away from our home. The warnings we had found on our own planet led us there to close the gaps. Tell me, they wouldn't know of us. We couldn't go home by the same route. It was closed, but also, we figured covering our trail was even a smarter plan to keep them away. We almost ran out of food and water. Our place of shelter wasn't safe there. We were on the closet planet to the red-dwarf-star M-4 when we found clues beneath the surface about their purpose—we tried to leave." Anna looked at Drew as if she had her fill with explaining about the Barnard M-4 Dwarf-Star system to last her a lifetime. With a bit of nudging from Anna, Drew took over in explaining.

"The Circle took us there…I mean to that other star system…" The others turned toward the vision of the Pyramid. We weren't supposed to find any clues recorded by those who left it, but Bella had this dream and knew where it was hidden. We used a time-spot to travel through that only showed a glitch of a second, something in writings showed us how. There was just that moment, and are timing had to be perfect. Bella told me when to move through the door. It had to be precise. We used the Kelvin measuring system, which cuts measurement errors to the exact Nanosecond. We synchronized it with their on-board computer. The portal left an opening to get us through, and then I took us through the door that was available. It was something we had to do to stop them from coming here—there were warnings through the markings on stones where we had previously found the other ship. The stones, once translated, showed warnings of an impending doom of Orbitus. The Clomends who spoke the only written language of that time, almost ten thousand years ago, had only one form of communication. We had found out at just the right time. We took the other members home before coming here. Those star-travelers of the past didn't know we had even been there because they weren't there themselves. The ship was the only thing left of a physical world that remained. Something happened to them—we couldn't figure out why they were gone. It was a world unprotected of any physical species. The Clodus fellowship was shipped there to work the ground for precious metals for the star-travelers—they were masters who made slaves of the Clodus fellowship. The planet holds no real value after they had stripped it of all its natural resources. No wonder they sought another world to live in. I believe that its close proximity to Orbitus gave the Clomends a heed speculation to warn others of the future. I'm guessing they weren't treated to well. We were only able to survive beneath the surface. We closed the gate behind us after coming back home."

Everyone sat in awe of this story of survival. Danica could hardly believe that her parents and the rest of their members had been imprisoned in the clutches of this time-loop, set up by this intelligent life form they didn't know much about. Danica sensed what they were safe for now, even if it now was going to be the ultimate challenge. Amen popped up out of his seat like someone zapped the tail end of him.

Argon said, "So, what do we do now?" Amen added a little surprise to the conversation.

"We need to find the Indian princess and the gifted and get the flock out of here." Ismael leaned over and shook Jacob awake and whispered in his ear. "Dude...wake-up and pay attention, we're up for a challenge." Jacob jerked forward and almost fell out of his chair. Amen looked over at the awakened dead.

"Have a nice nap?"

Danica turned around and Shhhh...Amen. Renee tapped their leader on the shoulder. Danica turned as her eyes focused. "Yes...what is it?"

"We've got company, and the watchers have trouble." Danica swung her head around toward Torack and knew he had inside information. David glanced Danica's way and suggested they take a certain aircraft not yet seen. David raised his hand with palm out as to stop them from going forward.

"If you would all follow me. I've a Stealth Helicopter that would be much more accommodating and packed with a punch—I think you'll like the modifications." Argon finally perked up.

"Now you're speaking my language!" Amen turned to view the meathead that hadn't spoken for the last hour. "I thought you were MIA...." Argon showed a certain awkward awareness, without comment. They walked quickly toward a ramp that led to the top of a hangar.

Amen replied. "Where's this wantabe chopper, and how fast does it fly?"

David thinned his lips into a hint of a smile. "Well young man, you're about to find out!"

Amen saw it first in the shadows of the hanger, all black and gray colors that infiltrated its rounded corners to hide its bulky bad to the bone image.

"Wow...dudes...hold you're linen and stop your grinin...that chopper is tight!" Argon insisted.

David pointed to the ramp that led up inside the helicopter. Resembling something out of soldier of fortune magazine. Argon gave

Amen a high-five as they crossed the entrance and began to buckle-up into seats connected to the sides all lined in a row. David stopped to explain the added gear and hardware on the Stealth-Helicopter.

"Listen up folks…this is a tornado waiting to happen. Quiet as a mouse, and we'll steal all the cheese out of the trap before the cat knows what hit him. The stealth lasers on this baby will light them up without letting her know you're even in the same vicinity. And added little gift I call a Q-bomb for the hearing impaired. Drop her quick, and she cleans up anything within a five-mile radius. Just make sure you have plenty of time to leave the area and bring a clean pair of briefs. Danica will take you through to the other side of safety. Load up…lets role!"

Amen bent over and whispered in his brother's ear. "What are briefs?" Ismael smiled and reached back to pull up on Amen's underwear, just enough to give them a little tug. Amen smiled and said what he was thinking out loud. "So—clean undies in case we have an accident?" Ismael raised his index finger to his lips.

David looked toward the boys and knew they had caught on.

The Stealth Helicopter had its own pilot and navigator ready and set to rock and roll. David closed the door and stayed behind as the Stealth Helicopter took to the air, just before Danica brought the helicopter right outside in front of their future ride, through one of her gifts many doors. The Pyramid sat there all shiny, glittering in the early morning sun, blending in with the local natives was a go. The helicopter hovered above five-hundred feet above the water. Then the pilot turned the helicopter quickly in a 180-degree pattern locked and loaded, ready to rock & roll on the enemy tailing in the distance…

16

The Guardian's Return

The Stealth helicopter banked so hard that Amen almost came out of his seat and flew across the fuselage. Argon leaned forward and grabbed Amen by the back of his jacket, and strapped him in, guessing he forgot to click the buckle. The ride was fast and furious, and Danica had a look of OMG, what's going on now?

The sky from the north showed an onerous black cloud moving toward them in hive like form. The watchers and Condorsorouses left the island's edge from the south slowly rising to greet them halfway. The Helicopter seemed to be riding on a wave of the wind caught behind them from the winged creatures at their back. Danica looked out the window southwest and noticed the three bright specks in the sky were much bigger now.

They were in a quagmire once again. She didn't see a way out. Each Circle member felt like sitting ducks. Danica looked over at her father. "What should we do?"

Drew glancing out the window had a look of concern etched in his eyes. "We can't stay here—we'll be sandwiched between them and the mountains coming up." Danica looked worried about the mass flying toward them too, and the certain doom of the asteroids speeding to earth from above in the southwest was still a concern too. It all seemed a mistake. She thought maybe it was time to leave, since it wasn't there fight in the first place. Besides, most of them from her Circle were still considered children, and those blackened winged creatures coming toward them looked unfriendly from what she could gather.

Anna gazed at her husband, and then said, "We should go—before it too late!"

Danica didn't wait for her father's approval. She braced her mind toward the other ship that they started their journey with from Skagway, Alaska. They, and this Stealth Helicopter, had disappeared into that hidden place pictured in her mind. Danica had taken them through a door.

The pilot of the helicopter felt a sudden change in cabin pressure. He veered the flight controls left and then right, surprised by their recent arrival some three thousand miles away from where they were originally—a battle of winged creatures of the fallen seemed to have been left behind in that other place. The pilot saw the drastic change of their surroundings. He looked quickly at all his gauges and ambient and barometric pressure readings, altimeter, wind velocity, and angle of flight. Everything appeared to be okay, and then Danica gave him directions toward the ship they left when first getting on this awful planet. It had been left under cover of the forested trees and deep twisting mountains of foliage, fog and rain. They were only a few miles where they had hidden it undercover. Suddenly, from the north another moving cloud drifted toward the helicopter. The pilot placed the helicopter into stealth mode while dropping quickly from the sky. This was one of the few places on earth that was still held together from the forested land that seemed untouched by destruction to the east. Danica looked down toward the earth from where she was seated in the chopper. This place still held beauty. It seemed to be a reminder that even once surrounded by destruction sometimes there still was a reminder of peace once dwelling here. A sudden peaceful calm came over her, as she gazed out into the land, a place once thought of beauty. She had learned from growing up that when focused, everything held purpose, similar to the cycles of storms or the change of seasons. This place was distinct in its own form. Danica's eyes began to water with emotion. She turned and looked at her father and mother. She saw in their eyes, something human that connected all of them. This place had been visited before by those of heaven, and she didn't know how, but she felt that presence of the past had a reason of being here. Drew yelled out to the pilot.

"Take us down and land just passed those trees!" The pilot immediately dropped down over a rushing river and lands just past the inside of a small clearing. Drew opened the side door and the Circle left the safety of the Stealth Helicopter. The helicopter took off toward the blackness of the night. Drew and the rest could hear the helicopter shooting its guns in the distance. Mayhem came from the clouds slowly surrounded them. Danica pulled her sword from its sheath. Anna prepared her bow, and Argon lit up his element-gun while flexing his muscles. It was time to make a stand...

Condac swung his club-like-weapon intensely between rows of the Fallen flooding the skies. The captain stayed with his friend closely knitted to his side, using the same type of weapon that Argon had. The Condorsorouses waged a pathway to death with the silhouettes of fire breathing dragons spewed from nostrils of a beast floating on air. Hellhounds rolled in numbers from the clouds pursuing their enemy. The captain put an Aquerian force-field around the few that were in his group left on the ground, dodging arrows and swinging swords at bad guys took some creativity. The watchers were a beast that these fallen had not yet met, and they were surprised by their strength needed to move about with agility, set in the pocket of leadership, conformed to their own style of ridding the air of their enemy. The watchers were skilled, reminiscent of God-Like creatures created by a God-Like-King, who found it entertaining to add a twist of improvement to each new member, each new strategy was part of this recompense. The legion of a thousand soldiers on the backs of a thousand dragon-like-steeds inflamed the circle around them, scorching and torching hundreds of fallen angels of heaven and those devil-hounds, lapdogs of purgatory. The circle grew tighter as those amassed for a redemptive nature pressed against them. The captain looked over at his friend who had been by his side for quite some time, an acquaintance for the last hundred years. He sensed them being pressed against the masses. There numbers were too many. The Fallen were taking it to the watchers with an over-whelming number, beating their unchained masses in numbers not comprehended of infinity. Condac picked up his pace to swing his arms in defiance against a warrior who had no heart, only vengeance pushed those creatures in the adrenaline of rage.

From where Danica and her crew had landed, back in Skagway, Alaska. Those blackened winged creatures of the air surrounded them, filling the sky with a heavy load of tension. It felt to suffocate the few of them, knowing not what to do next. They surveyed their positions of rank to be hostile at best. Danica raised her sword in defiance against a host that appeared to overwhelm every valley and hill, every tree and space of land pressed out away from them was filled with their numbers. She could see a sparkle of light coming from the forest, a good half mile above them hidden within a barrier of trees. Amen reached up and grabbed Danica by the shoulder and whispered in her ear.

"Look—it's there…we can reach it." Danica with the rest of her crew acknowledged a flint of light and realized their star ship was just up ahead hidden by the trees and force field set in motion by Torack their Aquerian leader. If only they'd realized the shadows of that darker world beforehand. Suddenly, a large figure broke out of the clouds and flew straight towards them landing just beyond their reach, with wings and attitude adding to his dimensions. This form moved in shadows of blackness lacking light. He had a presence of boldness set in his walk and stature. He seemed a bit amused by this small group of children that were before him. He approached with a smile and looked into familiar eyes of a father from several years back, from a time not forgotten by a past realm leader, one who leads in a way that breaks the bonds of friendship, the bonds of love, and family, and those that steal love from the heart are never forgotten. He stood for purpose that wreaks havoc and mayhem, one who destroys without consideration of the core. He stood as an example of how evil can find a way to corrupt. Drew saw the familiarity of the Fallen pulled from the third realm. He walked back and forth searching for words of shock. They stood in silence. Even Amen sensed this over-whelming force in front. The talons stuck out on the ends of twelve feet of wingspan. He was covered in a grayish muck that had camouflaged his body. The Circle of members were bemused, nowhere to go. The air was thick with the smell of blood and war, as evidence seen on those of a host that stood pressed closely with heavy breathing and stares of a thousand sets of eyes. This monster that stood before the Circle began to laugh. He looked into the eyes of this small inferior group before him while shaking his head. He stood before his captains and mocked their existence.

"We have a king that sends children to fight us!" This host of the fallen broke-out in laughter, Danica gripped her sword tighter and closed her eyes remembering to focus. The young warrior remembered the poem the unrealized is not what it seemed—a rhetorical mock as the wolves seen her, alone, vulnerable, a helpless state of being. Then this angel or leader, as he looked to address Drew, leader for leader, experience with experience, intellect against intellect. Drew stood his ground and stared into the eyes of his captor, as it appeared.

He had been through quite a lot the last few years with Anna, and he wasn't accepting defeat. He held on to his character, setting an example among children. This angel of the fallen finally addressed this rank of small soldiers. He had a smile on his face. With his penetrating stare he said, "You don't remember me boy?"

Drew remembered him but offered no honor of recognition. Drew said nothing. This massive being was in this for the thrill of introductions, for the sake of bringing fear toward this Circle, like bullies on an elementary playground.

"I'm Cornelius—leader of the sixth-realm—well, I used to be, but no more!" He said it loud and with a smile like he was proud of the loss. The Circle showed no emotion of intimidation.

Cornelius lost the smile while walking back and forth considering if he should slay the lot of them to set an example, in the face of his defiance or tease them emotionally until he had broken them.

"Why do I have to put up with such trivial matters that hold no bearing on this world?" Cornelius cuffed like he was a big cat flexing his muscles and claws of coercion. Amen being the smallest of all stepped forward, but his brother grabbed him quickly and pulled him back, the host of the fallen laughed. Drew stepped forward while placing his hands around Amen. Amen looked up at his devoted leader with a hesitating grin of concern. Danica gripped her sword even harder. Cornelius caught the tension in the air. The numbers of the Fallen seemed unmoved by the each member's adrenaline rush. What Cornelius didn't know was that they were not as ordinary as he considered. They were from Orbitus, a place of healing and strength, a place that helped them grow to be stronger, and a place where children grew-up to be warriors. A place that opened doors never thought possible. Cornelius continued his playful game of intrigue.

"You're the boy who was here before—some twenty years ago?" The giant angel said it like a question. Drew only nodded his head, not giving Cornelius any words to fight with him on a verbal plain.

"You have no words for me—boy?" Cornelius stepped closer, and then gave an account of what he saw.

"This is the day for the age of those Fallen of heaven. Time for man is gone. Your time is finished in just a day or so." Cornelius turned to try and see those three brightened streaks across the sky, but they were hidden beneath cloud and fog. He turned back and stared at this small warrior, who had aged a bit, as he could see speckles of gray throughout his hair. Cornelius standing frame towered over him as if he were just a boy, just a tiny speck left on the trails of humanity. A human left to the mercy of earth's finalization. He could see this leader stood without showing fear, which confused him a bit because he was seen as insignificant by first glance, but could there be more? He thought. This handful of mislead warriors weren't as powerful as his Dark-Angels, and certainly not prepared for such a force. He saw the small boys that stood around him, young, naïve when it comes to war, and had they ever seen death as in their youth? He thought of all other angles that his evil mind might have missed. There seemed to be none... "You're no challenge for me, you pathetic humans and your half-breeds of whatever you are."

Amen yelled, "You're the half-breed you black thing of the night— why would such a good King see fit to cast you from heaven!" Cornelius yelled back with his booming voice.

"Silence boy or I'll have you tortured!" Danica stepped forward and pulled Amen quickly back. The host of the Fallen laughed at this little demon that couldn't be controlled, who had to be physically subdued. Cornelius looked back at his captains and laughed.

"Look…the pet speaks!" Amen shot a hateful stare toward this creature of the night. This host of the fallen stood in a relaxed mocking stance—from the scene of a funny looking blue alien-boy showing courage.

Danica had remembered the wolves back on her planet, Orbitus, when the wolves over emphasized there position, and what the eyes saw. She remembered her training, her perseverance, her drive to always be one step ahead, one movement quicker than her adversary. Those black wolves with a dozen silvery eyes from her past had surrounded her were not prepared for their doom. In light of their position, she had to change her circumstance. A sudden vision came upon her. Danica moved quickly through a door and sliced off the giant angel's right hand, he screamed in agony. She had moved so quickly her enemy acted appalled, as an expression of bewilderment lay plastered on his face. Those of the fallen were so stricken by surprise they remained suspended by this alteration of impalement. Not believing at first that their leader had been deceived. This young warrior stood as a defiant force not recognizing Cornelius rein of power or might, she only considered her own abilities, not weighting them against a form such as these Fallen of heaven. Intimidation had not been considered by her Circle. They were taught to look past what it seemed to be the situation of what the eyes could see, like a Shepard boy defeating a giant. She only envisioned the path to take from what she had learned in her training. Danica yelled the words out.

"As a King has replaced your position of government in heaven's sixth realm, I cut your right hand off in witness to those warriors left to the Winds of Time as it takes you to the end of your days…you have lost your privilege to sit at his right hand, a privilege to those only of royalty!"

Cornelius tried to reach for his hand while Danica was still speaking, but it dissolved before he could grab it. He screamed a cry so loud and defiant toward all who could hear. This was not supposed to happen. Something was different in this sword swung by this smaller warrior, who appeared not to be of great skill or recognition—this child of blonde curls, a leader in her youth, who had given an unrealized stance toward this enemy, a Tomfoolery of existence. A mirage of despair flicked a crossed Cornelius eyes. He had been tricked beneath this illusion of her being small, insignificant. She had become unbridled, unmasked in the awakening of the proud and unprepared. This was no ordinary adversary. The ground licked up the blood from this violent move. Ten-thousand years gone by, of ten-thousands stares had awakened this giant of war. He knew he had a worthy challenge, a worthy enemy to contend with. He would not make the same mistake twice.

Drew pulled the Circle of members quickly through a door, which placed them right in front of the star ship that laid a half mile from where they were. The host of the fallen sprung forward, but to no avail… they had disappeared…

Cornelius looked in the direction of that sparkle from afar. He yelled at his legions.

"Go—drag them back to me before they flee!" Danica was quick to skip the physical door and made her own. They were all inside the star ship and a Aquerian force-field was placed around them as the darkness of the fallen had begun to overshadow…

The clouds broke open and a mighty host came from the brightness, it caused the fallen to pull back to take notice. Cornelius wound closed up where a hand used to be, but minus the hand. He was spitting obscenities at his captains as the clouds pushed back. He knew something was coming their way.

Condac and his watchers began to tire. The battle of flesh and blood and rage had taken its toll. When all seemed hopeless, the watchers and their winged beasts of the air continued to fight from strength of the healing planet. These dragons of fire staged winged frenzies toward their adversaries. They Thickened the air with smoke and burnt cinders cast across the face of barren land. The captain used his telekinesis to pull the blue healing-stone from a pocket and floated this bluish ore across the way to his friend. It hovered against Condac's forehead. The one-eyed watcher knew what was happening and let it happen. His friend for the past hundred years was communicating with him. He looked to his right and understood with a nod of his head and a gesture of his eye. The captain used the strength of his telekinetic gift. He reproduced the healing blue light from the stone from watcher to watcher, until a blue ray of light glowed throughout the ranks of watchers and Condorsorouses. This foreseen power of the healing-stone renewed their strength as rest and stamina was built back into their primary legion. The powers of the stone from the healing planet were systematically replaced. The soldiers of the battlefield raged on into the end of night. Condac acknowledged new strength as he sliced through another group of the Fallen as they flew toward him, yet they just kept coming, as the air became thick with the slinging of flesh and the drawing of blood. The smell of the dying left a trail not easy to erase, and endless mounting of wrath stored into the memories of those in the battlefield. From the distant atmosphere, the collective clouds began to move violently. An unconsecrated vortex waged its way forward from the sky binding those who were lost in this insidious fight of war and frigid air, picking up anything caught in its clutches. This mighty wind pulled on those lost in the focus of the fight.

The clouds of darkness and wind opened up a hole in the sky bringing down an immortal force of unnatural existence, pulling the enemy from the fight into blackness. A tumultuous tunnel was proclaiming those caught in its captivating grasp. The vortex was breaking through the ranks of the Fallen and avoiding the others. From the southwest, the sun was just ready to rise from an early morning sky. A reminder of those three streaks of light lit up the atmosphere in plain view. Everything of life became relevant of having an end at the end of the day. The end of all mankind was not in the hands of the Fallen, measured soldiers of the night, it was in the hands of a different fate to come. No hope left for those fighting for themselves. Left a blue planet not blazed in its own glory for millenniums hence. A fight of all fights no longer made any sense.

Earth... her current image, was at risk of being chased with fire from the skies, a place so close to come, but not so distant of hanging to far from reach. Making no connection of her history was to take the very essence that gave her life, without remorse of the damage impaled, without knowledge of her years of time gone by, or her ordered battles fought and won in the oblivion of lost memories, yet earths soft delicate breaths taken were as the pulse of each nation, she had not considered those of the innocent that have died by the wayside. Concerning earth, this was about love. Those of earth had showed a lack of love toward this earthen land which lights have dimmed in her history, reflecting some embittered moments, through her members. They could not give love back to her, to a world that had forgotten her through the ages, had left empty memories of a planet that scarred her surface throughout history, she was forgotten, lost in all the senses of love from her immoral deeds, to love her, meant to embrace her even though she had been hideous at times, which left the lonely or sick without comfort, or given no thought to the hungry mouth or the dying laid in her ditches of reality, her mistakes left behind, her ages of waywardness, her members were lost in the ability to love. This endeared planet left in the gloom of her finish.

As author and philosophical mind, Ayn Rand, wrote in one of her novels, Atlas Shrugged.

If you tell a beautiful woman that she is beautiful, what have you given her? It's no more than a fact and it has cost you nothing. But if you tell an ugly woman that she is beautiful, you offer her the great homage of corrupting the concept of beauty. To love a woman for her virtues is meaningless. She's earned it. It's a payment, not a gift. But to love her for her vices is a real gift, unearned and undeserved. To love her for her vices is to defile all virtue for her sake—and that is a real tribute of love, because you sacrifice your conscience, your reason, your integrity and your invaluable self-esteem.

So, this endeared blue-planet faced toward the eyes of her own demise, into the very souls that cut through rocks of the Rocky Mountains and trudged deeply making holes into her form. She finds those members that love, but not without a cost, not without looking past all the scars and nonconforming sacrifices, the greatest of all—humanity.

Skagway, Alaska was no ordinary place set into the mountains. With rain and fog and the cold drizzle masking her landscape, she showed mercy only on the Circle from hidden agenda of her surroundings. A storm had come down into their camp covering the area like a blanket. What could be seen in front of the eyes had become like the blind wandering masses. Suddenly, within the gloom, a warrior of heavens elite had given chase to something he could no longer see. Cornelius had his captains searching the surroundings of this bleakly fading night. Only the sounds of the forest could be heard in the quiet stillness of the unseen landscape.

The Circle stayed still and quiet inside the ship that sat in among the foliage of trees, calm, unmoved, like a lizard waiting for its victim to cross its path. Amen, not thinking of any danger looked out into the oblivion of the mist and whispered in his brother's ear.

"What about our night-vision goggles we have in the supply room— won't they give us sight?" Ismael looked over at his brother, and considered the statement, which seemed pretty reliable for the circumstances. He raised both eyebrows and tapped Danica on the shoulder, then whispered the same message. She smiled and moved toward a closed security door. Danica opened the sealed door just twenty feet away and pulled eight pair of night-vision goggles off a top shelf. The Aquerae had stored them in the ships supply cabinet. She handed out a pair to each member. Tory was already looking at some computer screen that showed red spots marking where the enemy was. Drew figured the Dark-Angels were wandering about the forest looking for them, in a hopeless effort. Moving the star ship through a door could only be done once they were in space, because of its enormous size. Drew or Danica couldn't move something this big through time and space unless they are in space itself, separate from all other physical entities that take up space. The ship would have to stay where it was for now, until the Fallen would leave this place. For the moment, they were stuck. Tory was entering a number of calculations into the computer system. She could estimate how many of the Fallen there were in a square mile by advanced math. She would multiply a certain number expressed by the Aquerae nation as a definitive equation, an advanced math learned from an Aquerian mind. By multiplying this by the square root of the definitive number, one could figure an almost exact number of the enemy within all the surrounding area. As she was waiting for the answer, she noticed everyone putting on the night-vision goggles or at least testing them out for a trip, soon to be taken outside, was her guess. They had to wait until the sun would rise, which would be in just a few minutes.

* * *

The Indian princess, from the seventh realm, stood in front of this massive ship. She pushed her legions passed the trees of cover without being detected by the enemy. The Circle leader couldn't believe what he was seeing. Drew went through a door meeting the Indian princess just outside the star ship. The guardians are pulled through another door inside the quietness of the ships main deck. James turned from a heavenly form to human form, and his Honorite to wolfdog. Three guardians of the seventh realm were finally here. The legions of angels surrounded this massive ship on all sides, like a cloak of cover as Conquerites hit the ground running, causing anyone standing outside to fall. They stood still once on the ground, surrounding the ship and protecting its borders as they were sent by a crown. Cornelius was thrown to the ground like the rest. Not knowing what had happened until seeing these Titans that had come from heavens elite. Something new that the fallen had never faced. Bringing them here was a shock to the system. Being an intimidation was their draw. Cornelius didn't know what to do, these were creatures that gave no quarter and could not be reasoned with or destroyed by any means made possible.

Inside the star ship, Amen reached over and ran his fingers through the wolf-dogs fur. The wolfdog returned a nudge of a cold wet nose, and some heart felt love. Skittles looked as if to smile, then Amen put his hands gently on his head, showing an inward acceptance.

James looked at Amen and understood the connection. "I think he likes you…I mean he seems to know of you, and who you are might even impress him." Amen wondered of the unwarranted expression and took it as a negative suggestion.

"I'm not a child like most of you view me. "He said." I'm the seventh member of membership…I'm a warrior like you and the Indian Princess… well, we're here to represent just like the rest of you." This caught Drew's ears as everyone swung around toward the smallest of members. Amen was curious why all eyes were stuck on him, becoming inquisitive of his sudden popularity. He kept shooting his stares around the room.

"What—did I miss something? Why are you all staring at me?" Thaliana stepped toward the youngest and put her hand out in introductions.

"Hello Amen. I'm the guardian of the seventh realm of heaven. It's nice to meet you."

Amen stuck his hand out with a bit of hesitation seen in his eyes, after considering his hands were alien to this guardian of heaven. He couldn't relate to one of such great importance.

"Oh, you're the princess? It's nice to meet you. I didn't think you would be coming so quickly. I mean to meet us like this. I thought you might have more important issues to deal with, besides facing the end of this planet!" Amen's words caused everyone to wonder what would come next from a boy so self-involved. Thaliana put her finger to his lips. Then turning to look back to James for moral support, since he knew all well the makings of a boy growing into his own. Then facing forward toward the boy so awkward she said. "What could be more pressing than the end of the world, and who said it was ending?"

Amen couldn't believe the sudden announcement of the up-and-coming obvious changes in the sky. "Well, the sky shows us of an end that can't be reversed by what we can tell."

Thaliana looked around and suddenly knew there was a big misunderstanding about the future to come. "Never judge the future by what is seen with the natural eye, as your young leader, Danica has learned from a wolf pack, the eyes can be quite deceiving of any future you think you see so clearly. For the workings of a King is always hidden from reality. Have you not learned your lessons given of those by inquisitive minds and thoughts. Has not a kings best intentions woven into the mind of a righteous man, who does not travel down any road of misconception. He dreams instead of the impossible as to be possible, that's truly how a King works. And don't you forget that young warrior."

Amen couldn't believe what he was hearing. His face suddenly lit up from the sudden reality that nothing was set in stone. "You mean this world is not set for destruction?"

"Do you think that a God of such greatness would destroy something that he created for us as all men to walk on, to see it's natural beauty, breath in the air and fill their minds with memories no one will ever forget. Would you, who were created in the image of such a King destroy what you meant to last forever?"

Amen's eyes fluttered from the implications of such words. "Well, no I wouldn't, I wouldn't let the devils of the sky take from me what was meant for good and meant for those pure of heart. This is that kings world of memories past, present and future. We have no right to judge the end before it is here."

"Well-spoken young warrior, a true visionary is what I see in you. So, listening to your heart is the key to everything that happens of any future we have not yet behold. Take up arms when your time comes, your heart will know the moment of courage will help you strike at the right time is in a king's workings."

Then Thaliana knew answers to many questions were still up in the air.

Argon was the second to ask a question, as if the current knowledge wasn't on his mind. "So, how do you change from angel of angelic form to your normal self?" It seemed to be a legitimate question. James wondered of the boy's frame of mind. With fluttering eyes in a bit of confusion put a hand on his shoulder. Argon looked up at him and continued his thought.

"Can they all do that...I mean change into humans from angels?" James developed a curious stare written in his eyes, "No...just my wolfdog and I are able to change...well, you see it's a story from long ago. I was given this honorary title by a king to help keep order outside the borders of heaven."

Argon asked. "Are there borders to watch outside of the pearly gates?"

"Of course, there is Argon, just like any kingdom surrounds itself with gates and walls to keep an enemy from a stone's throw away."

"I'm glad to hear it." Argon said.

"Well... to continue the thought of the Indian Princess, I will say, we don't know each moment of a king's plan or purpose. We'll know when we need too at the right time. I only know the fight is to continue, until we know of something else." Thaliana's eyes moved toward the spaceship door.

"Your time will come quickly young warriors. Your purpose and reason of being here is all a part of a master's plan. I'll tell you of its purpose when I am told, when the time is near of any future journeying is revealed." Amen reached up and wiped sweat from his forehead, before saying.

"And that means what in English?" Danica quickly grabbed Amen by the coat sleeve and thought to cover his mouth, but the Indian princess waved her off. She had dealt with many children from all walks of life seen of the seventh realm, but Amen was to be a new breed set apart... he was perceived to be put together a little differently than children wandering heavens communities of playful adventures.

Thaliana reached over and took the alien-boy's hand, to show him her attentions were of a good report. He could feel some type of soothing power leave her and run through his body, causing him to feel her strength just through her touch. Amen's bottom lip moved with emotion. Feeling something, he hadn't ever felt before. He knew somehow that this Indian-Princess was no ordinary guardian comforting lost boys of distant planets. She had taken on the role of a once young and beautiful Indian girl, who knew nothing about alien-boys of that distant place, beyond stars shot up into the heavens. Thaliana knew of something deeper in a young heart that beats with life. The Indian princess sensed this young alien-boy to be pure of heart. This brought a smile to Thaliana's face. She had all along been waiting for him. Amen had a purpose in this finale as everyone else, yet he remained set aside as having a key role in what seemed to be the end. A wave of emotion pierced at Amen's heart. He didn't know how to explain what he felt, but he knew it was a good and a pure process of why he was here. It was more than just some type of grand illusion. It was the best feeling ever. He began to think about it, with unsaid words just hanging in the distance. Amen, growing up, always had that prying mind that always searched for answers about life's questions, but at this very moment he held his tongue in silence, befuddled in this waking clasp of hands. His eyes were drawn in from the heavenly stare of an Indian princess. She seemed so right and loving in a way that young Amen was all bug-eyed and curious of her distant stare. Thaliana broke the transparent view she had on him by asking Amen a question. "You still have it...don't you?" Amen's eyebrow rose a concerning stare her way... about what she was asking him, and then it dawned on him she was referring to the courage stone so carefully stored in his pants pocket.

"Oh...yes, I have it right here!" Amen reached inside his pants pocket and pulled out the stone. From first impressions it didn't seem to hold much significance, if anything it appeared to be too small to hold any type of persuasive power in altering the end. But there it was sitting all sparkly in the palm of Amen's alien blue hand. Thaliana looked at Amen as if she could see past all the nasty little habits that young boys take too, and past his wayward tongue, and awkward movements, and only viewed the inward heart of a boy misconstrued. It was beating true to form from her perspective. Amen reached for Thaliana's hand—another surge of warming strength leaves her. Impressed by the expression that graced her face. He was a believer in everything about her, about her purpose and reasons of being here, right at this very moment. Thaliana smiled when she knew there was a connection between them.

Amen was the first to start conversation. "So, what's on the agenda of the day, and where do I fit in...to all this?" Thaliana's face lit up with a glowing beam of light.

"That's what I like...you're willing to challenge anything even in the dismal face of adversity!" Danica wanting to give of her opinion said, "Well, I don't think he understands the circumstances of the danger soon to confront us—Amen sometimes takes for granite that everything will be fine as long as everyone is present. He is just now learning that we can be vulnerable as anyone else, as we just recently experienced in the tunnels below." Thaliana looked into Danica's eyes and found the soul that made her pure.

"No...his innocence is what gives him strength for courage to come will come without meaning, it's taking the first step that holds meaning of a boy meant to be here is not of our time but of a kings." As all were focused on the perceptive words of wisdom. Amen suddenly got a goofy gait in his stride, wondering of being seen so valuable. He looked at the Indian princess.

"Well, you're to be much more important than I, in all this—what is our mission?"

Suddenly, at a distance, Argon had lost interest in all the princess dealings with young Amen, because he was staring at a mass that seemed to be headed toward the ship. Whatever it was he saw through the night-vision goggles didn't look to be friendly. Argon whipped back into a straight position and bellowed "They're coming…and they don't look like they're slowing down enough to consider us a threat!" James and the Indian princess go to the window from the main deck and look out into the blur of fog and rain. James was the first to inquire.

"I can't see anything…" Amen looked this leader up and down, wondering about his character. Amen replied, "Here, put these on… maybe they'll help you see what's outside." James looked down and knew of Amen's true intentions, saw the night-vision goggles and raised an eyebrow.

"Okay, I've got it now, night-vision goggles?" Amen shook his head not wanting to say what he was thinking to a guardian who was appointed by a king. "Yep…just strap it on the back like this, and turn these two nobs up here, until the blur becomes focused…got it?" Reaching to scratch his bottom lip while James placed the goggles over his head. They hugged his face and eyes like a glove. James started turning nobs and suddenly a mass form was seen moving quickly in front—this is what they needed all along. Amen interrupts those staring outside, "Why don't we take one of the hover cycles for a run?" Danica didn't know why they brought them along for the trip, but now it made sense.

"Since when do we have hover cycles on board?" Argon asked.

"Since a few weeks ago when I helped load them on the day we left." Ismael shook his head while explaining. "Torack said we would probably need them if we had to travel on foot too long, we would tire, their powered by small proton-cubes, so we won't need the sun."

Argon looked confused. "Why didn't we know about these three days ago Skippy…we wouldn't have walked fifty miles through the desert two days ago—and now you tell us?" Amen wrinkled his forehead. "I wasn't even here…remember I fell from the Condorsorous, I wasn't in your party, remember? And besides my brother knew."

"Oh yeah, I forgot you were lost squirt, pardon me, my bad." Argon admitted.

Amen said. "No problem, mistaken identity is all. But it wasn't my fault that no one considered looking for supplies in the star ship, how else can you have a good plan without knowing your supplies. I just assumed you guys weren't lug-heads, and would contemplate not everything at your fingertips, besides we need them more now than two days ago—unless you guys have any brighter ideas of averting those creatures outside, and bearing in mind the hover cycles will float in the air avoiding those creatures with ease. They are our main means of travel." Argon interjected his opinion of safety.

"Why don't you hold-up Skippy—that hasn't been decided yet, if we are to jet across the landscape on those...?" Argon didn't finish his statement. He was staring at Amen like he had an idea of what he needed to conform too.

Argon developed a twitch in his cheek while looking out the window. "Hold-up Ranger-Rick, we're not out of this mess quite yet, as you can tell our enemy hasn't made up their minds." Everyone turned toward the small window of opportunity.

James, with the night-vision goggles was trying to see what the Dark-Angels attentions were from outside the ship. Thaliana viewed the computer screen with Tory, who was still feeding calculations into the main frame, attentively focused on not only movement outside, but with their ships internal heartbeat of security. She didn't want those winged creatures to do any damage to the star ship. Even though it was covered by an Aquerian force-field—those winged beasts of the air weren't usually detoured by such things that got in their way. Thaliana turned to view Renee. She had this worried expression written in her eyes.

"Are you okay?" Thaliana asked. Renee blinked in response.

"I'm okay..." Renee said it like she wasn't worried about herself. She was worried about the Circle as a whole being outnumbered and surrounded like the Alamo in a Mexican stand-off.

"We don't...I mean we can't beat them by sword against sword... there's too many of them." Renee said, "We need to get to the other star ship."

Danica was standing at Tory's right shoulder while Thaliana stood on the left as they gazed at the computer screen, Renee was looking out of the main decks front window. She was staring off into space as if her eyes were glazed over.

Danica had noticed on the computer screen some darker colors of pixels were filtering into the picture. Tory was confused by what she seen on the screen, at the same time something else was happening on the screen not noticed from a visual perspective. Renee turned suddenly from her quick recognition of fright. She had envisioned a mass just below the star ship itself.

"They're trying to come in from below!" Renee said, "Turn on the star ships engines! I'm guessing to avoid the Conquerites." Danica reached over to a console and powered up the engines. Everyone heard a low rumble from below. "This should heat them up." Renee said, "We can't stay here any longer, they're on to us." Danica swung her stare back toward the Indian princess. "What about your legions of angels?"

"Don't worry about them, they'll be fine." Thaliana said. Something from around the ship started movement. Amen looked out the window and noticed them first. He turned to glance at James who caught his puzzled expression of surprise.

"Conquerites, soldiers of the seventh…their already moving about!" Amen shouted. He had remembered vividly the vision he had been forced to view, just a few months back. The Conquerites showed no emotion. Sixty feet high with glazed over color of gray, but in the moment, they were covered in ash. They were led by their natural internal instincts, not by words or deeds spoken by others. Argon wondered of their true intentions.

James said. "They're for your protection…you can thank the Indian princess for bringing them along. She thought they might bring quite the intimidation."

Amen's face lit up with excitement. "Yeah…boy…now you're talkin…Bam…take that you feathered freaks!" Everyone turned when hearing Amen's excitement. Ismael came up behind his brother and put his arm on his shoulder.

"Calm down Skippy…this battle hasn't even warmed up yet…"

Amen kept looking out the window with a glowing expression. "Yeah…but we get to see the main show…there's no turning back now!"

Ismael shushed…his brother, "Dude, control yourself!"

Amen developed a look of bewilderment. "No…what's wrong with getting excited?" The Conquerites can't be killed." Amen professed it like an omen.

Thaliana stepped forward to sway the little warrior with the big attitude. "Now, don't get carried away, time will tell…we've got a lot ahead of us."

Amen looked across the room at his brother. "Dude…really…you got to see this!" Amen was eyeballing Conquerites and what they were doing. Standing tall was just the beginning. Majestic in form sixty feet high, 12 in number all around. They were getting battle ready, wings abreast, talons hanging out on each expansion of wings. By what the monitors had showed on Tory's main computer it wasn't what she saw a minute ago. The Dark-Angels had stopped moving forward. James was the first to recognize this massive army had been frozen before them. They were waiting for instructions from their leader. Danica had assumed cutting off his right hand made the warrior of the Fallen from heaven to reconsider his position. Danica had caught him off guard. He never saw her coming. Twelve Conquerites stood in the stillness of fog and rain, waiting for some internal signal. Amen backed away from the window while wearing a pair of the night-vision goggles. The sun hadn't been an option of giving off light, as the early morning day remained dark.

Condac, and the captain, were exhausted from the onslaught of waging war on those demons of the air. The watchers were showing signs of exhaustion. Even though the Condorsorouses had scorched thousands of their enemy, they kept coming. Burnt cinders in the air was still thick with the flow of flesh and blood, quickly diminishing the circle. The captain sent a message with his mind to the young seer, Renee. He used the strength he had left to send this message, strong and clear. It seemed hopeless…until a flick of energy returned to his mind. Renee, being well informed in her gift now, was able to communicate back. Torack felt the keen awareness that she understood their demise…

Renee blinked with surprise as she felt an urgent message come to her mind from their well respected Aquerian leader's 2nd in command. She shouted across the room. "We have to go! The captain and the watchers are in trouble!" Everyone on the main deck of the ship turned to view Renee's insistence. Drew knew this was a mission for the younger group of members to complete on their own. He turned to look at his daughter and she saw the expression written in his eyes; she then knew.

"We all have to go!" Drew insisted, "All our members are going with you…Anna and I have learned quite a bit from our travels across the universe. Thaliana, her legions, and those soldiers of another kind will be right behind us." Danica didn't say a word. She took a few steps and hugged her dad and Anna. Then Thaliana spoke.

"Take James and the wolf-dog with you too." James turned to catch her view, knowing they would be better suited for the younger generations. Thaliana confirmed Drew's insinuation.

"Yes, our Circle needs to go...there's trouble in the sky beyond the limits of a full moon where you were a few hours hence. There's an underground place you need to visit before leaving this blue planet...there are a few chosen that are waiting to greet you." Danica pulled her members of the younger generation together to prepare for a trip unplanned.

They stood on the back loading-dock of the star ship, each Circle member placed on a hover cycle. A hover cycle was a light, fast moving air vehicle that could turn and move on a dime in midair flight. Their efficiency was one of grace with a glowing blue light placed in the center of the vehicle, shaped like a motorcycle without wheels, a hover cycle was a replacement, and speed and agility was its purpose. They were made for tight hair-pin curves and angles to not give a clue of direction. The Circle, with James and his Honorite disappear into the fog and rain. They were pulled through a door by Danica on the hover cycles each of them was riding, focused on the mission on their minds from one previously missing. They traveled quickly through a door fabricated by her gift.

They appeared into a mass of bodies above them, with the sound of breaking bones and the flowing of blood, swords and attitude ran rampage of a day gone wrong. The fight was above them scattered in unrelenting clouds as watchers and Condorsorouses hung heavy in the thickness of war. The stone around Danica's neck began to brighten. Amen felt the stone in his pocket heat up. James and his Honorite turned into their heavenly forms. Amen shot up directly into the midst of the battle as everyone else stayed below, he took his frame and hover cycles right into the heat of battle. The clashing of swords and clubs, and screams of death were amplified. James and his Honorite went flying after Amen. Danica screamed when she saw the movement of his blue glow pass everyone up into the chaos...

17

Detriment of Time

Danica's mind raced for those brief moments in time. She understood this to be the worst time to panic. She had remembered Amen finding her in the tunnels, and it was him that saved her from before. She'd been looking at their situation without accepting that Amen had a key role in all of this. There was a path to follow that the others could not go. But in all his innocence, Amen understood more clearly his purpose than anyone else. This was the time that Danica saw a clearer picture of Amen's journey. Reminded of his constant judgment on the others, always pushing them to think, pushing them to avoid mistakes, pushing them to stay focused. Somehow, she knew Amen had been critical for his own personal reasons, reasons she couldn't see until now, in the heat of battle, in a place far from what she considered home. Amen, in his whimsical sort of way saw purpose in perfection, reasons for his small gestures of judgments, his moments of discomfort he would express to the others. This was Amen's defining moment, a chance to prove he was worthy to be a part of this Circle of friends.

He shot above the clouds toward this mass of confusion. Taking the lead for a journey whirled into the moments of wind and war, into the spraying of blood, the tearing of flesh, and the breaking of bones, caught in a swarm of flailing creatures, like thousands of bees swarming to cling to the same hive. From Amen's perspective, this was a complete turnaround from anything measured as normal. This was his time—not to be held back by big brother or the others. It was time to be in his element where everything around him felt abnormal, because Amen was usually caught doing everything but normal. His normal was a flow of conformity without compromise or condition—but why this boy, and why someone that recognized not this place of being a personal refuge? A place that he couldn't call home, a place he couldn't recognize as good or worth his effort in making a sacrifice, a place of finality in the worst of ways.

The air above was almost too heavy to breathe in. Danica's mind couldn't imagine this boy of her youth slamming against bodies that would take him a part. She had developed a lump of emotion in her throat, and her eyes were past the point of staying dry. She was past the point of redemption, past the point of trying to find logic in why he had left them all behind. Tears began to flow causing her path to blur. The thoughts of her youngest Circle member leaving so quickly left her numb. The gap above her had been sealed up behind when Amen went through it. Danica wanted to slip through a door, but she couldn't move, and she didn't know what direction he would go. She couldn't leave her team behind. She was pulled into two directions. She had to focus.

Above her was a mist of rain that came down as she looked up, but it wasn't any rain she had ever experienced in all her life—it was a slow spraying mist of blood from the act of war. The darkened sky was full of it, from the slamming of swords against bones and flesh, it made her stomach churn. Danica remembered growing up in a protected environment. Living with love, freedom, goodwill toward others, but what she saw above appeared to be a dream she couldn't shake. Was there love sandwiched between bodies of the Fallen and creatures that didn't even belong here? Was there purpose in going this way, where even a Lion, a beast of his own kingdom would not consider this path? There was no clearer picture of death than what she could see above her. She started to understand the over-whelming ache that sunk into her very soul. There were many of those of this planet who seemed to lose hope, lose the ability to be able to survive, lost their ability to be able to last one final day. Families lost by the millions, many buried in memories that no longer existed. Her heart sank beneath the weight of guilt, the weight of shame she felt from losing her youngest member, in the oblivion of a thousand commonalities. She had hesitated for just a brief second to wipe the blood off her face. She had lowered her head enough to use her shirt to clear her eyes. Suddenly, a flicker of light came from the courage-stone hanging about her neck. Right then she knew what she was missing. Danica took a deep breathe while trying to relax her shoulders. The rest of her team pulled up around her, hovering about five hundred feet below a mass of the loudest fluttering of wings and crashing of swords they had ever heard. A tunnel above had begun pulling bodies and bones of the living and the dead just above them. Pulling these creatures into a confusing abyss, sucking the very life from them. A black hole they could not escape, erasing their memories. The black hole kept moving back and forth risking nothing for others to cross it's path, daring anyone to take a stand against it. It was pointless. What happened to having a master plan? Danica was thinking. It seemed hopeless.

She, and the rest of her members, saw the tunnel of blackness whirling towards the center of the battle. The cost was incomprehensible. The time was now—the Winds of Time held them all as having purpose. Showing its own free will, its combative sting. The stars above in the heavens were making room where others were thrown, making room for the new birth of stars. There was a reason of being, a reason for this destruction, a reason death was here, as it moved through the Winds of Time...

Danica looked into each set of eyes...they knew. She looked up before pointing her hover cycle toward the sky, shooting through a wall of blackness —urging the others to follow. Into the darkness they went...

The Indian princess readied her legions against those of the Fallen that lay in waiting. It was a time to face the enemy once again...a time no one thought would come again so quickly, but it was finally hear, in Skagway, Alaska. A place set out in a wilderness of this forgotten land.

The Guardian of the Seventh Realm pulled her legion of angels inside this massive ship and hovered above this place held secret. The Conquerites guarded the areas around the ship from the forces trying to get in.

Cornelius screamed a roar of defiance. "Go...kill them all!"

Thousands of the Fallen fell in silent ranks toward those of heaven. Swinging swords and shooting arrows in a vehement reign of terror. The Conquerites raised their swords and cut through the bodies of the dammed as they moved without recognition of brothers lost. Those of heavens elite gave no ground to those that had fallen of heaven. The sky became as a tumultuous twisting of swords and cries filling the air with death, whirling plunder of meeting an end. The Fallen were shooting towards the ship set to take off. Cornelius face was set into a stupor of rage. His blackened eyes fixed on his force to overcome, yet his masses could not penetrate their borders. The Conquerites stood their ground. It was not a matter of numbers. It was beyond the comprehension of strength over strength or sword against sword. It was about a king of glory that reined above with his own purpose, not to give away life from freedom of freewill was not a question of what to do, but who this was against. The shadows of evil could not overcome this place. Destiny was waiting for them. Sending them to a place of solitude and separation. A Great-Gulf that lies between the living and the dead. A place where comfort had lost her form, a place not to be recognized as a physical world.

Torack saw the blue-spark of light come from underneath. Amen was talking to him telepathically. Amen darted in and out of chaos moving as fast as he could. He saw the aged Aquerian leader trying to help clear a path in a circle of Condorsorouses breathing heavily in the act of war. He had ripped around a row of the Fallen on his hovercraft as his light of the courage-stone blinded them. Amen knew if he stopped the hover cycle he would be overtaken, so he kept moving in and out around them. He kept pushing his small cycle toward the black that lay in front, and only the courage-stone and Torack kept him toward an ecliptic edge, where those devils of the sky would usually not follow such a path. Amen wanting to believe there to be some greater purpose in this unorthodox way to go, which was pointing him toward the outer rim of the Great

Gulf, a place he had visited on one other occasion... Amen was propelled by a deeper mission that rose up inside, there was a higher calling set out on the edge of discontented space, where it was cold, and lifeless. Into the blackness he went, as the twirl of endless motion all around him moved him to move faster. He looked down at his speed and noticed he was at max. He could remember half a dozen other times courage had come to him, but not without the cost of knowing fear was the beginning before knowing it would end soon, something a boy so young usually had trouble with. But not Amen. Good things had happened for this boy of unrelenting facts. He didn't dare look behind him in an hour of this crazy mandated time of leaping before realizing what he had actually done. His pursuers would know soon enough they'd been duped by a boy so cunning without facts of retribution trailing behind him. Amen had to build-up enough courage to drive further into the path that lay ahead of him. It was this fixation that kept moving him, pushing him for time was of essence. His hands grew tighter on the grips, sweat ran down his face and on the back of his neck. There was no place to go once being trapped. The faster he climbed the harder it pulled him. The blackness held to its own set of rules of engagement, inflexible of any reasoning to a small boy of persistence, it's draw was perfect in leading him away from life. An infinite finality, an unknown origin sucked the small boy past all gates of return. All forms of communication would be lost once past a certain point. Nothing at the moment made any sense to Amen, but somehow eternally he knew he was destined by a king. There was an inept energy felt by Amen with not knowing its origin—he wanted to know if his Circle of members would soon be upon him, helping to assist him in this mission of insanity.

Amen not aware that something or someone was looking out for him, but all of a sudden, he felt a little unsure of his journey, so he considered talking to a king sitting in his glory or what he thought to be some non-physical body in the clouds above in the heavens—yet was there a solution? He paused for the briefest of seconds and then said, If your there...way up there beyond what I could understand...please help me to be courageous...help me not to disappoint...I want to know the way, even though I cannot see a path...please show me the way to truth... Torack felt the prayer go out from Amen's heart. He didn't ask for any personal strength or selfish desire, only courage was placed on the boy's shoulders of unrelenting facts, until the end would take him. Amen smiled as he was set aglow as if angels had followed him on this dismal day of retribution…he then held up the courage-stone as he was so generously taught. He noticed the deep glowing color of gold; it gave off light to a path showing Amen where to go. As the sky above lit up Amen beamed with courage and excitement that filled his bones and mind with strength, he thought to never have. He took the stone and led the Fallen into the blackness. Torack pulled back with Condac taking flight out and away from destruction just above them. There numbers were depleted to one-third. The fallen followed Amen into the blackness, as if led by the pied piper. Countless were led without really knowing why…

James led with his Honorite, as they struck forward into the flurried wings of war. Danica and the rest of the Circle followed closely after. James, Captain of the Guardian Angels, cut a trail above with his Honorite to make way for this Circle of the gifted to break through the ranks of the fallen blocking their path. Jacob's gift, being able to feel those around him in the darkness came second in line. He mimics a trail to follow for the others. Argon steered his hover cycle with one hand and lit up his Element-gun with the other, making a larger path to clear this quickly depleted of an abated hole. Renee, being the seer followed closely behind Jacob, who crossed every turn and curve in perfect symmetry. Ismael was next, sensing he better move quickly. Ismael used his telekinesis to push those blackened winged creatures to the left and right. Tory was after him and stayed closely knitted behind. Tory had broken ranks past the mass of bodies of the Fallen, with swords flaring, and the spraying of blood, with an unrelenting sight of merciless mayhem. The gap then quickly closed up behind them. They didn't stop there…they followed those of the fallen into this vortex of wind and weightlessness. Pushed by the churning of chaos, Danica pulled them toward Amen. Renee could see the light of the courage-stone attracting those of the fallen like a bug-light swimming in the brightness of lights and the callings of intonations of echoed sounds, a utopia of bug-bliss, and unrecognized odyssey of leading, like the Pied-Piper leading those of a reprobate of mind. This gap of time set in space between the living and the dead. Danica signaled everyone to stay together. Amen doused the light and blended through those of the fallen that were still coping with night-blindness from staring into the light. A blinding flurry of forgetfulness gave way to bad judgment on their part. Plus, the circle were wearing their night vision goggles.

Ismael pulled his brother toward him with the strength of his mind, connection of conformity, telekinesis of movement, brothers of a higher calling than being tricked by this devil of a loop. Danica could see Amen as they shot forward into this kaleidoscope of discontented space. Into the atrocity of weightlessness, waging their wills forward in the balance of the present and what used to be. This enemy flew past in a thousand streaming dreams of a thousand blinding stares, shot past them in this oblivion of discontented space. No realms to be harbored in this bottomless land of the dead. It was a place of no retribution, no compromise, a place not meant for those pure of heart. Danica closed the gap between the force of the Circle, and Ismael grabbed Amen by the back of his coat. He looked up around his collar with an air of surprise.

"Oh...it's you...thanks...it's about time you guys made it...I was beginning to have my doubts." Danica remained quiet as they joined hands and took the Dark-Angels to their doom. This Circle of members held together by the tight bond of love, the bond of friendship and purpose, the bond in the reality that they were the gifted, chosen by a king, set apart from ordinary beings to do a good deed. They flew through those fabrics of time that held together those fragments of space placed in the gaps of a world, a place saved for the dammed. The Oracles of the Great-Gulf left a trail of Dark-Angels behind. James, Captain, and leader pushed Dark-Angels aside, with the help of his Honorite, his wolfdog. Those who had fallen were of no power here in this tunnel of forceful wind and hypnotic blackness, a place where lost souls had gone from days gone by, just left within minutes. Eerily lurking in an unordered fashion. The Circle prepared their mental pathway back, a predestined journey to prove their innocence. The vortex that brought the evil here—a complicated monopoly of wind and weightlessness forced them to be caught into a mix of unwanted chaos, fused together, an inflection of a past —their memories were quickly erased.

They recognized together this place of the dammed right away. Those lost souls of the damned began to soak-up Dark-Angels as they were shot through this vortex that time forgot. James had covered the Circle with a cloaking device, protecting them from the eyes of many, an added little defense from the guardians. The Circle watched as thousands of Dark-Angels disappeared in the dark. They were to be no more. In the distance, the Circle could see the last of those creatures being closed in behind this gap between the living and dead. Danica took this small moment of opportunity to pull this Circle back through this Vortex in reverse with James and his Honorite. Tory opened the gate to let the Circle through before Danica swung open a door, which had reversed their direction, toward the world of the living. Danica pulled them through the door, which was only for a moment, a Nano second of precision, a door of last resort. Precipitously, a reversed kaleidoscope of colors appeared before their very eyes. Heterogeneous movement perceived by a receptive nature, recognized as colors for human eyes to behold. This wormhole projected forward heaved by massive force, turning in a three-dimensional direction. Several seconds had gone by before Danica and the others began to see a reflection of familiar light, trying to draw them nearer to a physical world holding a redemptive nature. On closer observation, they could tell the light was gold in color—shinning bright. Danica recognized that alien hand to be familiar, with its blue color and webbed hand. She shuddered with anticipation as they pulled through this last door closed behind. They had made it.

Danica saw the battle had left behind thousands of bodies in pools of blood, and the smell was unrelenting. Condac's face was bloody from the fight. He and his endeared warriors had suffered multiple abrasions and wounds, and their forces were reduced to a mare three-hundred watchers left standing when they had started with over a thousand, but the battle here was done as far as they could tell.

Danica looked up into the sky, seeing the three asteroid's headed for earth. Her nerves had almost taken her off her feet, and her heart was pumping out of her chest. She glanced over her shoulder toward her Circle and said, "Come on, it's time to go home."

Torack remained quiet, because he knew his fellowship and friends emotions had gone beyond what was expected of them. The smell of war in the air, and the taste of blood fresh on their lips—there were no words they could say that would convey a more exhausting message. Danica was thinking of those humans left behind in Ark-City. Still a mystery to all of them. They had lived in this fortress of darkness for three years now. Danica was considering the last three years of those that had suffered in the wake of almost being wiped off the face of the earth. She wondered of their frame of mind and able body strength left. She realized her team, and those watchers, and their steeds of the air had been the difference. She was on a mission. Danica looked at her team with an expression of concern.

"This is our fight now—we can't leave until we find those missing..."

David opened the gate as light of the early morning sun broke through the doorway for the last time. He was looking at this famous G-star as if a small amount of hope could be drawn from the beams of light that it cast. David had only met with the Indian-Princess twice in two years. She had limited her communication with him so not to be followed out of this secret place of Ark City. He was trying his best to seem cheerful, even with all the turmoil facing this city beneath the surface. He wasn't usually one to complain about conditions for his own accords, usually his small portion of food, and adequately furnished bedroom on Bunker-Mohave, upper south side of the hidden city. Ark City had been named by one of the three master builders named, Samuel Goodall... a tall older gentleman who used to design skyscrapers casting shadows in New York City, back in the nineteen eighties. Goodall had designed Ark City over twenty years ago when the U.S. government had hired him and two others in 2041. There had been two other underground cities in the United States. Three years earlier, they had been found out and destroyed by reasons unknown, by those devils of the sky, as he was told. Goodall had died two weeks before the last tunnels were dug from something incurable, he received in one of the tunnels. David had to have the project finished by an architect/contractor named Randy White. Mr. White was the brains of the project and had hired subcontractors with the only two branches of government that were still in operation. The main security system, designed by a company called Inter Tech-Security-Solutions, who suggested they had developed a full-prove security system that was a cut above the rest. No pun intended, but all the other competition had disappeared off the face of the earth, best or second best, at that point it didn't really matter. Inter Tech-Security-Solutions considered it to be their lucky day to receive this five-year contract from Randy White. Mr. White didn't see any other solution to this problem because no one else was left to take the job. In the end, when everything was said and done, Mr. White had seemed to have made a good choice because they somehow had survived, well up until now. Ark City was the last underground facility in the United States of a collapsed America, or to put it in the right context, the only underground city left on the planet. All other underground facilities were found and destroyed from Europe, Southeast Asia, and three underground food banks in China, also two in Russia. The ones in Russia, David had remembered from his notes. The first was called Northern Ridge X-Plant, and the second called the Saylyugem Mountains Food Bank, which also housed thousands of people below, yet now, none of that mattered. David just opened the south side entrance of this massive Hydraulic gate hidden behind canyon walls. The canyon walls were only separated by a hundred fifty feet of cliffs, jetting from the floor of the canyon to the top reached up to six-hundred feet. The angle above the top of the canyon, from a bird's eye view, didn't show the existence of its opening, it appeared to be hidden by the current angles of shadows and trees, and the deepness of the canyon floor. David remembered that the Indians that settled in this area back in the eighteen-hundreds, which they called, the water that rages. His best guess was that a massive river once flowed through this valley, but now it had become a dead riverbed of skeletal bones from once wandering thirsty predators, and now a riverbed of rocks and silt with a small amount of water was a brook compared to what used to run through this valley. All it had left to show from the past was the scars of water that had cut its way through this once healthy canyon. This part of Earth had basically dried up and died, and only small patches of greenery remained beyond, in hidden pockets covered and protected from the weather.

Suddenly, David dropped to the floor to avoid being slammed against a side rail he had been leaning on. This brownish-green winged-creature of an enormous size had flown in just past the gate, skidding in such a forward progress causing him to bowl over a group of soldiers.

David looked up and recognized this being a giant Condorsorous with a watcher attached on his back, but then quickly rolled to the side. David stood and yelled across the room for his soldiers not to shoot at these considered victims of war. Both, the Condorsorous, and the watcher, were in a saddened state, which were soon to be followed by three Dark-Angels coming from behind. The Dark-Angels were in such shock of this open passageway they were frozen. A soldier standing off to the side, back behind David saw the three Dark-Angels when first entering yet remained nervously in a rigid stance. The young soldier finished training two weeks earlier. He wanted to make a good impression on his superiors, but this was to be his first time confronting the enemy—he appeared to be confused by what he saw. David rolled underneath the guard-rail, ripped the gun from the youth's hands. David cocked the HK 416 and cut through the blackened winged creatures before they had a chance to advance. Some alarm went off and automatically triggered the gate to close. David approached the wounded watcher taking all precautions. Somehow this giant watcher knew he was in a safer place, a place he could rest or a place he could get his bearings. The Condorsorous lay in a fast-breathing heap of blood and smoke. Smoke was coming from his nostrils and blood from his side. From the looks of it, from what David could tell, this winged beast, and his master were not in any kind of shape to go one step further. It didn't take David too long to figure out this creature and his rider had been chased away from their fellowship, somehow lost in the confusion of war and chaos. David knew the only way he could communicate with this fifteen-foot-tall creature from what he had learned was telepathically, by touch. From afar, David reached up and touched this mammoth soldier. His line of communication began to open up between them. All David could remember in this transfer of thoughts was the gentle spirit of Condac character. The watcher had no identity to these humans. His only personal connection with all humans was only with the Circle members, who were nowhere near his present location. His only loyalty was to those he left behind in battle—his fellowship. He didn't seem to be focused on his pain or the temperament of any battle. He appeared to have changed his expression of comprehension. The watcher showed a calm clarity, attentive on those of this city, hidden beneath rock and soil. His purpose wasn't his own, but one that included those around him. He appeared to know this place of origin, as if in memory.

David, in the simplicity of things saw this creature had a job to do. He didn't appear to be absorbed on his own wounded condition. He was a simple guide. On a mission—worlds away from his natural home, here to lead those to a place of safety, lead them to a solid foundation of coherence, to give them hope, and provide them with a place of stability. David reached up and wiped sweat from his eyes. He understood that he was like this creature that was before him, just another guide to show others the way. A person or watcher in the simplest form of having a job to do, and only needing instruction to get through one more day, one more hour further down the road. David understood that they all as individuals had a profession to do, this was about rubbing shoulders with your brothers, giving a little more time to those who were left hopeless caring when no more compassion could be found. This was about saving the last of humanity from a dying world. A lump developed in David's throat when looking into the eye of the watcher, a sadden state and condition. David was here to help.

Skagway, Alaska had again become a place for those of heaven to be caught in the battle of heavens elite, a battle for position. Drew and Anna stood on the bridge of the star ship wondering about their condition. They were surrounded by Dark-Angels on all sides, and Cornelius, their leader missing his right hand seemed even more aggressive toward his enemy. The Indian princess looked across the main bridge at Drew and showed a hint of concern. Drew could see in her eyes that this fight was her assignment from the beginning, her place to be, why her training was so important. She grew-up in this forested land, remembering from her youth how she had left pieces of memory behind on this sodden soil. This was a land which her forefathers had defended their honor. Where she had defended the lives of those she had loved. Thaliana, a young girl of nineteen had died protecting her land and people. Now, an Indian princess from the seventh realm of heaven, she was a guardian, a protector of the Circle and guardian of an elite group of angels. Even though being small in size, she was here to represent. Destined to set an example for others to learn from and follow. She had purpose that superseded all other matters of this world concerning those of this small blue-planet, just a speck of light from a yellow-white G-star, third planet in order from the sun. A king saw something in a young Indian girl, who put a blessing on her life, and put her in a position of honor, a position saved for only a few. She had been trained to be a leader of the seventh-realm, one of a hand full of guardians. She was well informed about this land. Thaliana had four brothers and three sisters, who were more suited to fight, yet her past human-spirit had put her tears into her efforts, put her heart into everything she ever touched or created. It changed the pathway of her heart. She had forged a path from her efforts of courage by putting creativity and knowledge in all her works. Thaliana looked up past Drew and signaled her five captains that had come with her to head for the entrance. It was time for them to face the fiery that lay outside. Drew knew without words that he and Anna were to man this star ship to another place where others were hidden in the bowels of the earth. The Indian princess led her captains and her legions outside the star ship, with clashing swords and waging war against this defiant enemy. The Conquerites took to the sky...

18

Ark City

Drew and Anna flew toward the atmosphere on a breath of air, followed by seven Conquerites as blazing light, south a little over three thousand miles. The earth from below sat as a cold frigid spherical ball covered with a glowing blue glaze of quietness. It seemed dead from above, but somehow Drew recognized that earth still held a heartbeat with those beneath her shelter. Anna reached over and put her hand atop her husbands. They were caught between the sky and the view of three blazing lights cast in the darkened night. There remained a memory of what was to come in the blackness above the heavens. This was a race against time. An inward awakening began to rise up inside Drew and Anna's hearts, seeing the incessant presence of the earth below and heavens above. They were pushed to make history change. One last historic moment in time was all they wished for. Drew saw a tear trickle down Anna's face. She thought of that poem so many years before that had left an impression deeply embedded in her mind, from a Professor Rochester Furlong's book.

Memories that teach the soul not to regret...oh memories carried on the wings of the wind...

She knew in her heart that these were at the final hours of the end, but the end of what—humanity, the end of this earth forever? There was no logic to this nightmare facing humanity, no answers to the many questions that had crossed their minds. Nothing of finality made sense. For some reason, Anna couldn't find any purpose facing these blackened-winged-creatures of the night. Why even fight them... they were all going to parish in the end? She clung to her husband as if she could pull strength from the closeness of his touch, but nothing was drawn. While hovering above the heavens, Drew was looking at the stars that shot out before them in this vast cosmos. He felt the emptiness of space beyond. He thought of this star ship created by those of a different calling, of a different time, at another place—but why? This star ship hung floating in the orbit above this once beautiful planet...guided above the stratosphere into the cold darkness of unanswered questions. They had front row seats to the end of the world. The three asteroids blurred forward brilliant orange-golden light blazing streaks like a super-nova crossing their path. Their memories of this place left quite the impression on their internal souls, accepting a fate that drained the color of pigment from their skin. Drew guided the star ship down toward earth to a adequate clearing, showing the outline of what used to be the California coast-line drenched in cloud-cover. Going east, just before the mountains appeared, Drew saw a hundred and fifty-foot opening—a circle of hope came to his mind. Nothing above the clouds could be seen because of a previous storm, except this one place, this tiny clue of direction. Drew was guiding the star ship by a navigational system designed by the Aquerian fellowship, as the Circle had been taught of its technology. He was looking at a computer screen and watched the terrain change from mountains, to rolling hills, and rocks and trees, to a place he hadn't ever seen from this coastal city where he grew-up. A giant fissure had split the earth in a section of about three miles of barren land that lay atop of this mesa. This place couldn't be seen from VFR flight, visual-flight-rules, but Drew could make out the changes in terrain on a computer screen, through this three-dimensional NAV charts showing the star ship moving toward this strange looking fissure. The gap seemed not very wide between two canyon walls, well hidden from the naked eye. From the east side below were more mountains, higher but of the same likeness—yet something seemed different about what he saw? Anna had her arm around Drew as they stood on the deck of this aged star ship and stared at what was an opening. Something internally stopped him from going any further. Drew saw the terrain had changed, and Anna noticed a little bit of different movement below. From Anna's studies she understood the shadows of fog drifting off the top of what could only be water. The fog was the clue. Anna pointed toward the canyon floor and said, "It's down there Drew…look at the fog below…there's moisture collecting at the bottom of that canyon." She looked into her husband's eyes. "David had told us to look for the references of the land to find our way back, the fog is the key. I think the city is down there somewhere." Drew didn't question his wives motives. He lowered the ship toward the floor of the canyon wall and dropped in slowly beneath the cover of the canyons protection. This massive ship was camouflaged in stealth-mode. Suddenly, a rolling thunder past over the top of their ship startling Drew and Anna. Drawing focus, they determined this to be the Stealth-Helicopter left behind. It had barely flown sideways over the top of them with smoke spilling from the rudder. The pilot sat it down just past a grove of trees and turned off the engine while smoke billowed from the top. Drew saw the panic in Anna's eyes, but also saw the pilot and two other passengers get out of the helicopter and head in a direction toward the trees. Anna spoke quickly. "We need to get to the city before anything else happens!"

Drew nods before taking it lower, then suddenly seven Conquerites landed shaking the ground before Drew had a chance to set the ship on a hard surface. Once landing, they made their way out of the star ship and looked up toward those mammoth creatures, protectors of a crown. It was hard to believe at first that such creatures existed. Drew got the oddest feeling to reach-up and touch the first Conquerite, like they were silent Titans waiting for their masters call. The golden soft glow of their armor and what looked like their skin had the couple mesmerized. These protectors of a crown stood as a stoic reminder that heaven was not a myth, it wasn't a place held in secret, it wasn't a dream or fantasy of school children. What was really heaven to any of them? Something more beautiful and overwhelming that couldn't be explained by mere words was all that any one could say. As said so many times from writers across the globe…Heaven to us was about spending time together, learning of each other's strengths and building on them, and on a quiet part of a cooling day one could see heaven not so much in a physical form, but everyday life that draws the heart back to a place one calls home.

Drew had a thought. "Knowledge is what we seek, isn't that what the professor had told us…we need to know what's out there or otherwise there's no use in going forward—wouldn't you think?" Drew said it like he was waiting for Anna's approval, but she stayed silent. Anna knew Drew was searching for something within himself that couldn't be found without the help of one of these creatures that stood before him. He reached up and touched this warrior of heaven.

Immediately he had been pulled by a submission of his mind into a metaphysical world of coherence toward the beginnings of stars and planets, as they were born, as all things are born at one point in life. The clouds of gas that gave birth to protostars from early beginnings of a galaxy whirled in space above turned into an explosion of interstellar brilliance of movement, as if Drew was flying toward what seemed to be the other end of the universe. It took his breath away, like he was flying on the wings of the wind, but in a metaphysical sense, showing the age of all time in glitches of reverse—the cycles of life, touching the outer edges of the universe, before the beginning of all time, before the birth of millions of worlds shadowed throughout the cosmos, like the first birth of a baby from its mother's womb, or like the volcanic eruptions of earth formed from a new molted rock of heated changes, each with its inward violence of newness. A newness of organic mass in the vastness of space, as unborn stars clustered together in unity. Glitches of what used to be were moving through Drew's mind, forward through this barrier that opened up into a blackened hole into space. The heterogeneous vastness and colors of space had made him feel this allusive power moving from place to place without effort, as if he was given passage without understanding, passage through the fabrics of time and unfathomable space as time stood still. The restructuring of stars and perceived beauty and colors of perfection created before his very eyes. The brightness, the obscurity of colors had over-whelmed his senses. What was the purpose of him seeing this… and why was this Conquerite allowed to show him these things? Drew turned his head to look back, but realized nothing remained behind, and it brought him to feel small, insignificant for the moment. He felt only to be a speck, a small glitch of life flickering in the vastness of the universe. There seemed to be reasoning in all this, yet to be acknowledged. He was given this opportunity to view an unborn cosmos, a reflective nature of the past that he had concluded as not given to anyone else. He was an opportunist, not fearing the fear, leaning toward understanding, reaching for the stars as you would say, moving through doors he hadn't previously measured as having a divine purpose. Drew began to feel that even with all these cosmic happenings, he felt purpose for himself and those that were with him. The cosmic universe wouldn't be complete without the small parts that each member of his Circle had been a part of. The end had a purpose, as in the cycles of life, for the old to pass away and the new to be born. These Conquerites, protectors of heavenly realms as they are called, mystical God-like beings from heaven, from a place thought to be above or beyond deep space. A place thought to be of peace, a place where a weary heart could rest, or a place for newness. The Circle had found the Conquerites to have quite the library of knowledge to facts of their own history embedded in memory. Drew even considered that the knowledge he would gain would eventually point him toward this heart felt message—a purpose leading him away from the unknown and bring an equitable conclusion from many unanswered questions of the change of circumstances, yet from what he could tell—well from what he could see, nothing seemed to match-up to what he needed to know. For some reason this Conquerites vision was leading him far away from anything remotely close to what he needed to know. Yes, he was seeing creation around him, yes, it was beautiful and hard to fathom in the depths of what he could imagine, yet something was missing? What he wanted to know was why—not how?

Yet again, Drew deep inside knew the answers to life were not about the why's of the world…it was about the actual journey of each ones path where answers were found. A journey that each individual had to dream, and live, and experience, the why's weren't the answers to solving problems of this small planet, or about individuals having all the answers—the answers to life were acceptance of each ones journey, not always planned, not always dictated by each moment, but answers only come when each individual searches for certain answers with all their hearts, with intelligence, in wisdom, with unquestionable certainty there would be enlightenment. There can't always be inevitability of each goal, to each step taken forward, yet Drew was realizing by his own experiences to reach a goal one had to never stop dreaming, never stop moving forward, and never stop reaching for the stars per say, as this mighty warrior of heaven had to show. As the stars that shine in the heavens each one had their journey, and Drew's why's of his life were only answered at the right time and moment— He could only control small bits and pieces of his own personal universe, the journey was his to take, not the journey for those vast entities of stars that lay beyond. An individual with his own journey, his own reality, would continue each day as it leads to the next. He would have purpose.

Drew began to fight his way back from this mythological journey to where he first started— thinking a different tragedy than before, and it didn't include waiting for those three blurring rocks moving toward the earth. He had remembered Cornelius sharing about his opinion of the king, and how his own personal views had seen a different angle not thought out by other members. He remembered Cornelius saying that the only love this king had left for humanity was no longer there. Didn't he have his own opinions, wasn't he capable of finding out his own answers in life by continuing his journey? Didn't he have more pathway to take?

Drew raised his head—and smiled, gave Anna a hug while looking into her eyes he said, "Let's go make history!"

Once back from the Great-Gulf, the circle members met with Torack. It included a few hugs to each other and their devoted Aquerian leader. Condac, wasn't anywhere to be seen, until getting in past the gate. Amen was the first to see him. He gave a begrudging look toward the small alien-boy who thought to lay one on him, a hug or a kiss, or maybe that Aquarian smell that didn't set to well. Amen looked at the big, injured watcher and considered his frame of mind.

"Just give me a fist bump you big lug…I don't have cooties!" Condac held his fist out like Amen was about to electrocute him. With everyone staring. Something major happening with Amen's wild expression at first, yet he wasn't sharing. Too much had happened that day. Condac looked to having a begrudging attitude. Danica developed a smile while Amen's brother shook his head.

"Skippy's going to give Condac and ulcer." Danica swung her head to view Ismael's eyes. "No...I don't think so...he likes Skippy." Ismael developed a bewildering stare. "Like hemorrhoids...he does." Danica narrowed her eyes.

"TMI big-boy...I don't need a visual! Besides they've bonded quite well over the last few days...I can sense it."

"What-ever man...Skippy will get to him sooner or later. I'm glad he's irritating the giant watcher and not me." Danica continued an abraded expression.

"Cool-it Kilimanjaro...Skippy was the only one crazy enough to lead those creatures...we wouldn't be here if it wasn't for him. He's the only one that had enough courage to fly into that vortex!" Ismael twisted his lips to one side.

"Yeah, but he'll rub this in for a long time...I wish it would have been someone else." Danica appeared to be surprised that Ismael didn't have his brother's back on this one. Condac reached down and put his hand on top of Ismael's head like he heard and understood every word. Ismael's eyes met with the watchers. "You got that big fella...Skippy's going to make you regret this." A miserable grown came from Condac. He looked back at Amen.

Amen defended himself. "What's wrong big guy...cow tipping not your forte?" Condac sighed like a big cat cuffing who had acted forgetfully, pretending to have missed feeding a young lion cub. Amen reached up and scratched his bottom lip, showed a quirky smile while losing interest. Danica signaled her Circle to move on. They needed to start heading east on the hover cycles. After surviving the Great-Gulf they were ready for a little R n' R. Torack communicated with Condac for the last time. The watchers, with their Condorsorouses, were on a mission to go and guard the Pyramid star ship left three hundred and fifty miles south of San Diego. Condac nods in understanding. In the back of his mind, he felt someone calling to him. Condac turned with a blink of his eye and a curious stare. Torack saw his expression. He began to communicate by means of a mental suggestion. Condac was still recovering from injuries inside Ark City. Torack began to apply the blue healing stone almost right away. Condac's military fellowship took to the sky without his assistance. The Circle looked up and watched them disappear into an early morning sun. Floating amidst this left-over battle-ground Danica recommended to moving on.

"Come on...it can't be that far! We have a place to go and people to see." She shouts, as she led the way, they followed in the sequence of awareness, and Torack took up the trail behind them. Argon and Torack had locked and loaded their weapons...just in case they had more company of the miserable kind. Ismael saw Amen shoot past him like he was late to pick-up a belated birthday present. Ismael continued and irritated expression toward his brother. Tory viewed her miniature I-Pad before moving ahead of dark tunnels and more mystery ahead. Jacob, and Argon, only looked at each other while waiting for the others to pass to take the lead. Ten minutes later the Circle was walking down halls to a new welcoming of people they were soon to see. They moved through an open doorway one at a time.

The turned a corner when something delicious hit their nostrils. It was a welcoming smell. They looked tired, wanting to gain their strength back. Amen turned from the view of that long night behind them, and almost ran into the giant Condorsorous lying in a somewhat relaxed position just inside a large room. There was still evidence of blood dragged in off the concrete, and some left on the Condorsorouses skin. Amen could feel and smell his heavy aroma of breath and burnt flesh. He wanted to pinch his nose and not think of it. Then noticing one rider missing. Amen turned to view Danica as David came out to meet them. Amen asked.

"Where did he come from?" David showed a hesitant smile while he looked up past the smallest of Circle members.

"Well, the creature was pushed from his fellowship by a group of Dark-Angels. His rider is recovering from injuries suffered. Danica turned her glance toward David with a look of surprise.

"He's here! I mean...you have him in Ark-city?" David raised his glance toward Danica.

"Yes—he's resting from his injuries. I'm not sure where his fellowship ran off too. He lost a lot of blood, and well, we don't have blue blood to replace what he lost." Danica reached into a pocket and pulled out a small satchel with the healing-stones. David just looked at her, then said, "I believe your friend Torack, already applied those." She glanced back toward David.

"OH… I didn't know." David looked down to see what she had in her hand and noticed the stone.

"Those actually work?" Danica looked at him.

"Yes…they work…why…you need proof?" David's face held a curious stare, he looked tired or even overworked. His hands seemed a bit shaky, by what Danica could tell. He was slower in his movements. He held back some facial expressions. Then they were off. Each member of the Circle followed David toward a shuttle. They walked along a dim lit path with steel railing. They passed two soldiers standing in front of an office building, with the hanger behind and tunnels ahead. They were to shuttle to a place they could get something to eat.

The Circle sat quietly while the shuttle hummed along. It was dark and cold, and a metallic dampness drifted in the air. Amen stuck to Danica's side. She gave off a warming comfort. The lights in the tunnel flashed in flickering blurs as they crossed paths between darkness to light. Amen turned to look at Danica while her view drifted out the window. He saw the beauty of youth in her face. The long blonde curls drifting around her shoulders were a matted mess. The wind had tossed her hair about with dirt and soot, floating of memory from chaos left behind. He reached over and touched her hand. Somewhat startled, Danica looked down at him. Three times he had saved her life in the course of three days. Yes, he did have his own personal vices that seemed to get under her skin. Even though he had good intentions, not everything always turned out for the best. His motives were pure, and his heart in the game…but give me a break, was the look. Halfheartedly, she returned a reassuring nudge with a quivering smile. She sensed a little uneasiness in his manner. He sat in silence and felt a small flicker of doubt among his warrior friends. Danica turned to watch the lights fly by as the shuttle moved faster. They were pressed for time. She felt like life all of a sudden was too short. All her crew members looked tired, drained, more like it, by what they had experienced and seen. The rage of war and the memories of bodies lying in pools of blood were burned in memory, and cities that were just gone left her feeling empty. It made her feel so unimportant in the mix of things. Why had so many died? Was her thought, but nothing could change that. And they were the end results of everything else left. Ark-City was their last remaining hope, if there ever could be any. Everything had stopped spinning. It looked like the end of humanity. Danica reached over and put her arm around Amen. A slow tear trickled down her cheek. Her hands began to shake. The sounds of the road behind echoed off the tunnel wall. There was a chill in the drifting air. Jacob sat next to Tory. They both had their eyes closed. Argon was staring out his window with a distant stare of memories past. Renee had an expression of pain in her eyes. Ismael sat in the back of the shuttle, separating himself from everyone else. Danica turned her view back toward the front. She sensed time was the only valuable commodity they had left. Everyone sat, quietly, calm, distant, staring out into the blur of fast-moving glitches. David felt depleted and remained quiet. A heaviness hung in the shuttle. Amen kept looking from the driver to outside, and then back at Danica. The wind from the tunnel blew dirt inside the window. Danica reached up and closed the window. Ahead, the lights moved with people. The shuttle slowed down. Jacob, Renee, and Argon had fallen asleep, quickly woke up when the shuttle stopped.

David led the Circle of members down two flights of stairs before opening up a door to a large room about the size of a high-school gymnasium. Bluish curtains hung on stringed twine dividing rooms like in a hospital emergency center. Smells of the dying drifted into hospital beds of antiseptic walkways, which caused Danica's stomach to churn. Amen twitched his nose, sneezed, and then farted. David turned suddenly knowing little boy's sometimes can't control bodily functions. He looked offended.

Ismael sacked Amen on the back of the head, "Way to go Skippy!" Amen's face flushed a darker blue. Everyone else ignored the smells of antiseptic cleansing and what little boys ate from the day before. Danica saw the watcher by the shadow he cast through the curtains. He was unconscious, dreaming about something. His body twitched from time-to-time as he rolled slightly toward the outside of an over-sized bed, dreaming like he was still fighting. Amen reached up and touched him, then realizing it was Condac in the bed. The pain of the night slammed against two minds seeing the same thing. Amen could see what he saw. Death and blood with the rage of war, screams of the night, terror gripped him as he pulled away. Argon reached over and pulled Amen aside. Danica reached up and touched him while Condac slept.

The curtained room lit up with a light they had never seen. Danica saw a vision of a blue healing-stone changing the form of bruised ribs, swollen knuckles, and broken bones to better conditions. A doctor, two curtains down had been the only witness. Danica forgot people of earth had never seen the healing-stones and what they could do. Condac slowly opened his eye.

19

The Gifted

Argon put his arm around Amen and whispered in his ear. "Ignore your brother, he'll get over himself." Amen twisted his head to the side and scrunched his face by way of silent misunderstanding. David walked around several curtained doorways as the smell of the dying drifted among its victims. He stood there in disbelief as he watched this large creature sit up and smile. Danica took her blue healing-stone and started toward the next room. David tried to reach for her, but he hesitated before getting her attention. Amen knew of Danica's motive and took off after her. Everyone else stared at Condac in disbelief that he was awake. Amen grabbed Danica's hand from behind.

"Does that smell bother you too?" Danica turned to view her latest arrival and ignored him. Amen felt the need to be close to their leader as they walked past a doctor and two nurses into the next curtained room. An old pale thinly skinned man laid in a heap of bones while a young lady of bereavement stood over him. Danica didn't wait to get cozy with the young lady. She placed the blue healing-stone on the old man's forehead. The young lady bewildered by the rude interruption said, "Doctor...who are these people?" The doctor broke through the curtain and looked at the two. "What's going on here...you can't just barge in and take over!" Amen never short on sarcasm said, "Look doc... what would Jesus do?" The doctor was about to give Amen a piece of his mind, but this bright-blue-light grabbed his attention. Something was mesmerizing by this ecliptic blue sphere floating about this sick man's head in a wonder of light—the doctor sucked in air. Danica reached over and took Amen's hand, a connection of wills of a Circle of friendship bonded them together. He squeezed her hand in an approval. The old man's skin and complexion began to fill in his sunken in cheeks and added color to his face. The young woman leaped toward the awe-inspiring glow of her grand-fathers recovery was just short of a miracle. When the glow calmed to its normal light the elderly man sat up in bed. He rubbed his eyes and with a sense of confusion asked, "Is this heaven?"

Amen butted into an unwanted conversation. "Hey mister...not even close, you're still in Ark City, we thought you could use a little help." The young woman at his side had tears coursing down her face, she turned to thank them, but Danica knew they were limited on time, so she and Amen made their way into the next room, which was only twenty feet away, before the young lady could get the words out. Those of the gifted were passing out redemptive-new-life like lollipops to children. Amen looked up to see Danica's eyes. "Hey, how many rooms are there in this joint—this might take all day!" Danica looked down for the briefest of seconds and said as entering the next room, "I guess we'd better hurry then." The next room had two weeping parents straddled over a little girl that looked about Amen's age. Amen saw her condition and his heart sank, and even a tear or two leaked from the back of his eyes. Danica looked at both her parents and seen their disheartening condition and considered their thoughts of tender remissions and then Danica gently said, "I can help her if you would give me a bit of room." They turned in surprise but didn't question Danica's motives—somehow, they felt she represented something much greater than any mortal they had seen of any recent days. The young girl's face was set aglow that shimmered from the glow of the blue light. They moved aside as Danica repeated the process. The little girl's eyes moved with emotion, a dream like state of some peaceful place not ever experienced by any mortal eye. A smile developed on the corner of her mouth. A memory Danica thought perhaps having of a special time. Amen squeezed her hand in excitement. The little girl opened her eyes, surprised by her surroundings—seeing her parents before her all teary-eyed and taken back by the sight of her quick recovery. They cried tears of joy, hugs and kisses followed. Amen turned his head not wanting to be caught up in the emotion. He looked at Danica and knew this mission was right for now, and the most important part of the trip. In Amen's opinion this was perfect. Amen brushed back the thought of tears as they moved on to the next room. The parents turned and said thanking them as Danica and Amen left in a hurry. Swiftly, not far behind came the rest of the Circle, and the large watcher came stumbling after, ducking when he had too like a giant sloth dragging his knuckles on the ground. Amen looked over his shoulder and saw the over-shadowing image of the warrior from the Aquantice range and new he was here to represent—like back-up, a force to be reckoned with. Amen let go of Danica's hand slipping to the back of this conglomeration of Circle members and stood in front of this behemoth creature called a watcher. This one-eye wanderer of the dead-zone, tall and green, majestic in form and stature, a far cry from his distant fellowship. He stopped to consider his latest arrival. Amen looking like a lost child reaching up to take his big hand, as far as Amen was concerned this creature of mystery was one of them, as children do in accepting things in the innocence of a guiding hand. Somewhat surprised, Condac stood bewildered to no end that this small alien-boy would be so brave, yet having children of his own to guide, he understood. He cringed out a temperate smile to accommodate this smaller representation of life. A curious blue-boy with acquisitive stares—he wanted to know everything this mammoth creature stood for, determination, willful curiosity, bitten by a bug of bereavement, a giant among men. He held his hand even in light of their lack of likeness. Being that Amen was half Aquerae he could communicate telepathically. Amen stood their looking up into the eye of this awkward arrangement and began to see a world in a way he never imagined. Lights and color, and brilliance of memories flashed before him—it caused him to suck in air. What a beautiful heart this creature had was Amen's way of thinking. The life of this watcher flashed before Amen's eyes properly proportioned pictographs of a life unknown now transparent. He saw purity and perfection in a daily routine of giving and sacrifice. Never did a day go by that this mammoth watcher wasn't doing for others, always placing back his own needs of survival—Amen wondered if this was a true path for all to take. He considered his age to understand the blending of two minds. Then Amen let go and signaled for Condac to stay close by, just in case they needed him for moral support. Amen turned as if they had become good friends for now, while making a mental connection. Amen makes introductions to the rest of the Circle as they stand at the end of a doorway leading into another section of this underground hospital. With a raised finger Amen points, "Hey guys this is Condac?"

Argon rolled his eyes. "Tell us something we don't already know Skippy."

Then realizing Argon was right...he hadn't recognized the giant sloth. He looked a bit slimmer, and pale by what he could tell... how did he miss that? Amen improvised his train of thought so not to look silly. "Condac is one of the many redeemers left to draw the enemy away from the fellowship. The redeemers sacrifice themselves so that the younger watchers continue to survive. The redeemers are the elders of the watchers, but don't be fooled their also the smartest of them." Amen spoke like he was an expert of their species. The rest of the Circle looked up in surprise trying to find some commonality between them. Argon looked at the giant that came from the same place they did and said, "Sorry Condac, Skippy seems to be losing it."

Then David finally speaks again. "I assure you that these families are indebted to you for bringing their loved ones back to a healthy specimen, but we're not out of this dilemma you see yourselves in just yet—those evil lords in the sky are almost upon us—we need to make hast for the world has other plans not including our own." After leaving the hospital David led them to a restaurant two blocks away. This place was about the size of a Denny's restaurant, well decorated for the bit of moderation that was left, small but quaint, clean and bright, with chandeliers hanging over each table. With limited resources they sat and waited to be served as the conversation became serious about the conditions of the sky. David shared from what he had learned from this smaller solar system that lay just out beyond earths boarders. The Circle stayed attentive as David unraveled the secrets of a smaller portion of their galaxy. "Our planets delicate conditions have been thrown off from what is called the

Kuiper Belt, which is just beyond Neptune's orbit. Usually, Neptune is held in place that blocks an on slot of asteroids from passing earth's way, but Neptune has been pulled a good twenty-five hundred miles off its course of orbit leaving an open gap for asteroids to pass this way, that's what we are facing right now, and open space of a once closed door, our protecting natural shield has been compromised." Amen stared outside the window of the restaurant noticing Condac was sitting patiently against a wall, waiting to return to his fellowship most likely. Amen reflecting, wondering if he might be hungry. He looked at David and interrupted his conversation of details, holding no real significance to the boy lacking patience.

"Pardon me sir, but has anyone thought of feeding our friend out there? He looks quite weary from his travels?" David puzzled to be interrupted looked to the others and said, "Well, what does a watcher of his size eat?" Amen had to think about this for a moment before a sparkle of light lit up his face. "Well, I don't rightly know, but do you have any juicy Octus steaks or maybe a few turkeys might do." David raised an eyebrow of curiosity, wanting to ignore the last comment made by the boy who couldn't keep quiet. Amen looked back out the restaurant window and considered the one eyed giant with more of a good nature than anyone he'd ever known. Still sitting patiently against the wall. Amen replied, "He doesn't look like a vegetarian, he's got too many muscles…maybe a good Irish stew or a good leg of lamb, but maybe just left-overs might be sufficient." David reached up and clicked his fingers as the waiter came to lean in for his approval. David leaned over and whispered in his ear. The waiter nodded and left for the back of the restaurant. Ten minutes went by before anyone else saw the waiter again. He had rolled out a large flat cart on wheels with a big pot with something steaming that smells really good. Amen got up to volunteer his efforts of pushing the flat cart out the front door. A large wooden spoon set on the side, perfect for one of such size and shape. 'Meals on Wheels' made Argon smile. He covered his mouth so others wouldn't take notice. Amen pushed the cart out of the front door, towards this gentle giant. Condac looked up in surprise. The watcher reached out and touched Amen on top the head as he showed a sign of thankfulness…

Drew and Anna make their way toward the flock of trees following after the pilot of the stealth-helicopter in front. The wind began to whistle between the trees to warn them that time was almost gone. Anna reached for her husband's hand while feeling a chill in the air. She looked into her husband's eyes, and he knew what she was thinking. Drew opened a door, and they were suddenly inside the roll-up door of Ark city, with the pilot and his two passengers attached to their side.

David was there to greet them. "Good timing on your part." He said while extending a hand in gratitude. Drew gave a bleak smile even though he willfully meant it.

"So where are these gifted that everyone has mentioned but no one has seen?"

David gently rolled his eyes as his cheek gave a slight twitch. "The Indian-Princess has them in safe keeping. There in a place you haven't been yet."

"And where would that be?" Drew asked.

"A place like paradise, but different. Your younger circle of members have a chance to prove themselves once again. But before they do, the Indian-Princess has a dilemma that needs attention before moving on to the next mission that is appointed of a father who looks in waiting. And your daughter started a fight that needs to be finished, before any of you have a chance to go home...is this okay with you and your members of membership?"

This was a surprise to Drew. "What fight, and why does my daughter need to finish a fight that's way out of her league?"

David understood his protecting father radar just rose a few feet higher than normal.

Without answering Drew's question, he said. "We're all to meet soon, your children and those closest to them are almost done with a good meal we provided for them." David looks at his watch, quickly drawing Drew's attention of being on someone else's eternal clock.

"Uncle Drew!" Amen belts out. "When did you get here?"

Drew suddenly looked up and noticed Amen and his daughter and the lot of her crew walking toward them, settling among some park benches, a streetlamp lit up, with plants going down a cobblestone walkway. A golden color of light lit up the pathway. Amen got to Drew first and through his arms around him, then a hand on Anna's shoulder, feeling he really missed them, separated by war in the sky, seemed to have shed a little bit of light on fading confidence.

"Hey, you guys, how are you doing...?" Then Drew's words faded from his mouth realizing what they had been through recently.

Then Amen answers. "We're doing great Uncle Drew, we just finished rounds in the hospital, lots of people needing our help... problem solved though... Danica brought the healing-stones with her." Amen looked over his shoulder back a Danica who was walking toward her parents.

"...Anna...I'm glad your hear." Danica said. "The last three days were the toughest of my life."

She reached to hug her father and Anna joined in the hug. Drew knew she'd been through a lot, and then knowing she had bested a leader of the sixth realm was unexpected. He wondered her train of thought when jumping out in such a manner when all her circle was exposed to the danger surrounding them all.

Yeah, about what happened yesterday. What were you thinking?" Drew said.

Danica had that serious look she usually gets when being scolded by her father. "Yeah, well I just felt Cornelius was overstepping a boundary that I knew he would regret by not seeing us as a threat. I did what I had to do...and you know it was the right thing to do, in the circumstances.

You understand, don't you?"

Drew looked into her deep blue eyes and knew she was right. "I just worry you'll take this too far and not have a way out of a dilemma you create for yourself, knowing in your heart this is only meant for those with more experience young lady. It's a father's right to worry about his children. Something you will just have to get use too."

"I know father, but I was picked to lead these young degenerates, so if I don't take the lead, who will they follow?" Drew understood her calling would come with split second decision making sometimes, he just didn't like it being his daughter, putting herself in dangerous situations, that's the last thing he wanted for her.

"You knew the risks involved with leading such a team isn't for those with blind ambition, and weary hearts, it's for a warrior, keen with their thinking, well trained, and defiant against all enemies foreign and domestic... that was our training, remember?" Danica said.

"Yeah, don't get me started on the Aquerian way of thinking, I've had enough of their type of logic... my logic for you is to run, so to fight another day, especially when the odds aren't in your favor."

"I understand father, but when will you ever feel I have the upper hand? Our calling is not our own, we are commissioned by a king, in a king's good timing has nothing to do with how we feel, it's bigger than us... you know that they know that..." as she turned to look behind her pointing at her crew of members. "We were commissioned for a certain job and a specific time, and our time is now... there is no more time, as you know the wind comes without notice or warning. We go when we're commissioned to go, or fight when commissioned to fight. That's how it has always worked, without reason, without complaint we move as a team." Drew knew his daughter was well trained for her calling, and she was just as smart or smarter than him, and just as stubborn.

"Yeah, I get that...I just want you to make sure before jumping out on a limb that might be to thin to hold you up."

"I get your concern father, but I am not a child, and I have already proven myself in many ways... it's my time to set the mark. It isn't just in my hands, I have a backing of a king, and six members, plus the watchers on my side, so be sure I'm the best they got for the moment."

Drew didn't like hearing such words from Danica, small in stature, but beautiful like a mother lost so many years ago, even though Anna had filled a mother's shoes quite efficiently. Amen came around Danica's side suddenly, then nudged her like her favorite dog wanting a treat. She turned to look at him when realizing her favorite watcher was missing. Then she began to worry.

Time was of essence, and they needed a good plan or better, a good way out of the up-and-coming streaks in the sky. "The Indian princess I'm sure knows more than we have been told, for what we're told is only a few suggestions before implementing a king's mark." Danica said.

Her father wondered himself what was scheduled just ahead, but none of them knew, it was in a King's good timing, to say the least. Once everyone were standing or sitting on the park benches, David began to speak.

"Gather you belongings after this meeting, your time left here is short. Make no mistake, even though Amen lead over seventy percent of Cornelius's army in the world between the living and dead, they will regroup and come back our way."

"Duly noted..." Amen said, "But what's next on the agenda, the day has already been long, and those asteroid's in the sky are almost here."

David looked over and shook his head. "Yes, you're right young warrior, but your mission is not quite over. And there's people to pick up along the way."

Argon reached up to flick Amen on the back of his melon shaped head. Amen took the playful punishment knowing, he had bested those demons of the sky, he could handle a friendly flick from one of his friends. When seeing Amen didn't respond Argon didn't continue, he had gained a little respect of the boy who had way more courage than he'd ever shone.

David shared about the next few hours they had left. "Drew, Anna, and half the watcher's and their steeds of the air will split up, half with you, and half with your daughter and her crew. I want both star ships to have protection. Drew and Danica need to be split up so there is a way to open a door, going back to your time, separately. That's the only way both star ships can get back home."

"Ten four good buddy...we know how time travel works; we've already figured that part out."

Amen said. Danica reached over and put an arm around Amen's shoulder.

"It's alright Amen, let David say what he came here to say, and then we will be on our way."

Amen knew her interruption was to get him to back off a bit, so David wouldn't lose his train of thought.

"Oh, sorry sir, I'm just excited to get this day behind us...my bad."

A quivering twitch was seen in David's cheek, as he continued. "Then, Drew and Anna will go back to the Island, that's where the Indian princess will meet you. Danica and her crew have to finish a fight, they started back in Alaska where you originally started. Thaliana will send seven Conquerites with you, so to watch your backs. The key of getting home, is being at the same place you first started. This is why you have to be separated."

Drew didn't like the idea of his daughter going back into a fight he felt himself compelled to avoid, because they were outnumbered ten to one thousand. What were their chances of getting out of there alive, was still a mystery.

"Cool then… well-spoken!" Amen said. "We're there… just tell us when to go." David wondered of the boy's upbringing, yet said nothing, only stared."

Danica got up and started filling backpacks that had been replaced, food, some water in canteens given to them and started walking toward the shuttle. Drew reached up and grabbed Danica's shoulder before moving on.

"Be careful. And take Condac with you, I'm sure he'll come in handy." Danica hugged her father, looked at Anna, then left quickly with her team.

20

The Fight

Danica and her crew headed for the chopper. Amen grabbed his stuff and ran after her.

The rest of the circle were quick to follow along. Danica didn't look back because she didn't want to see the worried look in her father's eyes. The wind began to pick up as the three markers in the sky seemed closer than before.

The air suddenly felt heavy on Danica's lungs as she sat in the seat next to Torack as co-pilot. The chopper was set in stealth mode, avoiding those creatures of the sky. There was a mission on her mind from one preciously missing. Her hands began to shake, and her mind began to wonder of their coming event. Amen saw the worried expression in her eyes and knew she had to focus on anything but what was ahead. Tory was viewing an I-pad computer screen trying to connect dots of blue and green. Argon was checking all the weapons. Ismael leaned against his brother and looked at him. Jacob was wishing for anywhere to be except here. The sky was dark with a cryptic feel in the air. Everyone remained silent and still, not feeling the mood of what was to come. Suddenly,

Danica opened a door and brought all of them through it. Torack pulled the yoke left then right.

"A warning would be nice…" Torack said.

"Sorry, just didn't want to give away our position to anyone… thought it to be better this way." Danica said. Torack only nodded, just before seeing the dim light in the forest just up ahead. The Conquerites would be there when landing. They had a point of making a entrance despite ill-advised timing.

Torack pulled the yoke hard to the left just before landing. Everyone quickly got out and headed for the star ship. Torack suddenly felt a rumble beneath his feet. Everyone turned to look up behind them. The Conquerites were just on time as usual, bringing with them a strong sweep of air. "Wow!" Amen said. "Nothing like making an entrance."

Danica had placed a hand on her sword, then eased up when seeing them. The Conquerites remained with wings with an outward position. Then they looked down at her. Curious, she wondered of their motives and walked toward them. Then one of them spoke for the first time ever.

"Your time is now young warrior!" This caused her whole crew to turn around.

Danica couldn't hardly believe they were addressing her. Amen knew for some reason these colossal giants weren't at a point of holding back anymore. "There is no more time to make adjustments… you need to prepare yourselves quickly." The closest one said.

Danica looked back at the other's to let them know the warning was for all of them. The sky suddenly filled in with clouds of black and mystic form. Danica knew this would be the only warning they would get. The Conquerites headed for the star ship a quarter mile up the hill. She suddenly knew… she wasn't meant to run in any direction but to face what was coming.

The clouds opened up and a host like no other surrounded all of them. For some reason, Danica looked back and noticed the Conquerites were hidden from the view, as if to watch the scene coming next. She sensed they were backup. She wondered of a king trusting her so willingly. Somehow she felt that they still held the edge. Cornelius walked toward her then stopped twenty feet away. He was hiding the area of the hand now missing. She looked and noticed his stare was penetrating beyond normal measure. His captains stayed at close proximity all around. Danica could smell the place they had been, along with Amen, and knew them to be frauds. They were an allusion of what was to be the next world order.

The three marks in the sky were never looked at by them. This caused Danica to sense they held a higher purpose than just survival. Amen noticed from 30 feet away, behind her that Danica held a relaxed position with her arms folded in front. This confused him at first, but then he remembered something mentioned by her that the eyes see what they want to see, not what actually was. Amen knew wisdom had graced the girl well prepared for a mission just in front.

Cornelius wouldn't be so coy of giving away his opinions so quickly... he learned a lesson well when losing his hand, taken by the girl just in front.

Cornelius looked down at her and smiled. "Why is such a girl in a hurry to leave so quickly?"

Danica wondered of the words so strange meant to confuse her. "You have alluded my grasp young lady, but your time has passed, you will not be so lucky again." He said, like she would accept his intimidation so quickly. "I am not your enemy as you think... there are other's worse than I that could take you without your knowledge or your approval. They are but like mist to those of a human species." He said it like she was inferior to them in all manner, and she would have to worry about others besides those that stood in front. She wasn't buying his fraudulent words more than deceptive.

"And how have I missed your real reason of you being here, when what is seen in the sky will draw the very life from those remaining behind. Are you not what is left of this world, and the world to come doesn't even know of you...how's that make you really feel?" Cornelius suddenly lost the smile.

"But you lie young demon!" Cornelius spit out. He didn't like her lack of respect, as if he earned it. "You are but a devil without a home young warrior, where are those that represent you? I don't see any that support you like you should have confidence among victims of this world that has already been defeated."

"And you see me and my circle like victims? You are more deceived than you know…" Danica stated. Cornelius quickly moved toward her like he would overtake her, but Danica disappeared and came up behind him. Cornelius almost lost his footing before seeing she had alluded him without him knowing how. She had placed her boot in his butt and pushed him. This enraged him. Moving around he swung his wings quickly in her direction. She ducked backwards to avoid the sharp talons. Danica cut the back of his right heal with the same blade that took his right hand. He grabbed for it with a scream of rage. His captains jumped toward her, but she alluded them all by appearing just at the side of Amen. He was surprised to see her early arrival. She placed an index finger to her lips so Amen wouldn't give away their position. Then she jumped back into the fight when they were looking outward. Danica sliced off one of Cornelius's wings. He screamed in pain. His second in command leaped toward her, but she came up in front of his leader and drove her sword through his gut. Blood was quickly seen coming from his mouth. Cornelius eyes were full of unbelief. What had actually happened. Once Cornelius hit the ground his legends stood quiet, wondering of this girl that had taken their leader out so quickly. Danica disappeared and stood just outside the star ship. The Conquerites faced the legends on their own… heavy breath filled the fields of rain and darkness. Heaven's elite took over…

Danica, and her crew warmed up the star ship and headed for Ark city. Amen couldn't believe the fight was already ended. "Man, you whipped them good." Amen said. Danica didn't respond. She only looked outside the window wondering where those left of earth would be hidden. Amen was the first to speak. "Where do we go from here?" Danica looked confused.

"Where do you think… back to Ark city where we left other's behind."

"But I thought the Indian-Princess had others for us to take?" Amen said.

"I don't think so Amen, where else would anyone be hiding? Do you know of a place?"

Amen seemed puzzled. "No…I don't think so… then where else could we look?"

Argon butts in… "Maybe in a rift we haven't seen yet." Amen wrinkled his brow.

"I don't think so numb nuts! We would have found it by now… look at the sky, we're out of time."

Argon looks out a window and sees the three asteroid's even bigger than a few hours back. And the colors seemed more define. Tory suddenly, found a group of something on the third level of Ark city. "Hold up Skippy, I think I found them." Amen got up out of his seat to glance over Tory's shoulder. 'Holy batman crap!" Amen announced. "How did we miss that?"

Tory quickly glanced his way then back. "I don't know Skippy, but there on the third level now." Danica somehow sensed that Ark city was their only draw.

"Wait till my dad finds out… he'll be surprised." She said.

"He'll be surprised. I'm surprised!" Amen said. "Aren't you surprised? How about you Argon, are you surprised… how about everyone else, are you all surprised?"

"Cool it Skippy… that's enough…" His brother said. "We get the joke, okay?"

Amen developed a quirky expression… "Wait till I get home, I bet my dad will be surprised too…" Then they all laughed, even Torack smiled from ear to ear. The team as a whole began to sense their time here was almost up.

Drew was at the helm of the star ship when other's from Ark city started going through the front door two by two like during Noah's day centuries back during a certain flood. Anna was watching it all happen on a video screen in front. Drew was wondering how his daughter was making out on her present mission. Then suddenly, the other star ship came down from clouds of another place and sat right down in front of them. It startled him so much he almost closed the door on those coming through. Anna looked over and grimaced. "Are you okay?" She asked.

A quivering acknowledgment was seen on his face. She reached over to calm him. "There, there my dear husband, we're almost out of this mess."

Both Drew and Anna could see the younger members pile out of the Star ship while running toward the door of Ark city. Amen almost knocked down and elderly woman, then stopped and said… "Oh sorry oh elderly one, I didn't see you there…" Ismael couldn't believe his brother lacking proper words. "Amen!" Ismael yelled. "What's your malfunction?"

"Oh…I'm sorry…didn't know her name bro… would you like me to make you some S'mores?" Amen asked. Argon couldn't believe the little weasel was back to that subject.

"Dude… she doesn't want your congeniality fart face… she's a victim that needs our comfort and a ride back to a better life. Who knows what you would do to her clothing…"

Amen couldn't believe he was already on someone's bad side again. "What did I do?" Amen retorted. "I didn't cause all this." Suddenly, realizing the rest of the crew were leaving them behind. "Now look what you did…" Amen said. "Our crew took off to Ark city without us."

"Not my fault…" Argon said. "I'm just trying to get you not to be a moron."

Skippy's face turned hostel. "I'm not the moron, you are!" As the sounds of a perfectly good fight faded behind closed doors. Drew and Anna heard the whole thing and began to smile.

Once both star ships were full of the remaining people of earth… they took off toward the atmosphere and left those dark angels behind…

Amen looked over at Danica after clearing the earth's atmosphere and said. "What happened to the Indian-Princess?" Danica had a glinting sparkle in her eye. "I guess we didn't need her this time, because we were prepared for our mission on our own."

Amen felt proud of Danica, in how she had handle herself and those opposing her. "We all did good… hallelujah… thank you Jesus!" Amen said.

Argon was confused. "Why the sudden praise, Skippy?"

"I don't know Argon…do you think we did this on our own?"

The three blazing lights in the sky suddenly weren't there…

AFTERWORD

The series keeps moving back in time to another world. A Love story of an angel who was demoted and placed on this earth to help when ever he saw the need in doing so. He has secrets kept to himself to not draw attention. His son has the same gift that his father has. He doesn't tell him anything of his past. It involves a time when the world begins to fall a part when just getting started.

Jimmy is at the brink of the world showing, it needs a savior. Julia is disheartened when Jimmy has to leave to save his son from a world turned upside down. And Lena is the daughter who receives certain gifts, more powerful than anything Jimmy ever could imagine. But Jimmy makes a mistake, which almost cost his life.

And the world has another on going problem. Someone sets off 4 nukes that take out the people in power. Now, they have to start over, and the dollar is on shaky ground. Jimmy leaves for a vacation to Spain before all this could ever happen, where he meets Julia. Julia has had trouble with an ex that's left her behind, without cause or reason he was killed two years back. Julia's left with the questions that you feel when missing the love of your life.

Spain After Rain, it will take you by storm...